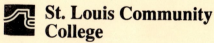

Critical Essays on
FREDERICK DOUGLASS

CRITICAL ESSAYS
ON
AMERICAN LITERATURE

James Nagel, General Editor
Northeastern University

Critical Essays on

FREDERICK DOUGLASS

edited by

WILLIAM L. ANDREWS

G. K. Hall & Co.
BOSTON, MASSACHUSETTS

Published 1991.
10 9 8 7 6 5 4 3 2 1

Library of Congress Cataloging-in-Publication Data

Critical essays on Frederick Douglass / edited by William L. Andrews.
    p.   cm. — (Critical essays on American literature)
  Includes bibliographical references and index.
  ISBN 0-8161-7301-X (alk. paper)
  1. Douglass, Frederick, 1817?-1895. 2. Douglass, Frederick,
1817?-1895. Narrative of the life of Frederick Douglass, an
American slave. 3. Slavery—United States—Anti-slavery movements.
I. Andrews, William L., 1946-   . II. Series.
E449.D75C75   1991
973.7'092—dc20
[B]   91-6426

Contents

◆

General Editor's Note

◆

This series seeks to anthologize the most important criticism on a wide variety of topics and writers in American literature. Our readers will find in various volumes not only a generous selection of reprinted articles and reviews but original essays, bibliographies, manuscript sections, and other materials brought to public attention for the first time. This volume, *Critical Essays on Frederick Douglass,* is the most comprehensive collection of essays ever published on one of the most important African-American writers. It contains both a sizable gathering of early reviews and a broad selection of more modern scholarship. Among the authors of reprinted articles and reviews are Margaret Fuller, J. Saunders Redding, Henry Louis Gates, Jr., Houston A. Baker, Jr., and Robert Stepto. In addition to a substantial introduction by William L. Andrews, there are also three original essays commissioned specifically for publication in this volume: new studies by Thad Ziolkowski, Ann Kibbey and Michele Stepto, and Deborah E. McDowell. We are confident that this book will make a permanent and significant contribution to the study of American literature.

JAMES NAGEL
Northeastern University

Publisher's Note

♦

Producing a volume that contains both newly commissioned and reprinted material presents the publisher with the challenge of balancing the desire to achieve stylistic consistency with the need to preserve the integrity of works first published elsewhere. In the Critical Essays series, essays commissioned especially for a particular volume are edited to be consistent with G. K. Hall's house style; reprinted essays appear in the style in which they were first published, with only typographical errors corrected. Consequently, shifts in style from one essay to another are the result of our efforts to be faithful to each text as it was originally published.

Introduction

♦

WILLIAM L. ANDREWS

Sometime during the spring of 1845 Frederick Douglass went to visit Wendell Phillips, a famous Boston abolitionist, in order to read aloud an autobiographical narrative on which Douglass had been working for several months. Recalling that notable day in a letter he wrote to Douglass on April 22, Phillips admitted that "when you read me your memoirs, I hardly knew, at the time, whether to thank you or not for the sight of them." Phillips knew that the laws of the United States made it "dangerous, in Massachusetts, for honest men to tell their names!"—particularly men who had escaped slavery and meant to stay free. Whether Phillips appreciated the intensely personal dilemma underlying Douglass's foray into autobiography—to be honest was to invite the dishonor of recapture—is not clear. But in the century and a half since Douglass's first autobiography came into existence, critical interest in the collision between personal expressive freedom and cultural authority in Douglass's writing has brought him to the forefront of contemporary reevaluations of American literary history.

Less than a month after writing his letter, Phillips's response to Douglass's narrative received the authorization of print. It appeared in tandem with comments by William Lloyd Garrison, the leader of the antislavery movement in New England, as part of the prefatory material to the *Narrative of the Life of Frederick Douglass, an American Slave, Written by Himself*. Both Garrison and Phillips were intent on introducing Douglass as a representative slave whose story, Phillips stressed, should be read for what it revealed about "the essential ingredients, not the occasional results, of the system" of human bondage in the American South. Maintaining that "the experience of FREDERICK DOUGLASS, as a slave, was not a peculiar one," Garrison went on to promise that what Douglass had written contained "nothing exaggerated, nothing drawn from the imagination," nothing, in short, that might reflect more of the individual himself than of the institution of which he had once been a commodified part.[1] Undoubtedly influenced by the assessment of Douglass

1

offered by both Phillips and Garrison, readers of the *Narrative* as well as Douglass's later autobiographies were slow to appreciate fully the individuality of Douglass's writing or its importance to the evolution of American narrative traditions. Partly as a consequence of this, Douglass's fame rested for a long time on his reputation as a man of affairs, not a man of letters, and on his accomplishments as a great nineteenth-century orator, rather than on his achievement as a writer of enduring cultural and literary import to America.

Probably the most widely read and important review that the *Narrative* received was written by Margaret Fuller, the well-known transcendentalist and feminist, for the *New York Tribune* on 10 June 1845. Fuller congratulated Douglass for infusing into his writing "the thoughts, the feelings and the adventures that have been so affecting through the living voice." She went on to say that she had never read a narrative "more simple, true, coherent, and warm with genuine feeling." Fuller's admiration of the "peculiar element" in Douglass's writing—his "talent for melody" and his "ready skill at imitation," for instance—says much more about Fuller's assumptions about "the African race" than about Douglass's literary abilities. Yet it was not unusual for even sympathetic reviewers of Douglass's *Narrative* to try to interpret his literary successes as somehow attributable to his racial heritage rather than to his individual mastery of the writer's craft. An occasional reviewer might observe the similarity of Douglass's style to that of John Bunyan or Daniel Defoe, but the major agenda of the reviews, particularly among the antislavery periodicals, was to stress what the *Narrative* said about slavery that could be used to further the abolitionist cause.[2]

Frederick Douglass's *Narrative* was an antebellum best-seller, a book much more widely read than Thoreau's *Walden,* for instance, or the first edition of Whitman's *Leaves of Grass.* Priced at 50 cents a copy, the *Narrative*'s first printing of 5000 copies sold out in four months. Four additional reprintings of 2000 copies each were brought out within a year to satisfy demand. Benjamin Quarles, Douglass's first scholarly biographer, estimates that by 1850 approximately 30,000 copies of the *Narrative* had been sold in the United States and Great Britain.[3] An 1846 Dutch translation of the *Narrative* and an 1848 French translation helped spread Douglass's fame on the European continent. By 1849 a reviewer of several prominent slave narratives, including Douglass's, stated that "the immense circulation" of these narratives had permeated the North, with the result that more people were becoming abolitionists by reading ex-slave autobiographies than by "all the theoretical arguments" against slavery mounted on the platform or in the press.

Perhaps because this reviewer, Ephraim Peabody, recognized the "very wide influence on public opinion" that narratives like Douglass's had, he took it upon himself to admonish Douglass publicly for the "violence and extravagance of expression" that Peabody found in the ex-slave's speaking and writing. Though most readers received Douglass's *Narrative* as a simple and unvarnished piece of personal storytelling, Peabody perceived a certain bothersome artfulness, a self-consciousness, in Douglass's literary manner. Peabody worried that Douglass's willingness to vent his emotions, together with his use of "extravagance and passion and rhetorical flourishes," indicated that Douglass might be "thinking more of his speech than of the end for which he professes to make it."[4] That Peabody objected to a black writer's attending as much to his style of expression as to the purpose for which he addressed his audience suggests that even the most sympathetic readers of Douglass in his own time were not prepared to take him seriously as a self-conscious literary stylist. Somehow a Douglass concerned with self-expression through "passion and rhetoric" made readers like Peabody suspect Douglass's wholehearted dedication to the cause of antislavery. This assumption that self-expressive rhetoric and self-sacrificing political commitment are mutually exclusive may help to explain why for such a long time Douglass's *Narrative* was not studied as a model of literary self-consciousness.

On 3 December 1848, Douglass launched the second phase of his literary career, publishing the first issue of his antislavery weekly, *The North Star,* from his Rochester, New York, press room. Douglass knew that many abolitionists believed that he was spreading his talents too thin and that he could do more good by concentrating on his antislavery speaking. To Douglass, however, the very idea that blacks should confine themselves to the role of speaker in the movement smacked of a certain patronizing attitude among whites, if not an assumption that blacks were somehow constitutionally better suited to speak than to write. That this prejudice was alive even among those who regarded Douglass highly can be seen in the words of David Bartlett, who included Douglass in *Modern Agitators: Or Pen Portraits of Living American Reformers* (1855) among such literary reformers as Whittier, Lowell, and Bryant. Bartlett labeled Douglass's paper "excellent," but opined, nevertheless, that "nature intended Douglass for an orator—not to be an editor." On the platform "he stands before an audience *a natural orator* [*sic*], like the African Cinque." Harriet Beecher Stowe's observation in 1868, five years after the cessation of Douglass's paper, that it bore "a creditable character for literary execution," represents the standard judgment of the time on Douglass the editor. Yet it is important to remember that William Wells Brown, the first African-American historian, maintained that Douglass's work as an editor had "done more for the freedom and elevation of his race than all his platform appeals."[5]

In August 1855, Douglass's second autobiography, *My Bondage and My Freedom,* was published by Miller, Orton, and Mulligan of Auburn, New York. Having lived in the North for almost 17 years (Douglass escaped from slavery in Baltimore on 3 September 1838), Douglass had much more to say about his experiences as a freeman in *My Bondage and My Freedom* than in his *Narrative.* In his second autobiography Douglass also elaborated many more details of his life in slavery, making *My Bondage and My Freedom* a much more comprehensive study of the mechanisms of slavery and a more thoroughgoing analysis of the evolution of Douglass's psyche than the *Narrative.* That *My Bondage and*

My Freedom is more than three times the length of the *Narrative* seems not to have deterred its readership. According to Quarles, the second autobiography went through three editions in three years, during which time 18,000 copies of the book were published.[6] In 1860 it was translated into German.

My Bondage and My Freedom won a favorable response from most reviewers for reasons similar to those that made the *Narrative* a best-seller. In the wake of the unprecedented popularity of Stowe's *Uncle Tom's Cabin* (1852), the *New York Tribune*'s reviewer saw Douglass's second autobiography as "one of the most striking illustrations of American Slavery, which either fact or fiction has presented to the public." Having read a good many slave narratives, the *Ohio State Journal*'s reviewer declared *My Bondage and My Freedom* in a class by itself because the narration did not require the reader "to supply the commentary" on the basic facts of slavery—Douglass fulfilled this need admirably. In the process he proved himself "a man of genius." The unusual scope and power of *My Bondage and My Freedom* was also cited in *Putnam's Monthly,* one of the prominent literary magazines of the era. Despite admonishing Douglass for writing "bitterly," the *Putnam's* reviewer granted the ex-slave preeminence among the most celebrated men of "genius struggling against adversity" in English literature. In the opinion of this reader, Douglass deserved his "unique" and "conspicuous" position on the international stage "both as a writer and a speaker."[7]

After the Civil War, Douglass's popularity as an orator enabled him to pursue lecturing as a career. Although he welcomed opportunities to agitate from the platform for the civil rights of African-Americans, he was most popular for his lecture on "Self-Made Men," which he wrote in 1855 and which became his mainstay during the Reconstruction years when he was most in demand as a speaker. Douglass's identification with the myth of success is one reason that Howard Carroll included Douglass's story in *Twelve Americans* (1883), a collection of biographies of public men who rose from "primitive surroundings" to exemplify "the astonishing social and material development of the Republic."[8] Douglass's third autobiography, *Life and Times of Frederick Douglass* (1881),[9] gave Carroll all he needed to conclude of his subject, "It is doubtful if any man, in any country, commencing so low, ever climbed so high as did Frederick Douglass."

Making only slight changes in the account of his early years given in *My Bondage and My Freedom* (except for inserting an explanation of how he escaped from slavery), Douglass added 12 lengthy chapters to his second autobiography, which made the *Life and Times* almost twice as large as its predecessor. The new material in the *Life and Times* was designed to show how Douglass's dedication to social justice and progress committed him to a "life of conflict and battle" not only in the tempestuous midcentury decades but thereafter, when his political activities and responsibilities as the spokesman of his people exposed him to a variety of black as well as white critics. Yet, Douglass affirmed in the conclusion of the *Life and Times,* his had also been a "life of victory, if not complete, at least assured." Ten years later, however, as he set about expanding the *Life and Times* for a final edition,[10] Douglass tempered his optimism somewhat in light of what he perceived as a rising tide of racism in the United States.

The *Life and Times* was the least popular of Douglass's autobiographies, selling only 463 copies in its first seven years of existence, according to Quarles. The expanded edition of 1892 did only slightly better, selling 399 copies in two years.[11] Few of the major literary magazines in the United States noticed the appearance of the *Life and Times,* although *The Critic* called Douglass's book "unique" and worthy of acceptance "without carping or criticism." Unfortunately, *The Critic*'s review hints that there is plenty to criticize in the *Life and Times,* from its poor printing to Douglass's "child-like self-complacency" in daring to publish his story "before there is five feet of good solid earth over him." A friendly word in a journal of public affairs like *The Independent* could not counter suggestions from other critics that Douglass's story was perhaps a bit passé. Turn-of-the-century white America may not have been disposed to read a book that, according to a well-meaning reviewer for the *Catholic World,* shed light on "a most important period in the history of the Republic," especially if that book revealed, in the *Catholic World*'s delicate phrasing, "those deeply hidden causes from which has sprung the present transition-state of the nation."[12] It is worth noting, however, that the *Life and Times* was published in England in 1882, in France in 1883, and in Sweden in 1895.

The first book-length biography of Douglass, Frederick May Holland's *Frederick Douglass: The Colored Orator* (1891), is distinguished by the intimacy between its subject and its author. This fact allowed Holland to print for the first time a number of Douglass's speeches and a wealth of anecdotes by Douglass's cohorts in the various reform movements in which he participated. Despite the title of his book, Holland also gives generous attention to Douglass's literary career. After Douglass's death in 1895, several eulogistic biographies appeared, among them a schoolroom text by Charles W. Chesnutt, a memorial volume by Douglass's second wife, Helen Pitts Douglass, and an account ghost-written for and attributed to Booker T. Washington.[13] Among these, the Washington biography of Douglass is noteworthy because it reflects the Tuskegeean's effort to legitimize his program by re-creating Douglass in his own image as a forerunner of Washingtonian accommodationism.

In 1908 Kelly Miller, a respected black academic and an incisive social analyst, published an essay entitled "Radicals and Conservatives," part of which attempted to reclaim Douglass's place in history as the antithesis—not the anticipator—of Booker T. Washington.[14] In this essay Miller identified Douglass as the intellectual progenitor of such "radicals" as William Monroe Trotter and W. E. B. Du Bois. Since Miller's essay, Douglass's alignment in the classic opposition of African-American "radicals and conservatives" has not been challenged, although the extent and the consistency of his "radicalism" have been debated. Literary critics of Douglass's writing have not often entered into these debates, however, preferring to study the matter and manner of his writing in terms of intellectual traditions such as humanism, literary modes such as romanticism, and discursive genres such as conversion narratives and jeremiads, rather than in relation to the right or left wings of African-American sociopolitical leadership.

During the first three decades of the twentieth century, Douglass's critical reputation languished, though his status as an exemplar of black achievement did not. In *The Negro in Literature and Art in the United States*, Benjamin Brawley, the most assiduous and widely read African-American literary historian of this period, paired Douglass and Washington in a chapter on the most distinguished orators of black America. By virtually ignoring Douglass's autobiographies, Brawley helped perpetuate the notion that Douglass was most appropriately remembered as a speaker not a writer.[15] In the 1930s, however, two critics, Vernon Loggins and J. Saunders Redding, rescued Douglass from critical neglect and provided the first sustained examinations of his place in the evolution of African-American literature. Loggins's *The Negro Author: His Development in America to 1900,* a copiously documented Columbia University doctoral dissertation published in 1931, named Douglass "the most important figure in American Negro literature before 1900" and gave ample evidence to justify this unprecedented claim.[16] Following the likes of Brawley, Loggins readily granted Douglass primacy among the great black orators of the nineteenth century. To Loggins, however, "the significance of [Douglass's] speeches lies in their intrinsic merit, not in the fact that they were created by a Negro." This led the critic to detail many rhetorical and stylistic reasons for Douglass's success as a speaker. Loggins went on to praise the *Narrative* for a rhetorical sophistication that could be easily overlooked because of its narrative pose of "childlike simplicity." He also contended that *My Bondage and My Freedom* was "in every sense a surer and bigger work" than the earlier autobiography. Despite the racial prejudice that sometimes subverts his attempt to apply unbiased scholarly standards to Douglass's writing, Loggins laid a foundation for the appraisal of Douglass the writer upon which innumerable critics have lastingly built.

For the most gracefully written critical essay on Douglass's entire literary career, J. Saunders Redding's compact but highly suggestive remarks in *To Make a Poet Black* still retain the foremost rank.[17] Redding and Loggins agreed on the fundamental premise that Douglass the speaker and Douglass the writer are an indivisible intellectual entity. Not content to applaud Douglass for his contributions to African-American literature, however, Redding boldly insisted that "the literary qualities of simplicity, interest, and compression of style" in Douglass's first three autobiographies were unexcelled in the history of American self-writing. Only the failure of white scholars to treat Douglass's books fairly and honestly kept him from his rightful deserts in the history of American letters, Redding concluded. Although few critics have endorsed Redding's preference for the 1881 *Life and Times* over Douglass's other narratives, the unstinting attention to Douglass among historians of American autobiography during the last two decades testifies to Redding's prescience and to the cogency of his criticism.

There was little published literary criticism devoted to Douglass in the 1940s and 1950s; nevertheless, several scholars made strong contributions to what became a Douglass revival. Among them were Marion Wilson Starling, whose path-breaking 1946 dissertation singled out Douglass's *Narrative* as the most important of all the slave narratives; Benjamin Quarles, author of the first scholarly biography of Douglass; and Philip Foner, who published in 1950 the first of his five-volume *Life and Writings of Frederick Douglass,* the first attempt to gather Douglass's speeches, editorials, and miscellaneous occasional writing together for students of Douglass. It was not until the publication of Quarles's scholarly edition of the *Narrative* by Harvard's Belknap Press in 1960, however, that Douglass's first autobiography, which had been out of print for roughly a century, made a dramatic reentry into the literary scene. During the 1960s Charles H. Nichols's *Many Thousand Gone* (1963), an interweaving of dozens of ex-slave texts into a composite slave narrative resonant with historical and literary import, helped to revive interest in Douglass. So also did the demand for Black Studies courses, which compelled the teaching of Douglass in curricula long unused to recognizing any nineteenth-century black writers. In 1968 the *Narrative* gained admittance into Henig Cohen's *Landmarks of American Writing,* perhaps the first sign that Douglass was on his way to becoming a canonical author in the history of American literature.[18]

The 1970s saw an outpouring of criticism on Douglass the writer. Virtually every genre in which Douglass worked received attention, so that in addition to the autobiographies, Douglass's journalism and his little-known experiment in fiction received solid critical analysis for the first time.[19] In perhaps the first essay to compare a Douglass autobiography to a classic text of American literature, William W. Nichols probed the differences between the treatment of self in *My Bondage and My Freedom* and Thoreau's *Walden.* The conclusion of Nichols's "Individualism and Autobiographical Art: Frederick Douglass and Henry Thoreau" portrays the latter as the more conventional in his allegiance to individualism while the "communal ethos" of *My Bondage and My Freedom* emerges as a valuable alternative to *Walden's* myth of "unrestricted selfhood." Despite Nichols's insights into the importance of *My Bondage and My Freedom,* criticism in the 1970s centered on the *Narrative.* Evidence of this trend emerged in Nancy T. Clasby's "content analysis" of the *Narrative* and in Jean Fagan Yellin's survey of Douglass's autobiographical writing in *The Intricate Knot* (1972), a study of black figures in antebellum American literature. That Yellin gave more space in her book to the writings of William Wells Brown than to Douglass suggests that the significance of the latter to "literature" was still by no means a settled matter. On the other hand, Stephen Butterfield's chapter on Douglass in *Black Autobiography in America* (1973) boldly proclaimed the author of the *Life and Times* "a superior literary artist," deserving appreciation as a rhetorician, a satirist, and a storyteller of major significance. While some scholars doubted whether political commitment sullied literary artistry, Butterfield asserted that Douglass's literary greatness was "mainly *because* of the demands made on him in his political life."[20]

Early in the 1970s, critics (like Butterfield) who wished to study Douglass as a literary figure began to point out some of the problems in trying to apply a traditional formalist esthetic to writing, such as the *Narrative*, which could be by turns ignorant of, indifferent to, or in clear rebellion against Eurocentric cultural assumptions about what art is and does. The first critic to offer an alternate theory of the cultural underpinnings of the *Narrative* and to extrapolate from that theory a sense of literary value appropriate to a text like the *Narrative* was Houston A. Baker, Jr. In *Long Black Song* (1973),[21] Baker set the stage for his discussion of Douglass's *Narrative* by offering a concept of a distinctive and vital black culture informed by a unique religious vision and a folklore that "stands at the base of the black literary tradition." This cultural contextualizing of the *Narrative* enabled Baker to comment with a specificity and confidence rare among critics of Douglass's writing. The result was an impressive cataloging of Douglass's "sophisticated literary techniques," ranging from his irony to his careful structuring of his story as a bildungsroman. Eschewing the traditional comparisons with Booker T. Washington, Baker named David Walker, a revolutionary contemporary of Douglass's, as a foil to the more reformist motives of Douglass himself. This helped to situate the *Narrative* in a sociopolitical milieu much more revealing of Douglass's antebellum cultural affinities than any discussion of him in relation to Washington had been able to offer.

Baker's examination of Douglass in *Long Black Song* proved to be a catalyst for a number of important articles and essays during the 1970s. H. Bruce Franklin found Baker's brief comments on animal metaphors in the *Narrative* to be quite suggestive. Franklin's study of the significance of animal imagery in Douglass's effort to define his "manhood" was published in *New Letters* in 1977. Baker's observation that the *Narrative* is a kind of spiritual autobiography in the tradition of Cotton Mather, Benjamin Franklin, and Henry Adams found fuller development in G. Thomas Couser's *American Autobiography: The Prophetic Mode* (1979). Here Douglass's secularization of the conversion theme is discussed in the context of spiritual autobiography, including Increase Mather, Franklin, and Adams. While Baker suggested that Douglass "was not interested in rendering the intonation and diction of oratory into written form," Robert G. O'Meally, in an essay on the influence of the black sermon on the form of the *Narrative,* argued that traditions of black oratory permeate Douglass's first autobiography, informing not only its religious themes but also its manner of self-presentation.[22]

Perhaps the most fruitful of the early essays engendered by Baker's discussion in *Long Black Song,* however, was Albert E. Stone's "Identity and Art in Frederick Douglass's *Narrative*." In Stone's view, Baker had not adequately reckoned with Douglass "as narrative artist and artificer of the self." Studying the *Narrative* as an artful text, Stone maintained, would not detract from its political significance but only enhance it, since the ideas of "freedom, personal identity, and self-expression" are all "fused" in the *Narrative* by the double perspective that pervades the book, a perspective that balances the slave's and freeman's view of American life. Repeatedly Stone pictures the *Narrative* as the locus of many competing, if not outright conflicting, claims and agendas, which Douglass skillfully manages in a creative tension. In the 1980s, criticism followed Stone's lead in investigating the dichotomies and oppositions inherent in the *Narrative*'s attempt to occupy, in Stone's words, "the territory between history and art, biography and fiction, memory and imagination." What Stone saw as Douglass's successful negotiation of these conflicting claims has become for some of his successors a more problematic issue, reaching to the basis of contradictions inherent in Douglass and/or the form of American autobiography itself.[23]

In 1980 appeared the first major biography of Douglass since Quarles—Dickson J. Preston's *Young Frederick Douglass: The Maryland Years,* the definitive study of Douglass's life in slavery based on exhaustive research into the available records and documents. In a review devoted mostly to Preston's book and an analysis of Douglass by the historian Peter Walker, Henry Louis Gates, Jr., praised Preston as the first biographer to penetrate the masks that Douglass assumed and the myths that he engendered in his autobiographies. The result is a "reevaluation of Douglass as a *language-using,* social, historical, and individual entity." This idea of Douglass as "a creature of language," who invented himself perpetually for myriad social and personal purposes, appealed to Gates as an alternative to a romantic, essentialist notion of a "knowable and unchanging black and integral self." He urged scholars not to accept black autobiography's myths of essence, but instead to examine the linguistic means by which those myths are constructed and at times deconstructed by the ironies inherent in black subscription to the form and ideology of Euro-American autobiography.[24]

In his second book of essays, *The Journey Back* (1980)[25], Houston Baker summed up the fundamental irony of Douglass's participation in the discourse of conversion and abolition that underlies his first foray into autobiography. Even as Douglass's *Narrative* seems designed to record his becoming conscious of his own being through access to language, that same *Narrative,* because it is structured by what Baker calls "white Christian standards," inevitably limits Douglass's freedom to define and express his sense of selfhood. "Unaware of the limitations" that subscribing to "the general public discourse about slavery" entailed, and lacking "a separate, written black language" through which to represent "the oral-aural community of the slave quarters," Douglass could not escape subjection to "the linguistic codes, literary conventions, and audience expectations" of white America. What his mastery of the art of rhetoric gave him—the power to fight slavery in the name of black selfhood—must therefore be balanced against what it demanded of him—a compromising of the "authenticity" of his own "prototypical black American self" as articulated and represented in his *Narrative*.

Much of the most important Douglass criticism of the 1980s debated the question implicitly posed by Baker: Does the *Narrative* signify Douglass's mastery of literary discourse—or its mastery of him? Most critics have argued that Douglass understood the pitfalls of the discursive conventions he followed as an autobiographer and that he found ingenious ways to subvert or revamp them to make them serve his individual literary and political purposes. This is the basic theme of Henry Louis Gates's "Binary Oppositions in Chapter One of *Narrative of the Life of Frederick Douglass*" and Robert B. Stepto's "Narration, Authentication, and Authorial Control in Frederick Douglass' *Narrative* of 1845."[26]

Gates begins with a discussion of the relationship of the *Narrative* to the European picaresque novel and sentimental fiction. He concludes that the *Narrative* is actually part of a "counter-genre"—the slave narrative—that should be interpreted as mediating between binary oppositions basic to antebellum American social structures and cultural values. In the first chapter of the *Narrative* Douglass acts as a kind of literary trickster, repeatedly reversing the hierarchies of nature and nurture, master and slave, human and animal that govern the worldview of the southern plantation. The art of the *Narrative* is in demonstrating that these oppositions, assumed by southern tradition to be fixed and natural, are merely man-made and arbitrary.

Stepto is also interested in the mediating function of the *Narrative*, though the tensions that he focuses on are an outgrowth of the relationship of Douglass's words to those of Garrison and Phillips, whose authenticating documents preface the *Narrative*. According to Stepto, Douglass fashioned his *Narrative* into genuine autobiography, in which his voice is dominant and sets the terms of the discourse among the documents that are published with it—an accomplishment that goes a long way toward distinguishing Douglass's from so many other slave narratives. The *Narrative* is thus a record of its author's triumphant achievement of the status of "articulate hero," who has won not only his physical freedom but also control over the text of his life. In a similar vein is Donald B. Gibson's "Reconciling Public and Private in Frederick Douglass's *Narrative*," which probes the tension between Douglass's personal and public agendas and the effect of this tension on his first autobiography. In the end of the *Narrative* Gibson finds a merging and reconciliation of the public and private dimensions of Douglass's identity, which anticipate his achievement of a similar balance in his narrating voice. Lucinda H. MacKethan's essay on Douglass's conversion of the slave narrator into a kind of "American poet," who "controls and orders national realities by his ability to name," is also linked to those studies that celebrate Douglass's *Narrative* as a sign of his mastery of the discourses of his era.[27]

The first critic to challenge this primarily celebratory view of Douglass the writer was Annette Niemtzow, whose feminist interrogation of the *Narrative* argues that the form and conventions of Anglo-American autobiography molded Douglass's into a black nineteenth-century version of Benjamin Franklin's success story. By the end of the *Narrative* Douglass the industrious worker, mesmerized by the wealth of New England and proudly displaying his marriage certificate, has met "the terms of the American male's dream in white, conventional limits—with a job and a wife." In two thoroughly documented essays, John Sekora concluded that the formal and ideological constraints built into the slave narrative itself prevented Douglass from writing autobiography per se and forced him to work "within the depersonalizing language of abolition." However, to Sekora, the *Narrative*'s adaptation to its generic and discursive circumstances is not fraught with such disappointing consequences as Niemtzow discovers. Following the example of Henry Louis Gates, Sekora stresses the *Narrative*'s masterful analysis and exposure of the inherent inadequacies of "the language of slavery." As a result, Douglass's slave narrative bears "a greater personal imprint, a wider historical compass, and a surer view of slavery than had ever been presented before."

Somewhere between Niemtzow's and Sekora's views of the *Narrative* is the conclusion of William L. Andrews in *To Tell a Free Story*. This work finds great rhetorical individuality in Douglass's portrayal of the brutal facts of slavery; but the author also believes that Douglass's freedom of expression was significantly hampered by the affiliation of his worldview with that of the American jeremiad. While agreeing with Gates that the *Narrative* demolishes the binary oppositions that maintained whites over blacks in the South, Andrews faults Douglass for trafficking in similar kinds of dualisms at the end of the *Narrative*, where he pictures New England as the antithesis of Baltimore, even though he knew from personal experience that racism united North and South in monolithic injustice. In a similar emphasis on the bifurcated discourse of the *Narrative*, Houston Baker's third major discussion of that text argues that "the tones of a Providentially oriented moral suasion eventually compete with the cadences of a secularly oriented economic voice" in Douglass's first autobiography. Revising the conclusion of *The Journey Back*, Baker concludes in *Blues, Ideology, and Afro-American Literature* that the more pronounced voice of the *Narrative* is not that of Christianized abolitionism but of an economic realism that adopts "a fully commercialized view of [Douglass's] situation" as a slave and freeman in capitalistic America. Thus Baker proposes in an ideological analysis of the *Narrative* a synthetic reading of the double-voiced character of that text that resolves some of the problems that are raised in *The Journey Back*.[28]

Interrogations of the *Narrative* in the 1980s have led some scholars to reinvestigate other important writing by Douglass to see whether the author found different ways of addressing the discursive problems that the *Narrative* posed for him. In "Storytelling in Early Afro-American Fiction: Frederick Douglass's 'The Heroic Slave,'" Robert Stepto suggests that writing his 1853 novella about a slave revolt constituted for Douglass a revision of his own 1845 autobiography as well as the first foray into fiction by an African-American writer. Through Stepto's formal analysis of *The Heroic Slave*, the embedded layers of storytelling and story-listening in that text display not only Douglass's literary art but also his answer to those white abolitionists who had called on him to tell his story but who were not willing to listen to it or him in an egalitarian and liberating manner. Building on this pioneering study of the literary self-consciousness exhibited in *The Heroic Slave*, William L. Andrews's "The Novelization of Voice in Early African American Narrative," a study of vocal experimentation in *The Heroic Slave* and in William Wells Brown's *Clotel*, suggests how Douglass's text problematizes the relationship of the factual and the fictive in order to empower this story as a novel, not as an autobiography. The recent publication of *The Heroic Slave* in *Three Classic African-American Novels*, edited by Andrews, places Douglass's novella in a context that should stimulate further research into this seminal African-American work of fiction.[29]

Eric Sundquist's "Frederick Douglass: Literacy and Paternalism" follows Stepto's lead in reading *The Heroic Slave* as a key to the evolution of Douglass's self-concept, but Sundquist's essay focuses on what *My Bondage and My Freedom* illustrates about Douglass's evolution as a writer and as an intellectual leader. In particular Sundquist is interested in the ways in which *My Bondage and My Freedom* registers a strategy of "self-fathering rebellion" on Douglass's part, which engages the ideology of the American Revolutionary fathers and the ideals of America's literary patriarch, Ralph Waldo Emerson, in order to inscribe an African-American significance onto them. Tracing this pattern through Douglass's second and third autobiographies, Sundquist finds in the black writer's ambivalence about Lincoln the climax of Douglass's oedipal struggle to fashion himself into a father, not a stepson, into a progenitor, not a product of "Romantic liberation" and "American freedom." Sundquist's suggestive and incisive examination of a leitmotif that knits together Douglass's three autobiographies is the most outstanding of several noteworthy studies in the 1980s. These efforts consider *My Bondage and My Freedom* as a text that represents Douglass's evolving and increasingly complex sense of self and literary mission, which makes the second autobiography different from but by no means inferior to the first. Thomas De Pietro's study of "Vision and Revision in the Autobiographies of Frederick Douglass" offers an evenhanded overview of the changing priorities that help to account for differing styles and emphases in Douglass's three narratives. William L. Andrews's analysis in *To Tell a Free Story* of *My Bondage and My Freedom* as a "culminating text" of the antebellum African-American autobiographical tradition argues that the narrative posture assumed in the second autobiography enabled Douglass to exploit his status as a marginalized figure in the 1850s. He thereby corrected some of the myths of himself that his *Narrative* generated, while also posing much more challenging questions about how he as a black freeman (no longer a fugitive slave) could both recover and invent a community for himself in and through his second autobiographical act. Drawing on his conclusions in *To Tell a Free Story,* Andrews's introduction to his annotated edition of *My Bondage and My Freedom* argues the importance of reading this work in the context of the so-called American Renaissance, in conjunction with and as an alternative to such canonical texts as Emerson's *Representative Men,* Fuller's *Woman in the Nineteenth Century,* and Thoreau's *Walden.*[30]

Criticism in the 1990s will undoubtedly continue to explore the breadth and depth of Douglass's writing in ways that will restore not only *My Bondage and My Freedom* and *The Heroic Slave* but also other key texts to their rightful place in the Douglass canon. But there is no danger of the *Narrative*'s suffering from critical neglect in the process. The three essays that conclude this volume, all of them published here for the first time, show that critics still have many unresolved questions about how this text works and to what effect. In particular, the problem summarized in Thad Ziolkowski's question—"What (if anything) is at stake in Douglass's use of hegemonic discourse as a mode of representation?"—may require much study among students of the *Narrative* before a consensus is reached.

Ziolkowski argues in "Antitheses: The Dialectic of Violence and Literacy in Frederick Douglass's *Narrative* of 1845," that what challenges Douglass is the problem of how to represent the full violence of slavery's reality while at the same time resisting the intellectual violation that comes from writing about that violence in the terms and postures of the dominant discourse, whether of the southern slaveocracy or the northern abolitionism. Ziolkowski notes several passages in the *Narrative,* particularly that in which Douglass describes the whipping of his Aunt Hester, that show the immensity of the distance that the mere act of writing could create between Douglass and the self in slavery that he wished to invoke. Yet through his experience of slavery Douglass learned key lessons in what Ziolkowski calls the "syntax of power," enforced through physical acts that climax in the well-known violent confrontation with Edward Covey. As a result, Douglass's recollection of his acquisition of the arts of language is steeped in a realization of the social and material origins and significance of that acquisition. This awareness enables Douglass to focus his discourse on the very questions of mediation and power—particularly as he comments on his reading of *The Columbian Orator*—that indicate his awareness of the dangers that his own literary art held in store for him.

Ann Kibbey and Michele Stepto also emphasize the language lessons that Douglass learned in slavery. Their essay on "The Antilanguage of Slavery" offers a detailed analysis of the ways in which referentiality is "fractured" in a master-slave economy. The result is not only the destruction of words' meaning but also the obliteration of the intersubjective relationship of speaker and hearer that is the social hallmark of linguistic communication. To Kibbey and Stepto, freedom entails not just the ability to break through the anti-language of slavery. Freedom for Douglass comes when he seizes the opportunity to address another for the purpose of establishing his own social reality. The process by which Douglass discovers how slavery denies him subjectivity—a sense of his uniquely human self expressed through language—opens out into a struggle to recover a liberating intersubjectivity, first with the slave community, then with the abolitionist community, and ultimately with the community of readers of the *Narrative* itself. Employing a Marxian analysis of the slave market as represented in the *Narrative*, Kibbey and Stepto identify the alienation from self and language as stemming from the marketplace and show how Douglass's awareness of the market's function in this regard helps to liberate him.

While Ziolkowski and Kibbey and Stepto stress Douglass's eventual liberation from the constraints of the discursive conventions in which he worked, Deborah McDowell raises serious doubts about Douglass's freedom from a gendered view of selfhood that privileges manhood at the expense of a nonobjectified view of women. McDowell's extensive feminist inquiry into the positioning of women in both the *Narrative* and *My Bondage and My Freedom* challenges not only the idea of Douglass's priority and predominance in the canon of nineteenth-century African-American literature, but also the very notion that some *one* writer, male or female, should be given this honorific status in contemporary criticism. McDowell's essay has a twin focus. She is interested in how Douglass's self-fashioning in his autobiographies made aggressive "manhood" identical with selfhood. She is just as interested in historicizing the process by which critics and literary historians have made Douglass into a "founding father" of African-American letters and a standard by which all other autobiographies by blacks might be measured. McDowell's analysis of the multiple strategies by which Douglass's equation of manhood and selfhood are effected (in the *Narrative* especially) ranges over many dimensions of his text. She moves from the voyeuristic way in which Douglass depicts the whipping of female slaves, to the gradual effacement of his mother in his three autobiographies, and leads finally to what McDowell calls "the thematics of literacy" in the first two autobiographies, in which the origins of Douglass the writer are traced back to his dependence on and affiliations with white male (southern and northern) models. To McDowell, even the critically celebrated struggles, both physical and literary, between Douglass and the likes of Covey and Garrison testify to an uncritical acceptance of an oedipal—and thus male-centered—model of intellectual and literary growth among African-American writers.

McDowell's call for another way of thinking about geneology in African-American letters—not a way that grants originary status to either male or female writers, but rather a way that focuses on the conditions that govern how and why writers are recovered and assigned prior status in literary history—concludes this collection of essays on a most appropriate note. If the study of Frederick Douglass can lead scholars beyond mere celebration of his literary achievement to a full, critical awareness of the cultural significance of the literary recognition chronicled and exemplified in this book, then

Douglass's importance to our understanding of American literary history, both in his time and ours, is assured.

Notes

1. Both Phillips's letter to Douglass and Garrison's comments on the narrative were reprinted in the original *Narrative* of 1845. See *Narrative of the Life of Frederick Douglass, An American Slave*, ed. Houston A. Baker (New York: Viking Penguin, 1982).

2. Fuller's untitled review of the *Narrative* is reprinted as the first review in this book. For excerpts from other reviews of the *Narrative*, see *Narrative of the Life of Frederick Douglass, An American Slave*, ed. Benjamin Quarles (Cambridge, Mass.: Belknap, 1960), xiv, and Marion Wilson Starling, *The Slave Narrative*, 2nd ed. (Washington, D.C.: Howard University Press, 1981), 251–54, 278.

3. Benjamin Quarles, ed., *Frederick Douglass* (Englewood Cliffs, N.J.: Prentice-Hall, 1968), 6.

4. See Peabody's "Narratives of Fugitive Slaves," reprinted in this book.

5. See David Bartlett, *Modern Agitators: or Pen Portraits of Living American Reformers* (New York: Miller, Orton & Mulligan, 1855), 45–46; Harriet Beecher Stowe, *Men of Our Time* (Hartford, Conn.: Hartford Publishing, 1868), 404; and William Wells Brown, *The Rising Son; or, The Antecedents and Advancement of the Colored Race* (Boston: A. G. Brown, 1874), 439.

6. Quarles, ed., *Narrative*, xiv.

7. The comments from the *New York Tribune* and the *Ohio State Journal* are taken from a list of excerpts from literary notices and reviews of *My Bondage and My Freedom* that appeared in *Frederick Douglass' Paper*, 1 February, 1856. The review in *Putnam's* is reprinted in this book as "The Life and Bondage of Frederick Douglass."

8. Howard Carroll, *Twelve Americans* (New York: Harper & Brothers, 1883), vii.

9. *Life and Times of Frederick Douglass* (Hartford, Conn.: Park, 1881).

10. *Life and Times of Frederick Douglass* (Boston: DeWolfe, Fiske, 1892).

11. Benjamin Quarles, *Frederick Douglass* (Washington, D.C.: Associated Publishers, 1948), 337.

12. "Frederick Douglass," *Critic*, 28 January 1882, 21 (reprinted in this book as "Review of *Life and Times of Frederick Douglass*"); *Independent*, 26 January 1893, 122; *Catholic World* 35 (1882), 287.

13. Frederick May Holland, *Frederick Douglass: The Colored Orator* (New York: Funk and Wagnalls, 1891); Helen Pitts Douglass, *In Memoriam: Frederick Douglass* (Philadelphia: J. C. Yorston, 1897); Charles W. Chesnutt, *Frederick Douglass* (Boston: Small, Maynard, 1899); Booker T. Washington, *Frederick Douglass* (Philadelphia: George W. Jacobs, 1907).

14. Kelly Miller, "Radicals and Conservatives," in *Race Adjustment* (New York: Neale Publishing, 1908), 11–27. A selection from this essay appears in this book.

15. Benjamin Brawley, *The Negro in Literature and Art in the United States* (New York: Duffield, 1930), 55–58, 62–63.

16. Vernon Loggins, *The Negro Author: His Development in America to 1900* (New York: Columbia University Press, 1931). Loggins's discussion of Douglass is reprinted in this book.

17. J. Saunders Redding, *To Make a Poet Black* (Chapel Hill: University of North Carolina Press, 1939), 30–38. *To Make a Poet Black* was reprinted, with an introduction by Henry Louis Gates, by the Cornell University Press in 1987.

18. Marion Wilson Starling, *The Slave Narrative: Its Place in American Literary History*, New York University dissertation, 1946 (published in 1981 by G. K. Hall of Boston and reprinted in 1988 by the Howard University Press); Charles H. Nichols, "Slave Narratives and

the Plantation Legend," *Phylon* 11 (1949), 201–10; Philip S. Foner, ed., *The Life and Writings of Frederick Douglass,* 4 vols. (New York: International Publishers, 1950–55) (a fifth volume was added in 1975); Charles H. Nichols, *Many Thousand Gone: The Ex-Slaves' Account of Their Bondage and Freedom* (Leiden: E. J. Brill, 1963). See finally, Benjamin Quarles, *"Narrative of the Life of Frederick Douglass",* in *Landmarks of American Writing,* ed. Hennig Cohen, (New York: Basic Books, 1969), 90–100.

19. See Patsy Brewington Perry's two important articles, "The Literary Content of *Frederick Douglass' Paper* through 1860," *CLA Journal* 17 (1973), 214–29 and "Before *The North Star:* Frederick Douglass' Early Literary Journalistic Career," *Phylon* 35 (1974), 96–107. Douglass's only known work of fiction, "The Heroic Slave" (1853), was introduced to contemporary readers in Ronald T. Takaki, ed., *Violence in the Black Imagination* (New York: Capricorn, 1972). In 1978 W. Burghardt Turner wrote the first bibliographical essay on Douglass, which appeared in M. Thomas Inge, et al., eds., *Black American Writers* (New York: St. Martin's Press, 1978), vol. 1, 58–72. In 1979 the Yale University Press published volume 1 of *The Frederick Douglass Papers,* under the general editorship of John Blassingame. This work is to be a comprehensive edition of all of Douglass's writings, to appear in three series: 1) Speeches, Debates, and Interviews; 2) Published Writings; and 3) Letters. To date, three volumes of series one have appeared.

20. William W. Nichols, "Individualism and Autobiographical Art: Frederick Douglass and Henry Thoreau," *CLA Journal* 16 (1972), 145–58; Nancy T. Clasby, "Frederick Douglass's 'Narrative': A Content Analysis," *CLA Journal* 14 (1971), 242–50; Jean Fagan Yellin, *The Intricate Knot: Black Figures in American Literature, 1776–1863* (New York: New York University Press, 1972), 160–67; Stephen Butterfield, *Black Autobiography in America* (Amherst: University of Massachusetts Press, 1973), 65–89.

21. Houston A. Baker, *Long Black Song* (Charlottesville: University Press of Virginia, 1973), 58–83.

22. H. Bruce Franklin, "Animal Farm Unbound: Or What the *Narrative of the Life of Frederick Douglass, an American Slave* Reveals about American Literature," *New Letters* 43 (1977), 25–46; G. Thomas Couser, *American Autobiography: The Prophetic Mode* (Amherst: University of Massachusetts Press, 1979); Robert G. O'Meally, "Frederick Douglass' 1845 *Narrative:* The Text Was Meant to be Preached," in *Afro-American Literature: The Reconstruction of Instruction,* ed. Dexter Fisher and Robert B. Stepto (New York: Modern Language Association, 1979), 192–211. For further information on religious influences on the *Narrative,* see Lisa Margaret Zeitz, "Biblical Allusion and Imagery in Frederick Douglass' *Narrative,"* *CLA Journal* 25 (1981), 56–64.

23. Albert E. Stone, "Identity and Art in Frederick Douglass's *Narrative,"* *CLA Journal* 17 (1973), 192–213. This essay is reprinted in this volume.

24. Dickson J. Preston, *Young Frederick Douglass: The Maryland Years* (Baltimore: Johns Hopkins University Press, 1980); Peter Walker, "Frederick Douglass: Orphan Slave," in his *Moral Choices: Memory, Desire, and Imagination in Nineteenth-Century American Abolition* (Baton Rouge: Louisiana State University Press, 1978); Henry Louis Gates, "Frederick Douglass and the Language of the Self," *Yale Review* 71 (1981), 592–611. Another important biographical study of Douglass that bears indirectly on his literary significance is Waldo E. Martin, *The Mind of Frederick Douglass* (Chapel Hill: University of North Carolina Press, 1984).

25. Houston A. Baker, *The Journey Back* (Chicago: University of Chicago Press, 1980).

26. The essays by Stepto and Gates appear in Dexter Fisher and Robert B. Stepto, ed., *Afro-American Literature,* 178–91 and 212–32, respectively. The Gates article is reprinted in this book.

27. Donald B. Gibson, "Reconciling Public and Private in Frederick Douglass' *Narrative,"* *American Literature* 57 (1985), 551–69; Lucinda H. MacKethan, "From Fugitive Slave to Man of Letters: The Conversion of Frederick Douglass," *Journal of Narrative Technique* 16 (1986), 55–71. See also James Olney, "The Founding Fathers—Frederick Douglass and Booker T.

Washington," in *Slavery and the Literary Imagination,* ed. Deborah E. McDowell and Arnold Rampersad (Baltimore: Johns Hopkins University Press, 1989), 1–24, which proposes a tension between the *Narrative*'s allegiance to both a Franklinesque and a Jeffersonian tradition in American autobiography.

28. Annette Niemtzow, "The Problematic of Self in Autobiography: The Example of the Slave Narrative," in *The Art of Slave Narrative,* ed. John Sekora and Darwin T. Turner (Macomb: Western Illinois University, 1982), 96–109; John Sekora, "The Dilemma of Frederick Douglass: The Slave Narrative as Literary Institution," *Essays in Literature* 10 (1983), 219–26, and "Comprehending Slavery: Language and Personal History in Douglass' *Narrative* of 1845," *CLA Journal* 29 (1985), 157–70; William L. Andrews, *To Tell a Free Story: The First Century of Afro-American Autobiography, 1760–1865* (Urbana: University of Illinois Press, 1986), 123–38; and Houston A. Baker, *Blues, Ideology, and Afro-American Literature* (Chicago: University of Chicago Press, 1984), 43–49.

29. Robert B. Stepto, "Storytelling in Early Afro-American Fiction: Frederick Douglass's 'The Heroic Slave,'" *Georgia Review* 36 (1982), 355–68 (reprinted in this book). See also Andrews "The Novelization of Voice in Early African American Fiction," *PMLA* 105 (1990), 23–34, and Andrews, ed., *Three Classic African-American Novels* (New York: New American Library, 1990).

30. Eric J. Sundquist, "Frederick Douglass: Literacy and Paternalism," *Raritan* 6 (1986), 108–24 (reprinted in this volume); Thomas De Pietro, "Vision and Revision in the Autobiographies of Frederick Douglass," *CLA Journal* 26 (1983), 384–96; Andrews, *To Tell a Free Story,* 214–39; and *My Bondage and My Freedom,* ed. William L. Andrews (Urbana: University of Illinois Press, 1987), xi–xxviii. See also Sundquist, ed., *Frederick Douglass: New Literary and Historical Essays,* forthcoming from Cambridge University Press.

REVIEWS

◆

[Review of *Narrative of the Life of Frederick Douglass, an American Slave*]

Margaret Fuller

Frederick Douglass has been for some time a prominent member of the Abolition party. He is said to be an excellent speaker—can speak from a thorough personal experience—and has upon the audience, beside, the influence of a strong character and uncommon talents. In the book before us he has put into the story of his life the thoughts, the feelings, and the adventures that have been so affecting through the living voice; nor are they less so from the printed page. He has had the courage to name the persons, times and places, thus exposing himself to obvious danger, and setting the seal on his deep convictions as to the religious need of speaking the whole truth. Considered merely as a narrative, we have never read one more simple, true, coherent, and warm with genuine feeling. It is an excellent piece of writing, and on that score to be prized as a specimen of the powers of the Black Race, which Prejudice persists in disputing. We prize highly all evidence of this kind, and it is becoming more abundant. The Cross of the Legion of Honor has just been conferred in France on Dumas and Soulie, both celebrated in the paths of light and literature. Dumas, whose father was a General in the French Army, is a Mulatto; Soulie, a Quadroon. He went from New Orleans, where, though to the eye a white man, yet as known to have African blood in his veins, he could never have enjoyed the privileges due to a human being. Leaving the Land of Freedom, he found himself free to develop the powers that God had given.

Two wise and candid thinkers,—the Scotchman, Kinment, prematurely lost to this country, of which he was so faithful and generous a student, and the late Dr. Channing,—both thought that the African Race had in them a peculiar element, which, if it could be assimilated with those imported among us from Europe would give to genius a development, and to the energies of character a balance and harmony beyond what has been seen heretofore in the history of the world. Such an element is indicated in their lowest estate by a

Reprinted from the *New York Tribune*, 10 June, 1845, 2.

talent for melody, a ready skill at imitation and adaptation, an almost indestructible elasticity of nature. It is to be remarked in the writings both of Soulie and Dumas, full of faults but glowing with plastic life and fertile in invention. The same torrid energy and saccharine fulness may be felt in the writings of this Douglass, though his life being one of action or resistance, was less favorable to SUCH powers than one of a more joyous flow might have been.

The book is prefaced by two communications—one from Garrison and one from Wendell Phillips. That from the former is in his usual over-emphatic style. His motives and his course have been noble and generous. We look upon him with high respect, but he has indulged in violent invective and denunciation till he has spoiled the temper of his mind. Like a man who has been in the habit of screaming himself hoarse to make the deaf better, he can no longer pitch his voice on a key agreeable to common ears. Mr. Phillips's remarks are equally decided, without this exaggeration in the tone. Douglass himself seems very just and temperate. We feel that his view, even of those who have injured him most, may be relied upon. He knows how to allow for motives and influences. Upon the subject of Religion, he speaks with great force, and not more than our own sympathies can respond to. The inconsistencies of Slaveholding professors of religion cry to Heaven. We are not disposed to detest, or refuse communion with them. Their blindness is but one form of that prevalent fallacy which substitutes a creed for a faith, a ritual for a life. We have seen too much of this system of atonement not to know that those who adopt it often began with good intentions, and are, at any rate, in their mistakes worthy of the deepest pity. But that is no reason why the truth should not be uttered, trumpet-tongued, about the thing. "Bring no more vain oblations": sermons must daily be preached anew on that text. Kings, five hundred years ago, built churches with the spoils of war; Clergymen to-day command Slaves to obey a Gospel which they will not allow them to read, and call themselves Christians amid the curses of their fellow men. The world ought to get on a little faster than that, if there be really any principle of movement in it. The Kingdom of Heaven may not at the beginning have dropped seed larger than a mustard seed, but even from that we had a right to expect a fuller growth than can be believed to exist, when we read such a book as this of Douglass. Unspeakably affecting is the fact that he never saw his mother at all by day light. "I do not recollect of ever seeing my mother by the light of day. She was with me in the night. She would lie down with me, and get me to sleep, but long before I waked she was gone."

The following extract presents a suitable answer to the background argument drawn by the defender of Slavery from the songs of the Slave, and it is also a good specimen of the powers of observation and manly heart of the writer. We wish that every one may read his book and see what a mind might have been stifled in bondage—what a man may be subjected to the insults of spendthrift dandies, or the blows of mercenary brutes, in whom there is no whiteness except of the skin, no humanity except in the outward form, and of whom the Avenger will not fail yet to demand—"where is thy brother?"[1]

Note

1. This review concludes by quoting the last four paragraphs of chapter 2 of the *Narrative*. [Ed.]

Narratives of Fugitive Slaves

EPHRAIM PEABODY

America has the mournful honor of adding a new department to the literature of civilization,—the autobiographies of escaped slaves. . . . The subjects of two of these narratives, Frederick Douglass and Josiah Henson,[1] we have known personally, and, apart from the internal evidence of truth which their stories afford, we have every reason to put confidence in them as men of veracity. The authors of the remaining accounts are, for anything we know to the contrary, equally trustworthy. We place these volumes without hesitation among the most remarkable productions of the age,—remarkable as being pictures of slavery by the slave, remarkable as disclosing under a new light the mixed elements of American civilization, and not less remarkable as a vivid exhibition of the force and working of the native love of freedom in the individual mind.

There are those who fear lest the elements of poetry and romance should fade out of the tame and monotonous social life of modern times. There is no danger of it while there are any slaves left to seek for freedom, and to tell the story of their efforts to obtain it. There is that in the lives of men who have sufficient force of mind and heart to enable them to struggle up from hopeless bondage to the position of freemen, beside which the ordinary characters of romance are dull and tame. They encounter a whole Iliad of woes, not in plundering and enslaving others, but in recovering for themselves those rights of which they have been deprived from birth. Or if the Iliad should be thought not to present a parallel case, we know not where one who wished to write a modern Odyssey could find a better subject than in the adventures of a fugitive slave. What a combination of qualities and deeds and sufferings most fitted to attract human sympathy in each particular case! . . .

These biographies of fugitive slaves are calculated to exert a very wide influence on public opinion. We have always been familiar with slavery, as seen from the side of the master. These narratives show how it looks as seen from the side of the slave. They contain the *victim's account* of the working of this great institution. When one escapes from the South, and finds an opportunity of speaking and has the power to speak, it is certain that he will have attentive listeners. Not only curiosity, but a sense of justice, predisposes men to hear the

Reprinted from *Christian Examiner* 47 (July 1849): 61–93.

testimony given by those who have suffered, and who have had few among their own number to describe their sufferings. The extent of the influence such lives must exert may be judged of, when we learn the immense circulation which has been secured for them. Of Brown's Narrative, first published in 1847, not less than eight thousand copies have been already sold.[2] Douglass's Life, first published in 1845, has in this country alone passed through seven editions, and is, we are told, now out of print. They are scattered over the whole of the North, and all theoretical arguments for or against slavery are feeble, compared with these accounts by living men of what they personally endured when under its dominion. . . .

The narrative of Douglass contains the life of a superior man. Since his escape from slavery, he has been employed as an antislavery lecturer, and is now the editor of a newspaper in Rochester, N.Y. He does not belong to the class, always small, of those who bring to light great principles, or who originate new methods of carrying them out. He has, however, the vividness of sensibility and of thought which we are accustomed to associate with a Southern climate. He has a natural and ready eloquence, a delicacy of taste, a quick perception of proprieties, a quick apprehension of ideas, and a felicity of expression, which are possessed by few among the more cultivated, and which are surprising when we consider that it is but a few years since he was a slave. In any popular assembly met for the discussion of subjects with which he has had the opportunity to become familiar, he is a man to command and hold attention. He is a natural orator, and his original endowments and the peculiarity of his position have given him a high place among antislavery speakers.

But while our sympathies go strongly with him, and because they go with him, we are disposed to make a criticism on a mode of address in which he sometimes indulges himself, which we believe is likely to diminish, not only his usefulness, but his real influence. We would not detract from his merits, and we can easily excuse in him a severity of judgment and a one-sidedness of view which might be inexcusable in another. We can hardly condemn one who has been a slave for seeing only the evils of slavery, and for thinking lightly of the difficulty of remedying them; but we have wished, when we have heard him speak, or read what he has written, that he might wholly avoid a fault from which a natural magnanimity does something towards saving him, but to which he is nevertheless exposed. His associates at the North have been among those who are apt to mistake violence and extravagance of expression and denunciation for eloquence;—men who, whatever their virtues otherwise, are not in the habit of using discrimination to their judgments of men or of measures which they do not approve. To him they have doubtless been true and faithful friends, and he naturally adopts their style of speech. But it is a mistaken one, if the speaker wishes to sway the judgment of his hearers and to accomplish any practical end. No matter what the vehemence of tone or expression, whenever a public speaker indulges himself in violent and unqualified statements and in sweeping denunciations, he not only makes it apparent that he is deficient in a sound and fair judgment, but what is worse, he creates in his hearers a secret distrust of his real earnestness,—a vague feeling that after all he is thinking more of his speech than of the end for which he professes to make it. When men are profoundly in earnest, they are not apt to be extravagant. The more earnest, the more rigidly true. A merchant, in discussing the politics of the day, about which he knows or cares little, freely indulges in loose, extravagant, and violent declarations. But follow him to his counting-room; let him be making inquiries or giving directions about some enterprise which he really has deeply at heart, and the extravagance is gone. Nothing will answer here but truth, and the exact truth. His earnestness makes him calm. It is seen in the moderated accuracy, as well as in the decision and strength, of his statements. Extravagance and passion and rhetorical flourishes might do when nothing which he greatly valued was at stake; but here is something too serious for trifling. Just so it is in other cases. A flippant, extravagant speaker, especially if he be gifted with the power of sarcasm, will probably be listened to and applauded, but nothing comes of it. They who applaud the most understand very well that this is not the kind of person whose judgment is to be relied on as a guide in action. His words are listened to with much the same sort of interest that is given to the personated passion of the theatre. A few sober words from a calm, wise, discriminating mind are, after all, the ones which are followed. Nothing is less effective, for any practical end, than the "withering and scorching" eloquence with which American speeches seem so to abound. It conciliates no opponent, and though it may light up the momentary passions, it gives no new strength of conviction to the friends of a cause. It is the last kind of eloquence to be cultivated by those who are heartily in earnest in their desire to promote any great reform.

We by no means think that these remarks apply peculiarly to Douglass. We make them, however, because we think that, more often than he is probably aware, he suffers himself to fall into this mode of speech. He has such ability to appeal to the higher and more generous sentiments, and such appeals do so much to win over enemies and to strengthen friends, he has such personal knowledge of slavery, and is so competent to make all he says effective, through candor and a just appreciation of the difficulties that beset the subject of emancipation, and is withal so much of a man, that we regret any mistake of judgment which tends to diminish his power as an advocate of the antislavery cause.[3] . . .

There are many passages in the narrative of Douglass which we should be pleased to quote, but it has been so long published and so widely circulated, that many of our readers have probably seen it. We would only say, in conclusion, that we feel a deep interest in his career. He is one of the living evidences that there is in the colored population of the South no natural incapacity for the enjoyment of freedom; and he occupies a position and possesses abilities which enable him, if he pursues a wise course, to be a most useful laborer in the cause of human rights.

Notes

1. In addition to Douglass's *Narrative,* Peabody refers to *The Life of Josiah Henson,* ed. Samuel A. Eliot (Boston: A. D. Phelps, 1849). [Ed.]

2. William Wells Brown, *Narrative of William W. Brown, a Fugitive Slave. Written by Himself* (Boston: American Anti-Slavery Society, 1847). [Ed.]

3. We have hesitated about making these remarks; and now, on reading them over, the sympathy which his narrative excites, and our respect for the force of character he has shown in rising from the depths of bondage to be equal associate of those who have possessed every opportunity of cultivation and refinement, almost make us erase what we have written. We would avoid giving pain to one who has suffered all that we should most dread ourselves, and who has risen above obstacles by which we should probably have been crushed. But still, whatever the past has been, he is now free. By his indisputable deserts, he has secured for himself an influential position. The course which he takes is important to others beside himself. Should he read this criticism, we hope that the internal evidence will be sufficient to show that it is written by one who rejoices in his usefulness. And in the faith that he may so read it, and that its suggestions may not be without value, we allow it to stand.

The Life and Bondage of Frederick Douglass [Review of *My Bondage and My Freedom*]

Anonymous

A third biography before us furnishes a still further contrast—the *Life and Bondage* of Frederick Douglass, the well-known fugitive slave, who has come to occupy so conspicuous a position, both as a writer and speaker. It details the incidents of his experience on the slave plantation of Maryland, where he was born, of his subsequent escape, and of his public career in England and the northern States. We need hardly say that it abounds in interest. The mere fact that the member of an outcast and enslaved race should accomplish his freedom, and educate himself up to an equality of intellectual and moral vigor with the leaders of the race by which he was held in bondage, is, in itself, so remarkable, that the story of the change cannot be otherwise than exciting. For ourselves, we confess to have read it with the unbroken attention with which we absorbed *Uncle Tom's Cabin*. It has the advantage of the latter book in that it is no fiction. Of course, it is impossible to say how far the author's prejudices, and remembrances of wrong, may have deepened the color of his pictures, but the general tone of them is truthful. He writes bitterly, as we might expect of one who writes under a personal provocation, taking incidents of individual experience for essential characteristics, but not more bitterly than the circumstances seem to justify. His denunciations of slavery and slaveholders are not indiscriminate, while he wars upon the system rather than upon the persons whom that system has made. In the details of his early life upon the plantation, of his youthful thoughts on life and destiny, and of the means by which he gradually worked his way to freedom, there is much that is profoundly touching. Our English literature has recorded many an example of genius struggling against adversity, of the poor Ferguson, for instance, making himself an astronomer, of Burns becoming a poet, of Hugh Miller finding his geology in a stone quarry, and a thousand similar cases—yet none of these are so impressive as the case of the solitary slave, in a remote district, surrounded by

Reprinted from *Putnam's Monthly* 6 (November 1855), 547.

none but enemies, conceiving the project of his escape, teaching himself to read and write to facilitate it, accomplishing it at last, and subsequently raising himself to a leadership in a great movement in behalf of his brethren. Whatever may be our opinions of slavery, or the best means of acting upon it, we cannot but admire the force and integrity of character which has enabled Frederick Douglass to attain his present unique position.

[Review of *Life and Times of Frederick Douglass*]

ANONYMOUS

An autobiography published in the lifetime of the author is rare enough to be remarked upon. Ordinarily men do not care to put themselves in a position where they will certainly be compelled to listen to a good deal of comment delivered with perfect freedom, possibly not tempered with good nature—to a good deal of criticism sure to be searching and not unlikely to be severe. An author may, like George Eliot, read or not, as he pleases, the reviews of his books on any other subject than his own life; but reviews of that, if he be in the flesh, he must read, whether he likes it or not, for they may require replies which the public, as well as his own reputation, has a right to demand. Here is reason enough why a man should wait till there is five feet of good solid earth over him before he provokes the world to talk about him by taking it into his confidence. The work before us is not indeed very likely to give rise to controversies, because, from the nature of the case, great allowances will be made, and provocations will be generally met, perhaps, with a good-natured "It is not worthwhile." But this, probably, did not occur to Mr. Douglass; and while his readers will be amused at his natural and almost child-like self-complacency, they will not fail to admire, often, his frankness and boldness.

Ordinary rules cannot properly be applied to the biography of such a man, written by himself and published in his life-time. The world may be glad that he can write his life at all, and quite content to receive it when it suits him, whether before his death or afterward. As his career is unparalleled, so his character is not to be measured in precisely the way that the characters of other men are measured. A man who was born a slave; who never had an acknowledged father; who only at rare intervals was permitted to see his mother; whose childhood was more desolate than nature dares allot to the young of any wild animal; whose youth was a period of almost unspeakable misfortune, of hunger, and cold, and nakedness, of scourgings, of beatings well nigh unto death, and of a despair to which death would have come as a mercy;—but a man over whose life, when manhood was reached, came a

Reprinted from *Critic*, 28 January 1882, 21.

marvellous change; who rose presently to be an orator so gifted that even enemies listened with delight; who came to have his share, neither obscure nor unimportant, in a great social movement which only the greatest civil war the world has ever known could bring to an end; and who came, at length, before he was an old man, to fill offices of dignity and trust in the capital of his country;—the story of the career of such a man as this may be written when and how he pleases, and the world may accept it without carping and without criticism, and be glad to get it. If free thought and free speech are not mere phrases and really belong to any body, they belong to Frederick Douglass. They are not denied in fable even to the beasts; surely a slave may earn them beyond all challenge if he achieves such a life as this one made for himself. Had he been of another complexion, the ages would count him among their heroes. Perhaps they will yet.

It is a pity that a work so unique, so altogether different from anything in autobiographical literature, has so poor a setting. It is not absolutely bad in type and paper; but in its binding, its scant margins, its press-work, and its illustrations it could hardly be worse. One must have a cultivated imagination to suppose that the impression on the cover is meant for the Goddess of Liberty and the American eagle, and not for a young woman preparing a dish of corn-meal and water for a large and evidently hungry spring-chicken. The illustrations within the covers are of that style of art belonging to the dime novel, suggesting to one who may casually open it that the book had better not be read, or, if read, cannot possibly be true. Had they been omitted altogether—excepting the portrait of Douglass, as a frontispiece—the book would have been attractive enough if left solely to the merit of the narrative.

ARTICLES AND ESSAYS

◆

Radicals and Conservatives

KELLY MILLER

When a distinguished Russian was informed that some American Negroes are radical and some conservative, he could not restrain his laughter. The idea of conservative Negroes was more than the Cossack's risibilities could endure. "What on earth," he exclaimed with astonishment, "have they to conserve?"

According to a strict use of terms, a "conservative" is one who is satisfied with existing conditions and advocates their continuance; while a "radical" clamors for amelioration of conditions through change. No thoughtful Negro is satisfied with the present status of his race, whether viewed in its political, its civil or general aspect. He labors under an unfriendly public opinion, one which is being rapidly crystallized into a rigid caste system and enacted into unrighteous law. How can he be expected to contemplate such oppressive conditions with satisfaction and composure? Circumstances render it imperative that his attitude should be dissentient rather than conformatory. Every consideration of enlightened self-respect impels him to unremitting protest, albeit the manner of protestation may be mild or pronounced, according to the dictates of prudence. Radical and conservative Negroes agree as to the end in view, but differ as to the most effective means of attaining it. The difference is not essentially one of principle or purpose, but point of view. All anti-slavery advocates desired the downfall of the iniquitous institution, but some were more violent than others in the expression of this desire. Disagreement as to method led to personal estrangement, impugnment of motive, and unseemly factional wrangle. And so, colored men who are alike zealous for the betterment of their race, lose half their strength in internal strife, because of variant methods of attack upon the citadel of prejudice.

. . . .

The radical and conservative tendencies of the Negro race cannot be better described than by comparing, or rather contrasting, the two superlative colored men in whom we find their highest embodiment—Frederick Douglass and Booker Washington, who were both picked out and exploited by white men as the mouthpiece and intermediaries of the black race. The two men are in part

Reprinted from Kelly Miller, *Race Adjustment* (New York: Neale Publishing, 1908), 11–12, 17–18.

products of their times, but are also natural antipodes. Douglass lived in the day of moral giants; Washington lives in the era of merchant princes. The contemporaries of Douglass emphasized the rights of man; those of Washington, his productive capacity. The age of Douglass acknowledged the sanction of the Golden Rule; that of Washington worships the Rule of *Gold*. The equality of men was constantly dinned into Douglass's ears; Washington hears nothing but the inferiority of the Negro and the dominance of the Saxon. Douglass could hardly receive a hearing today; Washington would have been hooted off the stage a generation ago. Thus all truly useful men must be, in a measure, time-servers; for unless they serve their time, they can scarcely serve at all. But great as was the diversity of formative influences that shaped these two great lives, there is no less opposability in their innate bias of character. Douglass was like a lion, bold and fearless; Washington is lamblike, meek and submissive. Douglass escaped from personal bondage, which his soul abhorred; but for Lincoln's proclamation, Washington would probably have arisen to esteem and favor in the eyes of his master as a good and faithful servant. Douglass insisted upon rights; Washington insists upon duty. Douglass held up to public scorn the sins of the white man; Washington portrays the faults of his own race. Douglass spoke what he thought the world should hear; Washington speaks only what he feels it is disposed to listen to. Douglass's conduct was actuated by principle; Washington's by prudence. Douglass had no limited, copyrighted programme for his race, but appealed to the Decalogue, the Golden Rule, the Declaration of Independence, the Constitution of the United States; Washington, holding these great principles in the shadowy background, presents a practical expedient applicable to present needs. Douglass was a moralist, insisting upon the application of righteousness to public affairs; Washington is a practical opportunist, accepting the best terms which he thinks it possible to secure.

Writings of the Leading Negro Antislavery Agents, 1840–1865

VERNON LOGGINS

Die on the field of battle,
Die on the field of battle,
    Glory to my soul!
Oh, I'm going to glory,—won't you come along with me?
Don't you see the angels beck'ning, and calling me away?
Don't you see the golden city and the everlasting day?
    O, Canaan, bright Canaan,
    I'm bound for the land of Canaan!

—Quoted in Harriet Beecher Stowe's
Uncle Tom's Cabin, 1852

By 1840, the movement for the abolition of slavery was being felt in every section of the United States. The mightiest struggle in American history was definitely begun, not to end until the slave was completely emancipated. The main thought of the age, becoming more and more fermented as the crisis of the Civil War was approached, centered about one subject—the destiny of the Negro. Under whatever disguises the great controversial issues of the day appeared before the public, whether they were social, political, economic, or religious, the place of the blacks in American life was usually the real theme of dissension.

The Negro was by no means passive in the stormy conflict which was waged about him. A chief among the Abolitionists, John G. Whittier, wrote in 1847:

With such examples of the intellectual capacity of the colored man as are afforded by L'Ouverture and Petion of Hayti; Dumas, of France; Pushkin of Russia; and Placido, the slave poet and martyr of Cuba, to say nothing of such men as James McCune Smith, Frederick Douglass, Henry H. Garnet, and Henry Bibb, in our own country, it is scarcely in good taste for white mediocrity to taunt

Reprinted by permission from Vernon Loggins, *The Negro Author: His Development in America* (New York: Columbia University Press, 1931), 127–132, 134–156.

the colored man with natural inferiority. Do not Toussaint's deeds for freedom, and Pushkin's songs of a great nation, waken within all hearts the sympathies of a common nature?

"There spoke our brother! Then our father's grave
        Did utter such a voice!"

In the colored man's follies and crimes, his loves and hatreds, his virtues and weaknesses, we but recognize our common humanity, and realize the truth of the inspired apostle's language—"God hath made of one blood all the generations of men."[1]

Working for the widespread recognition of the principle so voiced by Whittier formed one of the most important divisions of antislavery agitation. The Abolitionists were ever on the alert for the discovery of the Negro of extraordinary promise; and when he was found, he came under their encouragement and tutelage. Thus championed, the African race in the United States during the twenty years prior to the Civil War progressed with gigantic strides.

The attempt to provide the higher education necessary for the Negro leader occasioned one of the most extended and dramatic fights which the Abolitionists had to engage in, a fight marked with strange paradoxes. In 1833, Prudence Crandall was arrested for conducting an academy for colored girls in Canterbury, Connecticut; in the same year, Oberlin College was founded in Ohio as an institution admitting students of all colors on equal terms. In 1839, the Noyes Academy, at Canaan, New Hampshire, at which a number of colored boys were in attendance, was broken up by mob violence. The main building was wheeled away and dumped into a swamp, and the Negro students were given a limited time in which to get out of the town.[2] A number of them immediately repaired to the Oneida Institute, at Whitesboro, New York, a newly founded college under the control of Beriah Green, a celebrated Abolitionist who tolerated no distinctions because of color. Central College, located at McGrawville, New York, an institution of like character, employed during the late forties and early fifties at least three Negro professors—Charles L. Reason, George B. Vashon, and William G. Allen.[3] In 1841, Thomas Paul, a Negro, was graduated from Dartmouth.[4] Martin R. Delany, also colored, was accepted as a medical student at Harvard in 1851, after having been refused admission at the University of Pennsylvania, Jefferson College, and the medical schools at Albany and Geneva, New York.[5] Negroes in some way succeeded in being admitted into other leading colleges.[6] Yet Edward W. Blyden, perhaps the most distinguished of the Negroes who emigrated to Liberia, could not find a creditable college which would receive him as a student when, in 1850, he came to this country from his native home in St. Thomas, West Indies, in order to procure an education. Nineteen years later the honorary degree of Master of Arts was conferred on him by Lafayette College in recognition of his missionary and educational work in Africa.[7] According to a tradition, James W. C.

Pennington, one of the most noted of the colored preachers of the day, honored with the degree of Doctor of Divinity by the University of Heidelberg while he was still legally a slave, was refused admission as a regular student at Yale but was not interfered with when he stood outside the doors of class rooms in order to hear professors' lectures.[8]

Few of the prominent Negroes of the period were college-trained. The antislavery conflict, stirring up in its intensity the greatest extremes of sympathy and hatred for the colored race, provided in itself an education for the Negro. That he was insulted and buffeted by one element of the white public meant that there was another into whose companionship he was all the more freely and readily admitted. Frederick Douglass was extremely illiterate when he began his work for the abolition cause; but after a few years of close association with such Americans as William Lloyd Garrison, Wendell Phillips, and Theodore Parker, and with such Englishmen as George Thompson and Douglas Jerrold, he was developed into an exceptional orator, writer, and editor. When he took up his residence in Rochester late in 1847, he was held as a pariah by his fellow townsmen; but it has been said that such an American as James Russell Lowell never passed through the city without staying long enough to pay him a visit.[9] Because he was a Negro, Samuel Ringgold Ward was not permitted to take his meals in the public dining saloon of the Cunard vessel on which he crossed to England in 1853; but, as he tells us in his autobiography, the most distinguished passenger on board the ship, William Makepeace Thackeray, called on him each day for a conversation.[10] The Reverend James W. C. Pennington, although the holder of an honorary degree from one of the oldest and strongest of German universities, was forced to discharge his pastoral duties by walking over the great distances of New York City because colored people were not allowed to ride in public conveyances.[11]

The Negro was contending with such abuses as had never before been measured out to him, and at the same time he was receiving such support as he had never been privileged to enjoy. He fought the abuses, and he thrived on the support. In 1860, the colored population of the entire country was 4,441,830, of which the small minority of 438,970 was counted as free. The Negroes of the North, the only ones for whom abolition intervention could be of direct cultural benefit, were estimated at 225,274.[12] Included in this number were lawyers, physicians, politicians, officeholders, preachers, inventors, educators, manufacturers, and men holding responsible positions in business.[13] Few activities, not excepting the arts of music, sculpture, painting, engraving, and acting, were unengaged in by the Negro during the stirring years when his presence in the United States was considered the gravest of the country's problems.[14] He left few fields of literature unattempted. Among his publications we find newspapers and magazines conducted under his own editorship, letters and articles contributed to periodicals controlled by whites, speeches printed as pamphlets and reported phonographically for the antislavery and general press, sociological treatises, histories, books of travel and exploration, biography, literary criticism, the informal essay, poetry, the novel, the short story, and the drama.

Of the Negroes who tried authorship, none had such excellent opportunities as those employed as antislavery agents. The plan of operations decided upon by the American Anti-Slavery Society at its first convention, held in 1833, called for the engagement of agents to be sent far and wide for the purpose of lecturing, scattering tracts and pamphlets, receiving subscriptions for the antislavery newspapers, and spreading abolition propaganda in every way possible.[15] Such a plan was adopted later by other abolition organizations. The psychological effect upon the public of the Negro as an antislavery agent was soon recognized. By 1838, Charles Lenox Remond, a Massachusetts Negro, had begun his long career as an abolition agent for various New England societies.[16] In 1839, Samuel Ringgold Ward, born a slave in Maryland, became an agent for the American Anti-Slavery Society.[17] The number of Negroes so employed after 1840 grew in leaps and bounds. Fugitives from the South were especially in demand. Some when inducted into the abolition service could do no more than stand before an audience and relate the story of their experiences in slavery. Others, including both fugitives and northern Negroes born free, came to be classed with the foremost Abolitionists. The most distinguished, and the most valuable in their services to Negro literature, were Charles Lenox Remond, Frederick Douglass, William Wells Brown, and Samuel Ringgold Ward. In the battle for abolition all four stood as worthy and willing lieutenants for such generals with opposing views as William Lloyd Garrison and Gerrit Smith. All four began their work as lecturers. But, encouraged in every possible way by their sponsors, they soon learned to write their messages, to bring them before the public often in a most interesting and entertaining form.

. . . .

When he was on a lecture tour in the state of New York in 1843, Remond was accompanied by the Hutchinsons, the celebrated abolition singers, and by Frederick Douglass, who five years before had been a slave on a Maryland plantation.[18] The Hutchinsons were along to arouse audiences to tears by singing sentimental abolition verses, and Douglass was there for no other purpose than to relate the story of his experiences as a bondman. At that time his friends and promoters were not willing to allow him to attempt more on the abolition platform.[19] But within a few years the whole world knew that in Frederick Douglass the abolition cause had found the ideal orator, a fugitive able to describe with the most realistic detail the life of the Negro in slavery, and at the same time a speaker who could demand respect from any audience, not by the display of himself on the platform as a runaway black, but by the clean logic and intellectual vigor of his message. Remond's greatest service for abolition was in preparing the American and English public for Douglass.

Frederick Douglass was much more than an antislavery orator. He has been frequently called, no doubt with justice, the greatest of American Negroes. Certainly, no other American Negro has achieved such a high degree of success in so many fields of endeavor. And few Americans, white or colored, have exhibited such courage and common sense in living a life marked with the most phenomenal evolution. William Lloyd Garrison wrote as follows of his discovery of Douglass at a general antislavery meeting held at Nantucket in 1841:

> I shall never forget his speech at the convention—the extraordinary emotion it excited in my own mind—the powerful emotion it created upon a crowded auditory, completely taken by surprise. . . . There stood one in physical proportion and stature commanding and exact—in intellect richly endowed—in natural eloquence a prodigy—in soul manifestly "created but a little lower than the angels"—yet a slave, ay, a fugitive slave, trembling for his safety, hardly daring to believe that on American soil, a single white person could be found who would befriend him at all hazards, for the love of God and humanity.[20]

Before this time, Frederick Douglass had been for twenty-one years a slave in Maryland and then for three years a laborer in New Bedford, Massachusetts. During most of his time in bondage he had experienced the severest hardships; but he had been fortunate enough to serve for short periods in Baltimore, where he had at least learned to read and to write. As a fugitive living in New Bedford, he became acquainted with the significance of the abolition movement. But it was not until he met Garrison, who immediately employed him as an antislavery agent, that his serious training in the abolition school began. His rapid progress proved his genius, a sureness and quickness of mentality, which he was always gallant enough to regard as an inheritance from his African mother instead of from his never identified white father.[21]

For four years, from 1841 to 1845, Douglass was directly under Garrison's guidance, travelling extensively as an anti-slavery agent, repeating the story of his bondage before hundreds of audiences. From 1845 until 1847, he lectured in Great Britain; and, inspired by the broader and more practical views of the English Abolitionists, he grew in self-reliant thinking. Shortly after his return to the United States came the establishment of his newspaper, the *North Star,* which marked the beginning of the break with Garrison.[22] His tutelage was ended, and he was launched into his career as an independent advocate of the rights of his race. In 1851, he formally renounced the Garrisonian doctrines of disunion and aloofness from politics, and joined the Liberty Party, which was later to merge into the Republican.[23] He was now to remain what he was until he saw the extermination of slavery—editor and politician as well as orator. After 1865, editing, except for the brief period when he published the *New National Era* in Washington, was given up; but until the year of his death, 1895, he was strenuously engaged in lecturing, in contributing to newspapers and magazines, and in practical politics. Through-out his long public life, extending well beyond half a century, his was the Negro voice in America most respected by the whites and most venerated by his own race.

If all the writings of Frederick Douglass which were printed could be collected, they would fill a considerable number of lengthy volumes. But such a collection will in all probability never be possible. A great mass of his writings, including the only complete files known to have been preserved of his *North Star, Frederick Douglass' Paper,* and *Douglass' Monthly,* was lost when his house in Rochester was destroyed by fire in 1872.[24] Many other productions from his pen have no doubt perished with the loss of other antislavery newspapers. However, the published writings which are extant are enormous in quantity.

The earliest are open letters, printed usually in the abolition journals. In the issue of the *Liberator* for November 18, 1842, appeared the first, an overstrained and crudely written expression of Douglass' feelings in regard to the case of George Latimer, whose imprisonment in Boston as a fugitive slave claimed in Norfolk, Virginia, was then stirring the abolition North. The letter is concluded with an appropriate apology: "I can't write to much advantage, having never had a day's schooling in my life, nor have I ever ventured to give publicity to any of my scribbling before; nor would I now, but for my peculiar circumstances." Although this original effort shows little promise, three years later Douglass' letters became what might be called a regular feature of the antislavery press. They were usually printed first in the *Liberator* or the *National Anti-Slavery Standard,* and then were copied extensively in the lesser abolition journals. The majority of these communications, the style of which shows a constant improvement, are on his experiences as an antislavery lecturer, especially in Great Britain.[25] Characteristic of the letters at their best is one to Horace Greeley, written at Glasgow, April 15, 1846, and published originally in the New York *Tribune* for May 14, 1846. It begins: "I never wrote nor attempted to write for any other than a strictly anti-slavery press; but being encouraged by your magnanimity, as shown in copying my letter written from Belfast, Ireland, to the *Liberator* at Boston, I venture to send you a few lines direct from my pen." Then follows, in the tone of restrained invective of which Douglass was becoming a master, an answer to a charge made against him in the *New York Express* as a "glib-tongued scoundrel, running a muck in greedy-eared Britain against America, its people, its institutions, and even its peace." He says in beginning his defense:

> Of the low and vulgar epithets, coupled with the false and somewhat malicious charges, very little need be said. I am used to them. Their force is lost upon me in the frequency of their application. I was reared where they were in the most common use. They form a large and very important portion of the vocabulary of characters known in the South as plantation "negro drivers." A slave-holding gentleman would scorn to use them. He leaves them to find their

way into the world of sound, through the polluted lips of the hired "negro driver"—a being for whom the haughty slave-holder feels incomparably more contempt than he feels towards his slave. And for the best of all reasons—he knows the slave to be degraded because he cannot help himself; but a white "negro driver" is degraded because of original, ingrained meanness. If I agree with the slave-holders in nothing else, I can say that I agree with them in all their burning contempt for a "negro driver," whether born North or South. Such epithets will have no prejudicial effect against me on the mind of the class of American people whose good opinion I sincerely desire to cultivate and deserve. And it is to these I would address this brief word of explanation.

His assailant thus dismissed, Douglass clearly shows his position as that of an enemy of no American institutions except slavery and discrimination against blacks.

Equally strong is the letter in which he replies to an attack made by the Reverend Samuel H. Cox. In a communication published in the *Evangelist* (New York), Cox claimed that at a world's temperance convention at Covent Garden Theatre, London, in August, 1845, Douglass "lugged in Anti-slavery or abolition, no doubt prompted to it by some of the politic ones, who can use him to do what they themselves would not adventure to do in person." The insult was made all the deeper by the insinuation that Douglass was probably "well paid for the abomination." In his answer Douglass takes up each item of the charge and tears it to pieces. In the end he has shown that his irony was daring enough to meet the invective of a celebrated minister. The letter was so prized by the American Anti-Slavery Society that it was in 1846 printed as a pamphlet, entitled *Correspondence between the Rev. Samuel H. Cox, D. D., of Brooklyn, L. I., and Frederick Douglass, a Fugitive Slave,* probably the first of Douglass' long line of pamphlet publications.[26]

Douglass' last term of employment as an antislavery agent ended in 1847. In December of that year he began, in spite of the protests of Garrison and others, the publication of the *North Star,* for the founding of which funds had been subscribed by friends in England.[27] In setting out upon his career as an independent journalist he ended what might be conveniently called his apprenticeship as author. It was the time when he was perfecting himself in public speech as well as in learning to write. In addition to the open letters, a number of his orations were printed in the antislavery press.[28] But the most important production of his period of apprenticeship was the *Narrative of the Life of Frederick Douglass,* the first edition of which appeared at Boston in 1845.

Among the American makers of autobiography, Frederick Douglass is unique. Probably no other American, not excepting Benjamin Franklin, lived a life marked with such contrasts. George L. Ruffin said in his introduction to Douglass' *Life and Times,* originally published in 1881: "Up to this time the most remarkable contribution this country has given to the world is the author and subject of this book, now being introduced to the public, Frederick

Douglass. . . . For every other great character we can bring forward, Europe can produce one equally as great; when we bring forward Douglass, he cannot be matched." Such praise might on the surface be regarded as no more than the bombastic advertisement of a book. But if it is considered as Ruffin no doubt intended, we must agree that there is an element of truth in it. The intellectual and moral growth which Douglass attained, in spite of the long years which he spent as a slave and in spite of the lifetime of struggle which he experienced because of prejudice against his color, makes him a most remarkable figure among the celebrated Americans. And modern Europe has no match for him, simply because modern Europe has never known such violent racial discrimination as was practiced against the blacks in America throughout the period when Douglass lived. He recognized the drama in his career, and recorded it at appropriate times in four autobiographical works.

The first, *Narrative of the Life of Frederick Douglass,* follows in general the plan of the conventional slave autobiography, which had by 1845 become something of a distinct literary type. Its main difference is that it is immeasurably better than any previous narrative which we can without doubt ascribe wholly to Negro authorship. The book was hailed by the abolition public with enthusiasm. It was pronounced by the *Lynn Pioneer* "the most thrilling work which the American press has ever issued, *and the most important.*"[29] An anonymous writer in the New York *Tribune,* who saw in Douglass' style what he felt was the African rhythm and spontaneity responsible for the literary success of Dumas and Soulié, declared: "Considered merely as a narrative, we have never read one more simple, true, coherent, and warm with genuine feeling. It is an excellent piece of writing, and on that score can be prized as a specimen of the powers of the black race, which prejudice persists in disputing."[30] Within a little more than two years after the appearance of the book, a translation into French was in the hands of the printers.[31]

There is still interest in Douglass' *Narrative,* even considered apart from the fact that he, a fugitive, only seven years out of the degradation of slavery, produced it. His experiences as an abolition lecturer had taught him valuable lessons about holding and pleasing and convincing an audience. By nature strongly emotional, he had learned how to stir emotions in others. From the store of his memories of his intimate contact with slavery he selected details for his *Narrative* which at one moment provoke laughter and at the next, pity. They are always clear and concrete, and from them we build up a unified picture of Douglass' life from his infancy to the year in which he became an antislavery agent. Nothing argues more strongly for the precociousness of his mind than the detached perspective with which he looks back upon his wretched past even though removed from it by a very brief lapse of time.

The style of the *Narrative* is childlike in its simplicity. But it is marked with two effects, no doubt brought about unconsciously, which many writers labor vainly to obtain. One is evident in the following passage, illustrative of the manner in which a weight of feeling is compressed into very few sentences:

I never saw my mother, to know her as such, more than four or five times in my life and each of these times was very short in duration, and at night. She was hired by a Mr. Stewart, who lived about twelve miles from my home. She made her journeys to see me in the night, travelling the whole distance on foot, after the performance of her day's work. She was a field hand, and a whipping is the penalty of not being in the field at sunrise, unless a slave has special permission from his or her master to the contrary.

An equally difficult stylistic accomplishment is seen in the gracefulness with which Douglass mingles argument with incident. His sole purpose in writing his autobiography was to produce antislavery propaganda. Unlike the great majority of abolition writers, however, he possessed the ability to bring out his sermon without destroying his story. The following passage, which happens to be probably the first printed commentary made by a Negro on the folk songs of his race, preaches while it tells:

The slaves selected to go to the Great House Farm, for the monthly allowance for themselves and their fellow slaves, were peculiarly enthusiastic. While on their way they would make the dense old woods, for miles around, reverberate with their wild songs, revealing at once the highest joy and the deepest sadness. They would compose and sing as they went along, consulting neither time nor tune. The thought that came up, came out—if not in the word, in the sound;—and as frequently in the one as in the other. They would sometimes sing the most pathetic sentiment in the most rapturous tone, and the most rapturous sentiment in the most pathetic tone. Into all of their songs they would manage to weave something of the Great House Farm. Especially would they do this, when leaving home. They would sing most exultingly the following words:—

"I am going away to the Great House Farm!
O, yea! O, yea! O!"

This they would sing as a chorus to words which to many would seem unmeaning jargon, but which, nevertheless, were full of meaning to themselves. I have sometimes thought that the mere hearing of those songs would do more to impress some minds with the horrible character of slavery, than the reading of whole volumes of philosophy on the subject could do.

I did not, when a slave, understand the deep meaning of those rude and apparently incoherent songs. I was myself within the circle; so that I neither saw nor heard as those without might see and hear. They told a tale of woe which was then altogether beyond my feeble comprehension; they were tones loud, long, and deep; they breathed the prayer and complaint of souls boiling over with the bitterest anguish. Every tone was a testimony against slavery, and a prayer to God for deliverance from chains. The hearing of those wild notes always depressed my spirit, and filled me with ineffable sadness. I have frequently found myself in tears while hearing them. The mere recurrence to those songs, even now, afflicts me; and while I am writing these lines, an expression of feeling has already found its way down my cheek. To those songs I trace my first glimmering conception of the dehumanizing character of slavery. I can never get rid of that conception.

Those songs still follow me, to deepen my hatred of slavery, and quicken my sympathies for my brethren in bonds. If any one wishes to be impressed with the soul-killing effects of slavery, let him go to Colonel Lloyd's plantation, and, on allowance day, place himself in the deep woods, and there let him, in silence, analyze the sounds that shall pass through the chambers of his soul,—and if he is not thus impressed, it will be only because "there is no flesh in his obdurate heart."

Douglass' second autobiographical work, *My Bondage and My Freedom*, appeared in 1855, near the middle of the period of his maturity as an author, which we might say extended from 1848 to the close of the Civil War. Almost four times the length of the *Narrative*, it reveals in more respects than in size that it is the work of the mature Douglass. The introductions by Garrison and Phillips which served the *Narrative* give way to an introduction by a member of Douglass' own race, James McCune Smith. The dedication is to Gerrit Smith, who on account of his leadership in the Liberty Party had replaced Garrison as Douglass' idol among the Abolitionists. One of the earliest attacks which the Garrisonians made upon Douglass was that, by the act of permitting English friends to pay the price, seven hundred and fifty dollars, set upon him by his Maryland owner, he had recognized the legality of slavery as an American institution.[32] That his position as a free man could not be disputed when he wrote *My Bondage and My Freedom* was of great advantage to him. The book brings out in elaborate detail the story of his life as a slave, including minute descriptions of customs on a great Maryland plantation. What he did not dare say in the *Narrative* he now says with boldness. The book is in every sense a surer and bigger work than the earlier autobiography. While the style shows the same simplicity and compression, it is more accurate. If there is more argument, there is also more human interest, especially humor. The following description of a Christmas celebration among slaves is suggestive of the pictures with which the book abounds:

> Not to be drunk during the holidays, was disgraceful; and he was esteemed a lazy and improvident man, who could not afford to drink whiskey during Christmas.
> The fiddling, dancing and *"jubilee beating,"* was going on in all directions. This latter performance is strictly southern. It supplies the place of a violin, or of other musical instruments, and is played so easily, that almost every farm has its "Juba" beater. The performer improvises as he beats, and sings his merry songs, so ordering the words as to have them fall pat with the movement of his hands. Among a mass of nonsense and wild frolic, once in a while a sharp hit is given to the meanness of slaveholders. Take the following for an example.

> "We raise de wheat,
> Dey gib us de corn;
> We bake de bread,
> Dey gib us de cruss;

We sif de meal,
Dey gib us de huss;
We peal de meat,
Dey gib us de skin.
An' dat's de way
Dey takes us in.
We skim de pot,
Dey gib us the liquor,
And say dat's good enough for nigger.

Walk over! walk over!
Tom butter and de fat;
Poor nigger you can't get over dat;
Walk over!"[33]

In his autobiographical accounts as in everything else he wrote, Douglass seems to be speaking from the platform. His genius lay in his passion for meeting an antagonistic public with the spoken word. All of his writing is in the spirit of spontaneous and racy and stirring oratory. Reference has been made to the effect which his first convention speech made upon Garrison. Before he had ever written a line for publication, the newspapers were praising his power as an orator.[34] In 1843, he was named along with such abolition notables as Garrison and Phillips for a course of lectures in Boston.[35] In the same year an attempt was made by the Abolitionists of Ohio to secure his services as an antislavery agent exclusively in that state for a period of twelve months.[36] One who had heard him speak in Concord, New Hampshire, in 1844 wrote: "The close of his address Sunday evening was unrivalled. I can give no adequate description of it. I have heard the leading anti-slavery speakers, as well as the pro-slavery orators, and the great advocates at the bar; and I have never seen a man leave the platform, or close a speech, with more real dignity and eloquent majesty."[37] Even the enemies of the abolition principles which Douglass expounded in his early speeches did not hesitate to praise him. One wrote in 1845: "Pity so noble a specimen of man should have been spoiled by the miserable fallacies of the Garrisonian philosophy!"[38] The poems which were written in tribute to Douglass as an orator, especially by his English admirers, would make up a volume of fair size.[39]

Douglass' supremacy as a platform speaker was established by the time he returned from his first trip to Great Britain. There were few questions that arose in regard to his race during the succeeding eighteen years upon which we do not have a printed speech from him. A typical Garrisonian polemic against slavery is an address given at an anniversary of the American Anti-Slavery Society held in New York on May 11, 1847. Defenders of slavery in Baltimore saw in the impracticable program which it advocated what they thought was a suitable boomerang, and published it as a pamphlet, entitled *Abolition Fanaticism in New York: Speech of a Runaway Slave from Baltimore.* It was apparently the first of

Douglass' many orations circulated as pamphlets. A less visionary work, such as his opponents could in no way exploit, was a diatribe against Henry Clay and the American Colonization Society, spoken at Faneuil Hall, Boston, in 1849 and reported phonographically for the press.[40] Perhaps the best known of the orations devoted to the general subject of abolition are two addresses published at Rochester in 1851 as *Lectures on American Slavery.* Interesting for its irony is a Fourth of July speech published in 1852 as *Oration, Delivered in Corinthian Hall, Rochester,* the mood of which is suggested by the quotation—"What, to the American slave, is your Fourth of July? I answer: a day more than all other days in the year, the gross injustice and cruelty to which he is the constant victim."

At the commencement exercises of Western Reserve College in 1854 Douglass was a guest, and delivered before the literary societies of that institution his *Claims of the Negro Ethnologically Considered,* a soundly reasoned protest against the popular notion of African inferiority. The address was in the same year published at Rochester. A lucid defense of Douglass' desertion of Garrisonianism is *The Anti-Slavery Movement,* a lecture given before the Rochester Ladies' Anti-Slavery Society and printed in 1855. The same topic is discussed in a speech delivered at Canandaigua, New York, on August 4, 1857, in celebration of the anniversary of the emancipation of the slaves in the British West Indies. This address was published, probably in 1857, along with another, on the Dred Scott Decision, in a pamphlet entitled *Two Speeches of Frederick Douglass.*[41] One of the earliest of Douglass' many obituary orations on anti-slavery workers was the *Eulogy of the Late Hon. Wm. Jay,* delivered before a colored audience in New York and published in 1859. While in Great Britain in 1860, where Douglass took up temporary refuge after accusations had been made against him as an accomplice in John Brown's raid,[42] he gave a lecture at Glasgow, later printed at Halifax as *The Constitution of the United States: Is It Pro-Slavery, or Anti-Slavery?* It is a vigorous reply to an attack on his activity in American politics made by George Thompson, his chief supporter on his first visit to England.[43] Typical of the Civil War speeches is a rousing appeal for Negro enlistments delivered in Philadelphia in 1863 and published in *Speeches by the Hon. W. D. Kelly, Miss Anna E. Dickinson, and Mr. Frederick Douglass.*[44] Similar in mood is *What the Black Man Wants,* a plea for the full enfranchisement of the Negro delivered at Boston in 1865, and published the same year with speeches by William D. Kelly and Wendell Phillips in a pamphlet called *The Equality of All Men before the Law.*

The publication of Douglass' orations was continued throughout his third and final period of authorship, extending from 1865 to the year of his death. As representative as any speech which we have from him is *John Brown,* delivered a number of times before it was finally given at Harper's Ferry in 1881 in the form in which it was printed as a pamphlet. The occasion of its delivery at Harper's Ferry was dramatic. Andrew Hunter, who as a district attorney had prosecuted John Brown, was on the platform. The proceeds from the sale of the printed speech were to be devoted to the founding of a John Brown Professorship in Storer College, established at Harper's Ferry in 1867 mainly for the instruction of the colored.

Avoiding the apology with which he was wont to begin so many of his early speeches, Douglass gets into his subject with a sustained periodic sentence, such as the fashions of nineteenth-century oratory freely permitted:

> Not to fan the flame of sectional animosity now happily in the process of rapid and I hope permanent extinction; not to revive and keep alive a sense of shame and remorse for a great national crime, which has brought its own punishment in the loss of treasure, tears, and blood; not to recount the long list of wrongs inflicted on my race during more than two hundred years of merciless bondage; nor yet to draw, from the labyrinth of far-off centuries, incidents and achievements wherewith to arouse your passions, and enkindle your enthusiasm, but to pay a just debt long due, to vindicate in some degree a great historical character, of your own time and country, one with whom I was myself well acquainted, and whose friendship and confidence it was my good fortune to share, and to give you such recollections, impressions, and facts, as I can, of a grand, brave, and good old man, and especially to promote a better understanding of the raid on Harper's Ferry, of which he was the chief, is the object of this address.

Then follows a skillfully constructed summary, scarcely more than a page in length, of the events leading up to Brown's execution. The main theme is brought out in a few flash-like sentences.

> There is, in the world's government, a force which has in all ages been recognized, sometimes as Nemesis, sometimes as the judgment of God, and sometimes as retributive justice; but under whatever name, all history asserts the wisdom and beneficence of its chastisements, and men become reconciled to the agents through whom it operates, and have extolled them as heroes, benefactors, and demi-gods. . . . That startling cry of alarm on the banks of the Potomac was but the answering back of the avenging angel to the midnight invasions of Christian slave-traders on the sleeping hamlets of Africa. The history of the African slave-trade furnishes many illustrations far more cruel and bloody.

The body of the speech, in which the central idea is frequently repeated, is devoted to an account of Douglass' various meetings with Brown. There is a picturesque recital of the last conference between the two, held in a deserted stone quarry near Chambersburgh, Pennsylvania, just twelve days before the raid. There are occasional touches of humor, such as the reference to those who accused Douglass of being an accomplice of Brown—"Governor Henry A. Wise was manifestly of that opinion. He was at the pains of having Mr. Buchanan send his Marshals to Rochester to invite me to accompany them to Virginia. Fortunately I left town several hours before their arrival." After a tribute to Shields Green, the loyal fugitive slave executed with Brown, Douglass begins the peroration. He makes of it a restatement of his main theme. The Civil War, of which John Brown is named the first great hero, is proclaimed as the retributive justice which divine right had visited upon the slaveholder.

In spite of the flimsiness of the philosophy on which Douglass based the idea of the speech, and in spite of his faithfulness in following the standards of old-fashioned oratory, held in debasement by the taste of today, he produced in *John Brown* an oration that still stirs. Even in print, it seems warm and passionate. Fired by emotion, the message moves in a rhythm in which there is no hint of halt or hesitation. But Douglass in his maturity never allowed feeling to run away with him. The admirable structure of *John Brown* is an evidence of the exactness of his sense of logical symmetry. Each phrase, however sonorous it may be, has a definite and practical meaning. And *John Brown* is only one of a great number of orations of excellence which Douglass delivered and printed after 1847. Suggestive of the tributes paid to his genius as an orator when he was in his prime by many respected critics, including his enemies as well as his friends, is a statement made by Thomas Wentworth Higginson: "I have hardly heard his equal, in grasp upon an audience, in dramatic presentation, in striking at the pith of an ethical question, and in single illustrations and images, as 'For the negro the Republican party is the deck; all else is the sea.' "[45] In the oratory of Frederick Douglass, American Negro literature aside from its folk song has reached perhaps its highest plane. And the significance of his speeches lies in their intrinsic merit, not in the fact that they were created by a Negro who for the first twenty-one years of his life was a slave.

Douglass made the following statement in 1883: "If I have at any time said or written that which is worth remembering, I must have said such things between 1848 and 1860, and my paper was the chronicle of most of what I said during that time."[46] When he returned to the United States from England in April, 1847, he came with the determination to fight slavery through the press as well as from the lecture platform. After wavering for a few months, considering whether he was to become associated with the *Ram's Horn,* a Negro newspaper then being published in New York, or whether he was to confine his journalistic work to contributions to such broadly circulated publications as the *Liberator* and the *National Anti-Slavery Standard,* he at length decided to devote the gift of money tendered him by Abolitionists in England to the use intended by them, namely, the establishment of a newspaper of which he was to be the owner and the editor.[47] The name selected was the *North Star,* symbolical of the slave's guide to a land of freedom; and Rochester, New York, because of its remoteness from the fields of other strong abolition journals, was definitely chosen as the place of publication, after Cleveland, Ohio, had been considered.[48] One number appeared before the year 1847 was ended; and the journal lived as a weekly (known after 1850 as *Frederick Douglass' Paper*) until August, 1860. It was then merged with *Douglass' Monthly,* which had been begun in June, 1858, as a small magazine planned for circulation in England. A monthly in its last years, Douglass' paper continued until he was able to announce in its columns Lincoln's Emancipation Proclamation.[49]

Douglass began his journalistic venture conservatively. The obvious models for the *North Star* were the *Liberator,* the *National Anti-Slavery Standard,* and the *Pennsylvania Freeman,* all much alike in matter and makeup, even though differing in policy. The motto chosen for the *North Star* was "Right is of no sex—Truth is of no color—God is Father of us all, and all we are brethren." The object as stated in each number was "to attack slavery in all its forms and aspects; advocate universal emancipation; exalt the standard of public morality; promote the moral and intellectual improvement of the Colored People; and hasten the day of Freedom to the Three Millions of our enslaved Fellow Countrymen." The issue, like that of most newspapers of the day, consisted of four pages. Editorials, letters, brief notes, and copious extracts from the general and antislavery press brought to the readers of the *North Star* news of current abolition activities, as well as information on allied reform movements, such as women's rights, temperance, and better living conditions for laborers.[50] There was a poetry column, in which, as in the *Liberator,* verses on general as well as on antislavery themes were published. The *North Star,* except for contributions concerning Douglass himself, such as his manumission papers and the series of letters to Thomas Auld, his master when he was in slavery, was a general abolition paper. It contained little to identify it as a publication controlled and edited by a Negro, who at first had as his chief associates two other Negroes, Martin R. Delany and William C. Nell.

It was perhaps less a Negro journal when the name was changed to *Frederick Douglass' Paper.* The new title was adopted at the time Douglass became a publicly confessed convert to the abolition theories of Gerrit Smith. The *Liberty Party Paper,* which had been published at Syracuse under the editorship of John Thomas, was merged with the *North Star;*[51] and, since the policies as well as the organization of the paper were revolutionized, and also since, as Douglass afterwards declared, he felt that there were too many *"stars* in the newspaper firmament," the new name was decided upon.[52] What had been begun as just another antislavery paper was thus turned into a political organ, without the financial support of the party which it sponsored. Although it bore Douglass' name, and although he was the chief contributor as well as the editor, the discussion of Negro affairs found place only when not crowded out by Presidential messages, speeches in Congress, reports of party caucuses and conventions, Douglass' answers to the political enemies who were attacking him right and left, and his apparently endless defenses of the Constitution as an antislavery document. But however embroiled in politics it became, Douglass' paper remained the champion of the people of color. He went into politics as a Negro fighting sincerely for the welfare of his race; and the turn of events in the Civil War proved that in renouncing Garrison's radical doctrine of disunion he showed himself a more practical, farsighted, and useful fighter.

Maintaining a newspaper for such an extended period of time meant for

Douglass a trying struggle. Financing the enterprise was at first exceedingly difficult. The money subscribed by English Abolitionists, amounting to a little more than two thousand dollars,[53] was sufficient to begin the paper; but to keep it going he had to depend mainly on his own resources, especially on raising money by lecturing.[54] At the end of 1848, when one volume of the *North Star* had been completed, he issued a statement to the effect that the publication could not be continued without more subscriptions or donations.[55] Although articles were contributed gratuitously,[56] and the privilege of using extracts from other publications was almost unrestricted, the expenses were estimated at eighty dollars for the week.[57] When conditions were at their worst, Julia Griffiths, an Englishwoman, who in 1853 and 1854 edited and published in this country an antislavery annual, *Autographs for Freedom,* came to the rescue;[58] and through her aid the circulation of Douglass' paper was increased until an average of three thousand subscribers could be depended upon.[59] With such a subscription list, and with a fair income from advertising, the paper was financially stable until the John Brown troubles forced Douglass to seek a temporary refuge abroad, during which time the weekly publication of his paper was permanently discontinued.[60]

But financing was not the only stumblingblock which Douglass encountered. The more he became involved in politics, the more enemies he found. Those who had been his best friends became often his most scathing critics, members of his own race as well as whites.[61] In spite of all, Douglass fought and won. With the exception of the *Genius of Universal Emancipation* and the *Liberator,* his was the one abolition paper not sponsored and supported by an antislavery organization which survived for a considerable length of time and which exerted a broad influence towards the emancipation of the slave.[62] Since Douglass never attempted to make of it an exclusive organ of his people, it can scarcely be considered as belonging to the field of the Negro journalism of the time. But he, a Negro, was the very heart of its existence, and it was not inappropriate that during most of its life it was called *Frederick Douglass' Paper.*

After the Civil War, Douglass had no paper of his own in which to record his numerous speeches and communications to the public, except for the years from 1869 to 1872, when he conducted and edited at Washington the *New National Era,* a Negro weekly. But his final period of authorship was none the less productive. In a letter to Whittier, dated March 18, 1873,[63] he spoke of having lectured during the preceding winter "from Bangor to Omaha, and from St. Louis to St. Paul." There were few winters from 1865 to 1894 when he was less active on the lecture platform. Many of his later orations, like *John Brown,* were printed as pamphlets. In 1881 appeared his third autobiographical work, the *Life and Times of Frederick Douglass.* The fourth and final autobiographical account came in 1892, the *Life and Times* enlarged by more than a hundred pages. In either edition, the story related is a strange one, peculiarly American. A man who has been a United States Marshal, a Recorder of Deeds, a Minister to Hayti, looks over his dramatic past, back into the desperate years which he spent in servitude in Maryland. Occasional passages reveal the oratorical Douglass still brimming with emotion. An example is the tribute to Theodore Parker, introduced into a brief description of a visit to the graves of Parker and Elizabeth Barrett Browning in Florence.

> The preacher and the poet lie near each other. The soul of each was devoted to liberty. The brave stand taken by Theodore Parker during the anti-slavery conflict endeared him to my heart, and naturally enough the spot made sacred by his ashes was the first to draw me to its side. He had a voice for the slave when nearly all the pulpits of the land were dumb. Looking upon the little mound of earth that covered his dust, I felt the pathos of his simple grave. It did not seem well that the great American preacher should rest thus in a foreign soil, far away from the hearts and hands which would gladly linger about it and keep it well adorned with flowers. Than Theodore Parker no man was more intensely American. Broad as the land in his sympathy with mankind, he was yet a loving son of New England and thoroughly Bostonian in his thoughts, feelings and activities. The liberal thought which he taught had in its native land its natural home and largest welcome, and I therefore felt that his dust should have been brought here. It was in his pulpit in Roxbury that I made my first anti-slavery speech.

But the *Life and Times* is the work of an aging man. One finds in it verbosity and tediousness, not the compression which makes the earlier autobiographies very readable. Also in his last period came a number of contributions from Douglass to leading periodical publications.[64] He was the first of American Negroes to get into the company of the prominent magazine writers.

It is a relief to find his writings in the careful print of such a periodical as the *North American Review*. Most of the work which he produced in his prime, including his autobiographies, was evidently rushed through the press. There is at least one notable exception, "The Heroic Slave," an account of Madison Washington's mutiny, which appeared in 1853 in *Autographs for Freedom,* an annual remarkable for its artistic typography. To see Douglass' writing in such decent dress, when the great mass of it is in timeworn newspapers or cheaply printed pamphlets, makes one feel that justice has not been done to the greatest of American Negroes, the most important figure in American Negro literature before 1900. Douglass' extant writings are worth preservation in a complete and scholarly edition.

Notes

1. *National Anti-Slavery Standard,* Feb. 25, 1847.
2. See Alexander Crummell, *The Eulogy on Henry Highland Garnet, D.D.,* 1882. Crummell and Garnet were students at the Noyes Academy when it was broken up.
3. See William G. Allen, *The American Prejudice against Color,* 1853, Chapter II.

4. *Liberator,* Feb. 19, 1841.

5. Frank A. Rollin, *Life and Public Services of Martin R. Delany,* 1883, p. 69.

6. See Carter G. Woodson, *The Education of the Negro Prior to 1861,* 1915, p. 277.

7. *African Repository,* XLV, 298 (Oct., 1869).

8. Rollin, *op. cit.,* p. 39.

9. Frederic May Holland, *Frederick Douglass: the Colored Orator,* 1891, p. 226.

10. Samuel Ringgold Ward, *The Autobiography of a Fugitive Negro,* 1855, p. 235.

11. *African Repository,* XXIX, 82–83 (Mar., 1852). See also the *National Anti-Slavery Standard,* July 1, 1847.

12. *Negro Population, 1790–1915,* 1918, p. 57.

13. Woodson, *op. cit.,* pp. 271–273.

14. See Carter G. Woodson, *The Negro in Our History,* 1927, p. 274.

15. "Declaration of the American Anti-Slavery Society," adopted at the convention held December 6, 1833. Printed in *The Anti-Slavery Almanac for 1836.*

16. *Pennsylvania Freeman,* Sept. 20, 1838.

17. Ward, *op. cit.,* pp. 31, 50.

18. *Liberator,* Sept. 22, 1843.

19. Frederick Douglass, *Life and Times,* 1892, pp. 269–270. See also John Wallace Hutchinson, *Story of the Hutchinsons,* 1896, I,70.

20. *Narrative of the Life of Frederick Douglass,* 1845, p. iv.

21. *Cf.* Holland, *op. cit.,* p. 8.

22. *Ibid.,* pp. 161–165.

23. See the *Rochester American,* Dec. 9, 1853, and the *Liberator,* Jan. 27, 1854.

24. Douglass, *Life and Times,* p. 327.

25. Typical letters are to be found in the *Liberator,* Sept. 26, Oct. 3, 10, 24, Nov. 28, 1845; Jan. 16, 30, Feb. 27, May 15, June 26, Aug. 28, Nov. 27, 1846; Jan. 29, Apr. 30, June 4, 11, 1847; and in the *National Anti-Slavery Standard,* Oct. 15, 1846; July 23, Aug. 10, Sept. 9, 23, 1847.

26. The letter was first printed in the *Liberator,* Nov. 27, 1846. For press comment regarding it see the *Liberator,* Jan. 1, 1847.

27. *People's Journal* (London), Apr. 24, 1847; *National Anti-Slavery Standard,* July 8, Sept. 30, 1847, and Jan. 27, 1848. See Note 22.

28. Typical early speeches are in the *Liberator,* Feb. 6, 27, May 29, and July 3, 1846. Others are to be found in Frederick Douglass, *My Bondage and My Freedom,* 1855, pp. 407–418.

29. Quoted in the *Liberator,* May 30, 1845.

30. From a featured review in the New York *Tribune,* June 10, 1845. For varied press opinion on the *Narrative,* see the quotations given in the *Liberator,* May 23, 30, June 6, 20, 1845, and in the *National Anti-Slavery Standard,* June 19, 1845.

31. *Liberator,* Nov. 12, 1847. The translation, made by S. K. Parkes, appeared in Paris at the beginning of 1848 as *Vie de Frédéric Douglass.*

32. Garrison himself considered the attack absurd. See the *Liberator,* Jan. 29, 1847.

33. For varied press notices regarding *My Bondage and My Freedom,* see *Frederick Douglass' Paper,* June 20, 1856.

34. See the *Liberator,* June 17, 1842.

35. *Liberator,* Jan. 27, 1843.

36. *Liberator,* Nov. 17, 1843.

37. Quoted in the *Liberator,* Feb. 23, 1844, from the *Herald of Freedom.*

38. Quoted in the *Liberator,* Aug. 1, 1845, from the *Liberty Press* (Utica).

39. Typical of the verse tributes are the poems published in the *Liberator,* July 11, 1845; Mar. 27, May 1, Nov. 27, Dec. 4, 1846; Jan. 15, Feb. 5, May 14, Nov. 19, 1847; and in the *National Anti-Slavery Standard,* May 27, 1847.

40. Printed in the *Liberator,* June 8, 1849.

41. The pamphlet bears no publication date.

42. An interesting development resulting from Douglass' precipitated flight in 1859 was that for a lecture for which he had been engaged in Concord Henry David Thoreau appeared as his substitute. See the *Atlas and Bee* (Boston), Nov. 2, 1859, and the *Liberator*, Nov. 4, 1859.

43. For an earlier reply to Thompson's attack see the *Liberator*, Jan. 2, 1852.

44. A more direct and stronger appeal for Negro enlistments is *Men of Color, to Arms!* Written as a speech but possibly never spoken, it was printed as a broadside in 1863.

45. Holland, *op. cit.*, p. 313.

46. Douglass, *Life and Times*, p. 328.

47. *People's Journal* (London), Apr. 24, 1847; *Liberator*, June 4, 25, July 9, 23, Aug. 20, Sept. 24, 1847; *National Anti-Slavery Standard*, July 8, 1847, Jan. 27, 1848. See Note 27.

48. *National Anti-Slavery Standard*, Sept. 30, 1847; Douglass, *My Bondage and My Freedom*, p. 395.

49. The last issue of *Douglass' Monthly* which I have been able to locate is that for November, 1861. Douglass himself referred to it as still being published in March, 1863 (see *Life and Times*, p. 414).

50. See the *North Star*, Aug. 11, 1848.

51. See the *Liberator*, July 4, 1851.

52. Douglass, *Life and Times*, p. 325.

53. *National Anti-Slavery Standard*, Jan. 27, 1848.

54. *Frederick Douglass' Paper*, May 18, 1860.

55. *North Star*, Dec. 22, 1848.

56. Manuscript letter from Douglass to I. C. Kendall, dated Jan. 3, 1854. In the New York Public Library.

57. Douglass, *Life and Times*, p. 324.

58. See Janet Marsh Parker, "Reminiscences of Frederick Douglass," *Outlook*, LI, 552–553 (Apr. 6, 1895).

59. Douglass, *Life and Times*, p. 324.

60. *Frederick Douglass' Paper*, May 18, 1860.

61. See the *Liberator*, Sept. 5, 1856. For the attack of a Negro on Douglass, see the letter by Robert Purvis published in the *Liberator*, Sept. 16, 1853.

62. *Liberator*, July 4, 1851.

63. Manuscript, in the library of the New York Historical Society.

64. Typical magazine articles are "The Color Line," *North American Review*, CXXXII, 567–577 (June, 1881); "The Condition of the Freedmen," *Harper's Weekly*, XXVII, 782–783 (Dec. 8, 1883); "The Future of the Colored Race," *North American Review*, CXLII, 437–440 (May, 1886); and "Reminiscences," *Cosmopolitan*, VII, 376–382 (Aug., 1889).

Let Freedom Ring

J. Saunders Redding

Among the great personalities who achieved eminent personal success during the period from 1835 to the turn of the century none was greater than Frederick Douglass. No man of his time achieved in so many fields through so many difficulties. No man of the time was better known than he, and only Lincoln was more honored (and more reviled) and better loved. His personality, so essential to the effectiveness of his work, flows through the times like a strong, calm tide.

Frederick Douglass was born a slave in Talbot County, Maryland, in or about 1817. For twenty-one years he remained in slavery, first on the plantation of Thomas Auld and later as a hired-out boat caulker in Baltimore, where he lived in the home of a relative of his master's. Here Douglass learned his first letters. Through the kindness of the mistress of the household he was taught to read along with the young son of the family, until the master of the house put a stop to it. Afterwards he was largely self-taught, ingeniously beguiling the young white boys of the neighborhood into telling him letters and words he did not know. When he came into possession of *The Columbian Orator,* a popular school book of the time, he felt that he had discovered a treasure. In his *Narrative* he tells us that the speeches of Sheridan, Lord Chatham, William Pitt, and Fox "were all choice documents." But even so, when he escaped to New York and settled in New Bedford, Massachusetts, in 1838 he was still far from literate. He learned to read more easily at the same time that he absorbed the abolitionist doctrine in the pages of the *Liberator.* "From this time I was brought into contact with the mind of Mr. Garrison, and his paper took a place in my heart second only to the Bible. . . . I loved this paper and its editor." It was not until he met Garrison in 1841, however, that Douglass definitely entered into the abolitionist movement.

His rise was rapid. By 1842 he had begun his first writing, letters that were published in numerous antislavery journals. The chief characteristics of these early letters were their dignified scorn and calm and their humorless censure of the slavers and the slave institution. Many of them were autobio-

Reprinted by permission from J. Saunders Redding, *To Make a Poet Black* (Chapel Hill: University of North Carolina Press, 1939), 31–38.

graphical. Later he was forced to use these open letters as instruments of defense against newspaper attacks that were made upon him. By 1845, when the first long autobiographical account appeared, he had had to make at least four vigorous defenses of himself. That he did so with dignity is attested by the letters themselves, especially the one to Dr. Samuel Cox, one of the foremost churchmen of the day, who had stupidly attacked him.

The 1845 autobiography, *Narrative of the Life of Frederick Douglass,* came at a time when the writing of slave narratives, real or fictitious, was popular propaganda, but Douglass's book is in many ways too remarkable to be dismissed as mere hack writing. Contemporary criticism spoke in glowing and even extravagant terms of it. Modern criticism, though more conservative, is certainly warm. In utter contrast to the tortured style of most of the slave biographies, Douglass's style is calm and modest. Even in this first book his sense of discrimination in the selection of details is fine and sure. The certainty of the book's emotional power is due in part to the stringent simplicity of style and in part to the ingenuous revelation of the author's character.

Because his freedom was endangered by the publication of the *Narrative,* in 1845 Douglass went abroad where he lectured in England, Scotland, and Ireland for two years. It was now that his letters to the press began to appear regularly not only in the antislavery organs, but in such exemplary papers as the *New York Tribune,* the *Brooklyn Eagle,* and the *London Post.* This experience in written debate sharpened his logic, and was to serve him importantly when he later established his own newspaper. Those months abroad were fruitful for Douglass, months of enlightenment. He made new and strong friends for himself and his cause. The same dignity with which his letters answered malicious attacks or set forth his arguments marked his speeches. Indeed, reading his letters now, one feels that they were written for speech, that Douglass made no difference between the written and the spoken word. Before his return to the States, the English Society of Friends had undertaken to raise seven hundred and fifty dollars for the purchase of his freedom.

That Douglass's outlook had broadened is reflected in his decision to discard the principle of disunion and to adopt the policy of freedom and union. His changed views meant the loss of friends and the closing of many channels, but he endured this without bitterness. It meant a break with Garrison, under whom a faction of abolitionists took the view that slavery should be destroyed by splitting the union. Douglass's view, stemming from England, held that the union should be preserved. Garrison's faction was strong. To give himself freer scope, Douglass moved to Rochester, New York, and established his own paper, *The North Star,* a weekly which was published as *Frederick Douglass' Paper* for thirteen years.

Except for work from the pen of Douglass, *The North Star* differed but little from other antislavery journals. Because of the force of Douglass's personality the paper won a high place in the field, but a great deal of the editor's energy was spent in securing funds to maintain publication. He mortgaged his home to that purpose. Strenuous programs of speechmaking engaged him, and many of his editorials were abstracts of his speeches. He grew greater as a speaker than as a writer. The speeches he made between 1849 and 1860 were never equaled in logic, in emotional force, or in simple clarity. His peculiarly stony denunciation, the calm bitterness of his irony, and his frequent use of the simple and emotional language of the Bible make the speeches of this period memorable examples of the oratorical art. His speech on American slavery, perhaps his greatest, delivered in celebration of Independence Day at Rochester, July 5, 1852, is an example:

> Why am I called upon to speak here today? What have I, or those I represent, to do with your national independence? Are the great principles of political freedom and of natural justice embodied in that Declaration of Independence extended to us? And am I, therefore, called upon to bring our humble offering to the national altar, and to confess the benefits, and express devout gratitude for the blessings resulting from your independence to us? . . . What, to the American slave, is your Fourth of July? I answer; a day that reveals to him more than all other days in the year, the gross injustice and cruelty to which he is a constant victim.

He says further, quoting the 137th Psalm: "We hanged our harps upon the willows in the midst thereof. For there they that carried us away captive required of us a song; and they that wasted us required of us mirth, saying, Sing us one of the songs of Zion. How shall we sing the Lord's song in a strange land? If I forget thee, O Jerusalem, let my right hand forget her cunning. If I do not remember thee, let my tongue cleave to the roof of my mouth."[1]

When *The North Star* became an organ of Gerrit Smith's Liberty party and was thereafter called *Frederick Douglass' Paper,* Douglass was still burdened with financing it. His entrance into politics was the one further step which he saw as a means of helping his people. By the late 1850's he had come to the conclusion that the abolition of slavery was not enough; that, when abolition did come, the Negro must have the right to vote in order to be completely free. "Liberty is meaningless where the right to utter one's thoughts and opinions has ceased to exist; and what more tangible evidence of that right can be found than in the ballot?" From this time on his expressions from the platform and in the press are more and more burdened with this thought.

In 1855 the autobiographical *My Bondage and My Freedom* was published. His style, still without tricks, proves surer. Considerably longer than his first book, its length is amply justified by its matter. Though the first part follows in general the simple plan of the *Narrative,* he acquaints us more intimately with slavery and expresses his more mature thoughts on the problems which he faced. It is evident, especially when he writes of his English trip, that his knowledge of men had grown. Equally evident in the logic and sincerity of his arguments is the growth of his knowledge of issues. Garrison's charges are here fully answered. *My Bondage and My Freedom* is the high mark of the second stage of Douglass's career. Indeed, though for many years after 1865 he was active as both speaker and writer, and though his thoughts steadily matured, he did not exceed the emotional pitch of this second period. As his intellectual vigor increased (and became, it may be said, a little warped by the over-development of his capacity for irony), his emotional and artistic powers fell off. By the 1880's he was not an orator speaking with a spontaneous overflow of emotion: he was a finished public speaker, more concerned with intellectual than emotional responses.

Douglass's aroused powers of thought made it possible for him to do a work that grew steadily in importance. Emotionally drunk, men had become intellectually blind to the true status of the Negro. A great many people seemed to think that abolition was a calm bay through which the black race would sail to some safe harbor. Few saw that harbors had yet to be constructed. It was this task that Douglass now engaged in. He accepted abolition as a future certainty and looked far beyond it. The material of his speeches, many of which were printed as pamphlets, shows the new tack he had taken. In 1854 he spoke on the Negro from the ethnological point of view. The next year in his paper and on the platform he sought to interpret the Constitution, climaxing his efforts with a reasonable argument that the Constitution is antislavery in a pamphlet entitled *The Constitution of the United States: Is it Pro-Slavery or Anti-Slavery?* Late in the fifties his pamphlet dealing with the epochal Dred Scott Decision was published. Douglass continued this line when he fled to England in 1860 after President James Buchanan sent agents to arrest him for the part he was supposed to have played in John Brown's uprising. And after the Civil War (during which he had helped to organize the Fifty-fourth and Fifty-fifth Massachusetts Negro regiments under Colonel Shaw), he argued that complete enfranchisement of the Negro was the logical end of freedom.

After the presidential campaign that resulted in Lincoln's election, Douglass threw himself more and more into politics. He was a prominent figure in the Philadelphia assemblage of the National Loyalists' Convention in 1866, having been elected to represent the city of Rochester. Resolutions passed at that convention after Douglass's speech in favor of Negro enfranchisement had their bearing upon the subsequent passage of the Fifteenth Amendment.

From this point in his career onward, Douglass became not only the intellectual leader of the Negro, but the political leader as well. He remained active as a speaker, but a great many of the speeches of this period were run-of-the-mine political speeches and commemorative orations. His work as editor of the *New National Era* from 1869 to 1873 and the work on his third book, *Life and Times of Frederick Douglass,* absorbed his best energies. *Life and Times* was published in 1881. Its interest comes authentically from the man's life and thought. It has been called properly the most American of American life stories. Unconsciously, with no fanfare of self-satisfaction, the story develops the dramatic theme from bondage to the council tables of a great nation. It is written with the same lucid simplicity that marks all of Douglass's best work, but there is still the lack of differentiation between speaker and writer. *Life and Times* is his best book.

It remained for him to do yet one other book. Between 1880 and the year of his death his political activities brought personal rewards, which he used to benefit his people. Three presidents—Grant, Garfield, and Harrison—appointed him United States Marshal, Recorder of Deeds, and Minister to Haiti respectively. In 1886 he visited England, Ireland, and Scotland for the third time. He took part in celebrations, demonstrations and protests, and was in the van of movements calculated to improve the position of American Negroes. All of these experiences went into a larger edition of *Life and Times,* which was issued in 1892.

This final work is slow and repetitious. His powers had waned, but he was still aware that all was not finished. He had mellowed with only slight decay; grown into acceptance without resignation. To the last, he wrote as he spoke.

> I have seen dark hours in my life, and I have seen the darkness gradually disappearing, and the light gradually increasing. One by one I have seen obstacles removed, errors corrected, prejudices softened, proscriptions relinquished, and my people advancing in all the elements that make up the sum of general welfare. I remember that God reigns in eternity, and that, whatever delays, disappointments, and discouragements may come, truth, justice, liberty, and humanity will prevail.

The literary work of Douglass is first important as examples of a type and period of American literature. Many of his speeches rank with the best of all times and are included in collections of the finest oratorical art. That at least two of his books, *My Bondage and My Freedom* and the first *Life and Times,* have not been recognized for what they are is attributable more to neglect than to the judgment of honest inquiry. Certainly no American biographies rank above them in the literary qualities of simplicity, interest, and compression of style. They delineate from an exceptional point of view a period in the history of the United States than which no other is more fraught with drama and sociological significance. By any standard his work ranks high.

That he was easily the most important figure in American Negro literature at the time of his death goes without saying. He was the very core of the For Freedom group,[2] fitting his art more nearly to his purposes than any of the others—and suffering less intrinsically for doing it. Without him the For Freedom group would be destitute of true greatness, Negro literature would be poorer, and American literary fields of oratory and autobiography would be lacking a figure in whom they might justly claim pride.

Douglass died in February, 1895, at Anacostia, D. C. His home there has been converted into a shrine, and the citizens of Rochester, New York, for twenty-five years his place of residence, have erected a public monument to him.

Notes

1. "Speech at Rochester, July 5, 1852," Carter G. Woodson, *Negro Orators and Their Orations,* Washington, 1925.

2. In the "For Freedom group" Redding discusses, along with Douglass, Charles Remond, William Wells Brown, Frances Ellen Watkins Harper, and James Madison Bell. [Ed.]

Identity and Art in
Frederick Douglass's *Narrative*

ALBERT E. STONE

"America has the mournful honor of adding a new department to the literature of civilization—the autobiographies of escaped slaves." This announcement by the Reverend Ephraim Peabody, a New Bradford minister and abolitionist, appeared in the *Christian Examiner and Religious Miscellany* for July 1849, prefacing a long discussion of five slave narratives which had been published during the preceding four years. The personal histories were those of Henry Watson, Lewis and Milton Clarke, William Wells Brown, Josiah Henson, and Frederick Douglass. "We place these volumes without hesitation among the most remarkable productions of the age—" Peabody continued, "remarkable as being pictures of slavery by the slave, remarkable as disclosing under a new light the mixed elements of American civilization, and not less remarkable as a vivid exhibition of the force and working of the native love of freedom in the individual mind."[1] This appreciation of the emotional power and cultural significance of slave narratives was indeed prophetic. Though successors have widened his frame of reference and modified some of his genteel judgments, Ephraim Peabody remains one of the first white critics to pay serious attention to a new form of autobiography in America. Some years later in 1863, one of the new black writers he had discussed became himself an annalist of the Negro. In *The Black Man: His Antecedents, His Genius, and His Achievements* William Wells Brown cited these narratives as the first black voices in American literature. Moreover, like Peabody, Brown singled out Frederick Douglass as the master of this new literature. "The narrative of his life, published in 1845, gave a new impetus to the black man's literature," he wrote. "All other stories of fugitive slaves faded away before the beautifully written, highly descriptive, and thrilling memoir of Frederick Douglass."[2] Peabody and Brown announce early what history has since confirmed: the *Narrative of Frederick Douglass, an American Slave, Written by Himself* is at once an important cultural document and an unusual work of autobiographical art.

From *CLA Journal* 17, no. 2 (December 1973): 192–213. Reprinted with the permission of the College Language Association.

By 1849 the slave narrative had already become one of the more popular forms of political literature in the North. Peabody reinforced but did not create Douglass's fame. The *Narrative* had already gone through seven editions and Benjamin Quarles has estimated that by 1850 it had sold some 30,000 copies here and in the British Isles.[3] Brown's narrative had sold 8,000 copies by 1849 and Henson's *Life* was soon to become even more famous—and notorious—as a result of the publicity linking him as "the original Uncle Tom" to Harriet Beecher Stowe's best-seller; within Henson's lifetime the three versions of his autobiography would sell 100,000 copies.[4] Well before the appearance of *Uncle Tom's Cabin,* thousands of American, Canadian, and British readers had already formed impressions of chattel slavery in the Southern states by reading these personal histories as they appeared in magazines, in twenty-five-cent pamphlets, and in books costing a dollar or a dollar and a half. As Charles H. Nichols points out in *Many Thousand Gone,* the definitive history of the slave narrative, these were the first American autobiographies widely read by a popular audience—and for some of the same reasons which have made *The Autobiography of Malcolm* X a best-seller today.

Since the slave narrative flourished in close connection to the abolition movement and appeared (and declined) chiefly in the three decades before the Civil War, the modern reader tends to be concerned, as Nichols is, with the historical context of these books—their composition and publication, their reception and impact, their claims to historical truth or accuracy. Douglass and his fellow fugitives did indeed create an important literature of protest and propaganda. But to assert this is also to recognize that historicity cannot be divorced from other considerations equally important in assessing the permanent cultural value of these works—consideration of literary style and rhetorical strategy, of psychological revelation and motivation. As autobiographies, the *Narrative* and other similar works occupy the territory between history and art, biography and fiction, memory and imagination. When the ex-slave asked the question (or was urged to do so by a white sponsor or collaborator) which all autobiographers ask: "Why am I writing the story of my life?" the immediate answer was plain: to describe the experience of being a chattel and then *not* being one so vividly that the white reader would be moved to destroy the oppressive institution. To this end, the most effective means was to create a convincing impression of historical veracity and verisimilitude. Thus the editor of Douglass's second autobiography, *My Bondage and My Freedom,* declared: "the reader's attention is not invited to a work of art, but to a work of FACTS. There is not a fictitious name or place in the whole volume . . . ; every transaction therein described actually transpired."[5] Telling the unvarnished truth about verifiable experience and re-creating thereby the self in relation to time, history and change, is an aim of all authentic memoirs, but one which had a particular value for the writer and editor of slave narratives.

Yet all history is, as J. H. Hexter has shown, a deliberate artistic creation.[6]

Slave narratives like Douglass's exhibit a variety of literary devices for recording a past, persuading belief, and motivating action. Capitalizing FACTS above is one simple instance of such a rhetorical tactic. Other techniques were devised for the strategy of "sticking to the facts," for in recording the bare details of life as a slave—including the pathos and tragedy of slave auctions and family separations, and drama and excitement of escape to freedom—the writer could hardly avoid the appearance of fiction or the atmosphere of melodrama. Thus the line between autobiography and fiction became a fine one, as is suggested not only by the title of Josiah Henson's second autobiography, *Truth Stranger Than Fiction* (1858), but also by the early appearance of actual romances or pseudohistories like Richard Hildreth's *The Slave: or Memoirs of Archy Moore* (1836). The later novels of Mrs. Stowe and William Wells Brown derived much of their force from the reader's realization that actual life histories existed to authenticate what the novelist had imagined.

If historical truth could have an effect stronger and stranger than fiction, one way to achieve this effect was not to explore the whole system of slavery but instead to exploit the natural focus of autobiography upon private experience and the single self. This, too, provided a fiction-like perspective. How the individual slave became a man in the act of escape was both plot and moral of the slave narrative. In this respect Douglass's *Narrative* is the exemplary work in the genre. By forging a portrait of himself, rather than simply writing history or abolitionist propaganda, Douglass reveals himself a true autobiographer. He also distinguishes his achievement from that of other ex-slave writers like Harriet Jacobs, author of *Incidents in the Life of a Slave Girl* (1861) and Charles Ball, author of *Fifty Years in Chains* (1837). Harriet Jacobs, with assistance from Lydia Maria Child, dramatizes the experience of slavery by means of fictional names, dialogue, sentimental language, and a melodramatic plot of fear, seduction, and flight; hers is personal history under the influence of sentimental romance. Ball's account, on the other hand, reads more like history than autobiography, for its tone and perspective draw attention away from the narrator and his developing identity, toward the generalized facts of life under the brutalizing institution. More successfully than either of these, Douglass saw and exploited the crucial difference between autobiography and its allied forms, history and fiction. As I shall seek to demonstrate, he would have agreed with modern critics of autobiography like F. R. Hart who emphasize the distinctive aim of autobiography. Hart observes that "in understanding fiction one seeks an imaginative grasp of another's meaning; in understanding personal history one seeks an imaginative comprehension of another's historic identity. 'Meaning' and 'identity' are not the same kind of reality and do not make the same demands."[7] Identity through history and art, self as the container of meaning—in these terms, I would argue, lies a proper understanding of Frederick Douglass's *Narrative*.

Though later readers have followed Peabody and Brown in accepting the preeminence of this slave narrative, nevertheless the true artistry of the *Narrative* has yet to be fully analyzed and appreciated. This is surprising in light of Douglass's fame as a public figure, which has been recorded in several biographies. Among the critics and literary scholars who have contributed to a richer realization of Douglass's achievements as writer are Vernon Loggins, Benjamin Brawley, Arna Bontemps, Charles H. Nichols, Benjamin Quarles, Jean F. Yellin, and Houston A. Baker, Jr.[8] Each has illuminated certain aspects of the *Narrative;* none, however, has exhausted its deceptive richness of language, style, and structure. A typical recent discussion is Jean Fagan Yellin's in *The Intricate Knot.* It is, she affirms, "a classic American autobiography" with a narrative style which combines sparcity and aptness of symbolic detail with a dramatic pace and structure. "Douglass' *Narrative* is not a flawless work of art," she concludes, "but it expresses more than the boundless incident and passion of the other slave autobiographies and of the contemporary plantation and abolitionist fiction."[9] Unexceptionable as these judgments are, they occur in a three-page commentary—too brief to do justice to their implications. A fuller discussion is Quarles's introduction to the John Harvard Library edition of the *Narrative,* but this essay never gets around to the closer look at narrative strategy and style which is promised; the historical and biographical background takes up most of the space. The fullest, most sensitive reading which has so far appeared is Houston Baker's in *Long Black Song.* Even this shrewd analysis fails, however, to define precisely and explore adequately all its insights. Baker is correct in seeing the *Narrative* as "sophisticated literary autobiography" and he admirably describes the characteristics of Douglass's prose style—the understated, visualized narrative, the dry, humane irony, the deft characterizations, the adroit use of animal imagery, antithesis, and the agrarian setting. But Baker's linkage of Douglass as a "spiritual" autobiographer to the tradition of Mather, Franklin, and Henry Adams is debatable on several points, for he admits Douglass is never centrally preoccupied with inner experiences of conversion, salvation, or confession. As the appendix indicates, Douglass's Christianity was a practical, public, moral matter. Baker also sees Douglass as "something of a mythic figure" but fails to suggest evidence in the text—rather than in the minds of black or white readers—for this self-mythification; the weight of Baker's discussion, in fact, works against a mythic reading of the *Narrative.* Moreover, Baker simplifies the movement "from a cruel physical bondage to freedom" narrated and psychologically explored in Douglass's book.[10] The achievement of a prior, inner freedom in the fight with Edward Covey is recognized but unrelated to other episodes and patterns of metaphor. Nevertheless, Baker's provocative discussion opens new issues and suggests the need for a careful examination of Frederick Douglass as narrative artist and artificer of the self. To look at the *Narrative* in these terms—at once literary, historical, and psychological—should not detract from the author's polemical purposes. For the more clearly and fully we see the man *and* the writer—the man revealed in the act of discovering and recreating his own identity—the more we acknowledge the force of his argument for an end to slavery's denial of individuality and creativity.

I

Douglass's identification of self begins with the title and prefaces, which establish conditions of the autobiographical contract between black writer and white audience. *Narrative of the Life of Frederick Douglass, an American Slave, Written by Himself* has a directness later replaced by the more figurative title *My Bondage and My Freedom,* in the 1855 version and then in 1892 by the final, historical *Life and Times of Frederick Douglass.* Probably the most meaningful part of the title to the reader of 1845 was *Written by Himself.* The phrase reverberates with *An American Slave* to suggest the poles of Douglass's experience—his past as dependent slave, his present as independent author. The practical need for these phrases was doubtless the attacks in the pro-slavery press on the authenticity of slave narratives as not simply biased but untrue because ghostwritten by white abolitionists who knew nothing of slavery. Like the earlier case of the *Narrative of James Williams,* Douglass's *Narrative* was labeled a fraud soon after publication.[11] In a letter to the Delaware *Republican* A. C. C. Thompson challenged the author and publishers. "About eight years ago, I knew this recreant slave by the name of Frederick Bailey (instead of Douglass)," wrote the ex-slaveholder.

> He then lived with Mr. Edward Covey, and was an unlearned, rather an ordinary negro, and am confident he was not capable of writing the Narrative alluded to; for none but an educated man, and one who had some knowledge of the rules of grammar, could write so correctly; although to make the imposition at all creditable, the composer has labored to write it in as plain a style as possible; consequently the detection of this first falsehood proves the whole production to be most notoriously untrue.

Douglass's rejoinder, in the 1846 English edition of the *Narrative,* made effective use of Thompson's charge to stress the central theme of his story—self-transformation. "You are confident I did not write the book," he observed.

> the reason of your confidence on this point is, that I was, when you knew me, an unlearned and rather ordinary negro. Well, I have to inform you, that you knew me under very unfavorable circumstances; . . . For if any one had told me seven years ago that I should ever be able to *dictate* such a Narrative, to say nothing of *writing* it, I should have disbelieved the prophesy. I was then a mere wreck; Covey had beaten and bruised me so much, that my spirit was crushed and

broken. Frederick the Freeman is very different from Frederick the Slave . . . Freedom has given me a new life.[12]

Whereas Douglass's title asserts the identity and responsibility of its black author, the first pages of the *Narrative* are devoted to guarantees by white sponsors. The preface and introduction by William Lloyd Garrison and Wendell Phillips are double assurances by two of abolitionism's greatest names of the book's authenticity. Virtually every nineteenth-century slave narrative carried such seals of white approval. Indeed, the practice has persisted long after Emancipation, as Dorothy Canfield Fisher's introduction to *Black Boy* (1945) and M. S. Handler's to *The Autobiography of Malcolm X* (1965) both attest. At the time Douglass wrote the practice was well established; one principal purpose was to state openly the circumstances of authorship and the degree of editorial assistance. Despite accusations from antiabolitionists, these accounts, with their sometimes condescending but explicit introductions, are less dishonest forms of American autobiography than many present-day ghostwritten lives of Hollywood or SuperBowl celebrities.

What immediately distinguishes the *Narrative* from most other slave accounts is Douglass's skill in using the introductions for his own purposes, so that what is elsewhere an extraneous essay becomes part of a unified form. The first advantage, of course, is a dramatic presentation of himself by another, thus dealing at once with the reader's possible imputation of vanity. "In the month of August, 1841," Garrison begins,

> I attended an anti-slavery convention in Nantucket, at which it was my happiness to become acquainted with FREDERICK DOUGLASS, the writer of the following Narrative . . . I shall never forget his first speech at the convention— the extraordinary emotion it excited in my own mind—the powerful impression it created upon a crowded auditory, completely taken by surprise—the applause which followed from the beginning to the end of his felicitous remarks. (*Narrative*, 3-4)

As Garrison proceeds to praise Douglass also as a writer his own style as writer-orator becomes sharply contrasted to that of his black protegé's. "Mr. Douglass has very properly chosen to write his own Narrative, in his own style," he continues,

> it is therefore, entirely his own production; . . . He who can peruse it without a tearful eye, a heaving breast, an afflicted spirit,—without being filled with an unutterable abhorrence of slavery and all its abettors, and animated with a determination to seek the immediate overthrow of that execrable system,— without trembling for the fate of this country in the hands of a righteous God, who is ever on the side of the oppressed, and whose arm is not shortened that it cannot save,—must have a flinty heart, and be qualified to act the part of a trafficker "in slaves and the souls of men." (9)

An introduction has turned into a speech and the personal subject largely lost in oratorical emotion. Though briefer, Wendell Phillips, too, falls into similar pulpit language and righteous regional feeling. These fulsome outpourings are deftly counterpointed by Douglass's own style and language throughout the *Narrative*. His final paragraph brings the reader back full circle to Garrison's opening one, but the Nantucket event is now re-created with the quiet authority of his own and not the white man's voice:

> I had not long been a reader of the "Liberator," before I got a pretty correct idea of the principles, measures and spirit of the anti-slavery reform. I took right hold of the cause . . . I seldom had much to say at the meetings, because what I wanted to say was said so much better by others. But, while attending an anti-slavery convention at Nantucket, on the 11th of August, 1841, I felt strongly moved to speak, and was at the same time much urged to do so by Mr. William C. Coffin, a gentleman who had heard me speak in the colored people's meeting at New Bedford. It was a severe cross, and I took it up reluctantly.
> The truth was, I felt myself a slave, and the idea of speaking to white people weighed me down. I spoke but a few moments, when I felt a degree of freedom, and said what I desired with considerable ease. From that time until now, I have been engaged in pleading the cause of my brethren—with what success, and with what devotion, I leave those acquainted with my labors to decide. (153)

Here the whole movement of the autobiography is succinctly recapitulated—the desire for freedom but the sense of being a slave, speaking out as the symbolic act of self-definition, Douglass's quiet pride in his public identity. Though the appendix apparently undercuts the symmetry of this ending, this afterthought on religious hypocrisy also asserts his independence of official white institutions. Thus the original contrast is maintained throughout: while the white men, Garrison and Phillips, argue a cause and point to this extraordinary black man as proof, Douglass's own account creates the image of a man, and this act of identity authenticates the cause of abolition.

The process from first to last is the creation of an *historical* self. "I was born in Tuckahoe, near Hillsborough, and about twelve miles from Easton, in Talbot County, Maryland." (23) So begins his story, which ends on an equally matter-of-fact note: "I subscribe myself, FREDERICK DOUGLASS. Lynn, Mass., April 28, 1845." Both statements sound flatly conventional but carry a special meaning. Under slavery, man possesses no such historic identity as name, date, place of birth or residence usually provide. Douglass has *achieved* these hallmarks of historicity, has attached himself to time, place, society. Therefore he shows no wish to escape from history. As soon as memory provides them, and it is safe to do so, he gives names, dates, titles, places—all the usual evidence of existence which many slaves are denied. Yet Douglass never loses himself in memoir, as do many slave narrators, by making his account merely factual or typical. To be sure, the *Narrative* records many experiences and emotions shared by other fugitive slaves, but these are stamped with Douglass's own imagination.

This individual vision develops gradually, but can be seen even in the first primal scene, the flogging of Aunt Hester, "a woman of noble form, and of graceful proportions" who has aroused the passions and ire of the master. Douglass terms his initiation "the blood-stained gate, the entrance to the hell of slavery, through which I was about to pass,"(28)—apt imagery for the violent emotions of master, slave woman, and the terrified child in the closet. The metaphor of "blood-stained gate" is typical of Douglass's language. Tradition-ally Christian on one level, it also communicates more private and inchoate feelings about birth, sexuality, violence, dark mothers and white fathers. To deal with such emotions and forces the boy has little of the family love or religious consolation available to other ex-slave writers like J. W. C. Pennington or Solomon Northup. Instead, like many slave children, he can recall nothing of his father except that he was reportedly white, and remembers seeing his mother only by night, for she lived on another plantation. The child's sense of isolation and his ultimate response are both neatly connected in his explanation: "It is a common custom," he observes dryly, "in the part of Maryland from which I ran away, to part children from their mothers at a very early age."(24) His later experiences—as house servant and field hand, in Baltimore and on plantations large and small, with brutal masters and some kind ones—continue his personal history in terms also representative. However, Douglass prefers the personal and seldom goes out of his way to dramatize situations which his readers are expecting but which are not actually part of his own remembered past. When he does refer to the sufferings of other slaves, these are carefully identified. The result is a narrative with less violence but more authority than many works in this genre.

The gradual enlargement of perspective in the *Narrative* is made natural and appropriate by Douglass's autobiographical point of view. He does not limit himself to the growing child's impressions but, like Benjamin Franklin (with whom, Alain Locke has noted, he has several parallels),[13] writes both as experiencing boy and experienced adult. This double vision is managed with considerable skill throughout the book. On the opening page he contrasts himself as a young slave whose only birthday is an animal's—"planting-time, harvest-time, cherry-time, spring-time, or fall-time"(23)—with the grown writer whose present identity shares the anonymity and ignorance of slavery. "The nearest estimate I can give makes me now between twenty-seven and twenty-eight years of age. I come to this, from hearing my master say, some time during 1835, I was about seventeen years old."(23–24) Like Malcolm X and Claude Brown, Douglass is a very youthful autobiographer, with a young man's vivid memories instead of an older writer's diaries or reminiscences as resources.

Other means of juxtaposing past and present selves in order to dramatize change and continuity are even more arresting and effective. Speaking of his childish sufferings, he remarks: "I had no bed. I must have perished with cold, but that, the coldest nights, I used to steal a bag which was used for carrying corn to the mill. I would crawl into this bag, and there sleep on the cold, damp, clay floor, with my head in and feet out. My feet have been so cracked with the frost, that the pen with which I am writing might be laid in the gashes."(51–52). Still more striking is the memorable description of the slaves' songs he remembers hearing on the road to the Great House Farm. He writes first from his present perspective. "I have often been utterly astonished, since I came to the north, to find persons who could speak of the singing, among slaves, as evidence of their contentment and happiness," (38) he remarks. Then he recaptures his past emotion: "those wild notes always depressed my spirit, and filled me with ineffable sadness." Finally he returns to the present to drive home his point: "I did not, when a slave, understand the deep meaning of those rude and apparently incoherent songs. I was myself within the circle; so that I neither saw nor heard as those without might see and hear."(37) His message is clear, but more complex than with most slave narrators. Neither the slaves themselves nor a sympathetic outsider—like, say, the sympathetic English actress Fanny Kemble who could not fathom the significance of the slave singing on her Georgia plantation—is in a position to tell the truth about this music. Only by being *black* and *becoming* free has Douglass earned the rank and right of interpreter. It is a message whose precision Stephen Crane would have understood.

Douglass's departure from Colonel Lloyd's plantation provides another occasion for dramatizing the double perspective. Embarking for Baltimore, the young boy, who symbolically scrubbed all the dead skin from his knees and donned his first pair of trousers, placed himself "in the bows of the sloop, and there spent the remainder of the day in looking ahead, interesting myself in what was in the distance rather than in things near by or behind." Only in retrospect (54) does the traveler see the significance of this preliminary escape to the city, which opens another "gateway, to all my subsequent prosperity." Contrasting that boy "in the galling chains of slavery" with himself now "seated by my own table . . . writing this Narrative,"(55–56) he nevertheless affirms, as do all true autobiographers, a deep continuity between the two selves. "From my earliest recollection," he writes, "I date the entertainment of a deep conviction that slavery would not always be able to hold me within its foul embrace."(56) This same sense of himself as two persons yet one self is likewise expressed in Douglass's various names and aliases; though at different times he becomes Bailey, Johnson, and Douglass, he never relinquishes Frederick. "I must hold on to that, to preserve a sense of my identity," (148) he declares near the close of the *Narrative*.

Among later episodes which express this writer's evolving identity, the crucial ones are his learning to read and write. Expression is at the core of selfhood for Frederick Douglass. In Baltimore, Mrs. Auld's assistance is soon halted by her husband, but young Frederick is not daunted. Their white repression awakened "sentiments within that lay slumbering,"(58) and he turned to the white boys of the street for help in reading. "When I was sent of errands," he relates in language that suggests Franklin," I always took my book with me, and by going one part of my errand quickly, I found time to get a lesson before my return. I used to also carry bread with me . . . This bread I used to bestow upon the hungry little urchins who, in return, would give me that valuable bread of knowledge." (65) The climax of this process of discovery came when he was twelve, at a time when "the thought of being *a slave for life* began to bear heavily upon my heart."(66) Then he discovered the *Columbian Orator*. This book becomes a key link between boy and man, slave and abolitionist, for its full *The Columbian Orator: Containing a Variety of Original and Selected Pieces; Together with Rules; Calculated to Improve Youth and Others in the Ornamental and Useful Art of Eloquence* by Caleb Bingham.[14] "Among much of other interesting matter," Douglass recalls, "I found in it a dialogue between a master and his slave." He continues: "In the same book, I met with one of Sheridan's mighty speeches on and in behalf of Catholic emancipation. These were choice documents to me. I read them over and over again with unabated interest."(66) Though memory has played him slightly false (the actual speech is not by Sheridan but is a *Speech in Irish Parliament by O'Connor in Favor of Roman Catholic Emancipation, 1795)*[15] a glance at its contents proves the wisdom of masters and mistresses in trying to keep such books from the eyes of slaves. Here, for instance, the boy read a *Discourse on Manumission of Slaves* by the Rev. Samuel Miller, *Slaves in Barbary: A Drama in Two Acts* by Everett, and a dialogue about civilization between an Indian and a white man.[16] The most suggestive excerpt, perhaps, to the young reader was the one remembered, the *Dialogue between A Master and a Slave* by Aiken, which appears just before O'Connor's speech. Here is a sample of the ideas the boy encountered:

MASTER: Now, villian [sic]: What have you to say for this second attempt to run away? . . .

SLAVE: I am a slave. That is answer enough.

MASTER: I am not content with that answer. I thought I discerned in you some tokens of a mind superior to your condition. I treated you accordingly. You have been comfortably fed and lodged, not over-worked, and attended with the most humane care when you were sick. And is this the return? . . .

SLAVE: Providence gives [the robber] a power over your life and property . . . But it has also given me the legs to escape with; and what should prevent me from using them? . . . Look at these limbs, are they not those of a man? Think that I have the spirit of a man too.

After the Master has freed his Slave, the latter addresses him:

> Now I am indeed your servant, though not your slave. And as the first return I can make for your kindness, I will tell you freely the condition in which you live. You are surrounded with implacable foes, who long for a safe opportunity to revenge upon you and the other planters all the miseries they have endured . . . You can rely on no kindness on your part, to soften the obduracy of their resentment. You have reduced them to the state of brute beasts; and if they have not the stupidity of beasts of burden, they must have the ferocity of beasts of prey. Superiour force alone can give you security . . . Such is the social bond between master and slave![17]

In the *Narrative* itself one may see the ultimate effect on the young boy of discovering how the aspirations and realities of his slave's life could find adequate expression. "The reading of these documents enabled me to utter my thoughts,"(66) he recalls with characteristic understatement.

But to reach this point he needed to write. This decisive step towards his present identity as a free black man occurred under circumstances which are recollected in detail: "The idea as to how I might learn to write was suggested to me by being in Durgin and Bailey's ship-yard, and frequently seeing the ship carpenters, after hewing, and getting a piece of timber ready for use, write on the timber the name of that part of the ship for which it was intended." (70) Specific details like these have a deceptive simplicity. Learning to write in a shipyard bearing in part his own name is both an historical and a symbolic event. In recording an actual occurrence, one which connects the twelve-year-old boy to the present writer in Lynn, he continues a pattern of event and image linked together to articulate his autobiographical identity. For Douglass's association of learning to read and write with ships and shipyards is not accidental. It recalls earlier and later moments when boy and man are seen in terms of ships, shipbuilding, and sailing across the water. We have already noted the first such occasion—placing himself in the very bow of the sloop sailing towards Baltimore and eventual freedom. Another moment is the famous apostrophe to the ships on the Chesapeake:

> Those beautiful vessels, robed in purest white, so delightful to the eye of free-men, were to me so many shrouded ghosts, to terrify and torment me with thoughts of my wretched condition . . . I would pour out my soul's complaint, in my rude way, with an apostrophe to the moving multitude of ships:—
> You are loosed from your moorings, and are free; I am fast in my chains, and am a slave! . . . You are freedom's swift-winged angels, that fly round the world; I am confined in bands of iron! (95–96)

Beneath this awkward rhetoric are some powerful personal associations linking ships and sails not simply to freedom, adventure, and literacy, but also the color white and the word "angel" with Mrs. Hugh Auld, his white preceptress who started him on the voyage to a free self and then betrayed him. In less emotional language, Douglass records another event in this complex when he describes his last act of self-assertion as a Maryland slave—his fight in Gardner's shipyard with the white apprentices. In his memory and imagination Douglass identifies freedom with both learning from and fighting with whites; both relationships are often associated with ships or their construction. Thus though we do not learn so in the *Narrative,* but only later in *Life and Times,* it is fitting that this young plantation slave escaped to the North disguised as a sailor. What the *Narrative* does tell us is that an Irishman on a wharf asked him first the vital question: "Are ye a slave for life?" (69) Here manifestly is a rich mixture of persons, places, sights, acts, and emotions which have combined in the autobiographer's memory to become what James Olney would call a "metaphor of self." Douglass's deepest impulses towards freedom, personal identity, and self-expression are fused and represented in these memories and images of ships and the sea. Therefore it is wholly appropriate that the final act by which selfhood is confirmed in the *Narrative* is speaking at the meeting on the island of Nantucket. Far more so than animal imagery, I believe, this pattern is central to Frederick Douglass's first autobiography for it connects and defines all stages of his personal history. "The following of such thematic designs through one's life," writes Vladimir Nabokov in *Speak, Memory,"* "should be, I think, the true purpose of autobiography."[19]

II

These literary strategies of self-presentation—the symmetry of Garrison's opening and his own closing paragraphs, the unity provided by the double perspective and by repeated experiences and images of ships, shipbuilding, and sailing across the water—set Douglass's *Narrative* apart from other artful accounts by ex-slaves like Henry Bibb, Solomon Northup, and Harriet Jacobs. But one must not forget that autobiography depends upon memory as much as on imagination. All remembered events do not fit readily into neat structural or imagistic patterns, no matter how many emotional needs are satisfied by trying to make them do so. Furthermore, one should not lose sight of Douglass's polemical purposes or the expectations of his readers. These readers, some of them unsophisticated and many suspicious of too much artistry, would be won over more immediately by a *story* than by a *point of view* or a *pattern of imagery.* Hence Douglass's emphasis upon exciting narrative, hence his climax in the gripping fight with Edward Covey. This event, he tells us, was the turning-point of his life. It occupies the same central place in the *Narrative.*

"You have seen how a man was made a slave; you shall see how a slave was made a man."(97) Everything in the re-created life of Frederick Douglass builds to and leads away from this declaration. The fight between the sixteen-year-old boy and the white farmer occurs in chapter 10—nearly at the end of the *Narrative*. In content, this chapter is a microcosm of the whole *Narrative*. The events described cover exactly a year—1833 in the young man's memory but amended to 1834 in later editions—and thus possess some of the symbolic unity of *Walden*. In becoming the clumsy field hand sent out with the equally clumsy oxen, Douglass is thrust back into the animal's place, easily brutalized there by Covey's whip. But like the oxen he, too, kicks over the lines, will not finally be broken to the yoke. The inspiration to rebel, interestingly enough, is not clearly understood—"from whence came the spirit I don't know" he confesses; "I resolve to fight."(103)—but it follows the sight of the sails on the Chesapeake and derives obvious support from the offer by the superstitious slave Sandy Jenkins of the magical root as a protection. After the fight, which lasts two hours, his transformation is sudden and complete: "It rekindled the few embers of freedom, and revived within me a sense of my own manhood . . . It was a glorious resurrection, from the tomb of slavery, to the heaven of freedom. My long-crushed spirit rose, cowardice departed, bold defiance took its place; and I now resolve that, however long I might remain a slave in form, the day had passed forever when I could be a slave in fact"(104–105).

The remainder of the chapter completes in narrative terms the rebirth here announced. From Covey's hell he moves to the comparative heaven of Mr. Freeland's. The new master's name—like the earlier one, Mr. Severe—is emblematic of Douglass's fortunes. However, a slave's life even under a "good" master cannot be heavenly, as the brutal disruption of his Sabbath school and the betrayal by a fellow slave of his attempted escape both prove. Nonetheless, he affirms, "my tendency was upward."(116) The chapter closes with the young slave back in Baltimore and earning a good wage, which his master appropriates. "The right of the grim-visaged pirate upon the high seas is exactly the same" (133), observes Douglass, and again we note how readily his indignation employs the imagery of the ocean.

As in narrative form and content, so in style is chapter 10 representative of the whole work. It exhibits his two voices with characteristic clarity. The dominant one is the unassuming prose narrator who can set a scene, describe an action, or portray a person with forceful economy. This, for instance, is Edward Covey:

> Mr. Covey's *forte* consisted in his power to deceive. His life was devoted to planning and perpetrating the grossest deceptions. Every thing he possessed in the shape of learning or religion, he made conform to his disposition to deceive. He seemed to think himself equal to deceiving the Almighty. He would make a short prayer in the morning, and a long prayer at night; and, strange as it may seem, few men would at times appear more devotional than he. The exercise of his family devotions were always commenced with singing; and, as he was a very poor singer himself, the duty of raising the hymn generally came upon me. He would read his hymn, and nod at me to commence. I would at times do so; at others, I would not. (93)

Such a description characterizes both the individual and an institution—here the "religion of the south." Thus the balanced antiphonal structure of many of Douglass's sentences is wholly appropriate. A sentence like "The longest days were too short for him, and the shortest nights too long for him" (94) reveals Covey as slave-driver and also as self-driven Southern Protestant, and does so in rhythms strongly reminiscent of the Old Testament, particularly the Psalms. Once attuned to this cadence, the reader recalls how many of the work's aptest aphorisms obey this pattern. "What he most dreaded, that I most desired. What he most loved, that I most hated," describes Hugh Auld's opposition to his learning to read. "I was ignorant of his temper and disposition; he was equally so of mine," is another comment which also reveals the psychological inspiration for this balanced style. The ex-slave sees himself from the start on equal and opposite terms with the white world of slavery. The shape as well as the content of his sentences expresses this equality and energetic opposition. Hence the formal fitness of the *Narrative*'s key sentence: "You have seen how a man was made a slave; you shall see how a slave was made a man." Douglass's story rests and rocks upon that semi-colon.

Douglass has, of course, another voice—the rich periods of the pulpit and platform, which sound so inflated and indulgent to modern ears. However, Alain Locke has warned that Douglass was "by no means the dupe of his own rhetoric."[20] Like his fellow abolitionists, he knew that readers as well as conventioneers expected large doses of sentiment and pathos. In chapter 10 the only instance of this style is the apostrophe to the sailboats. An earlier, lengthier one, which reads almost like a parody of John Pendleton Kennedy's *Swallow Barn,* is the bathetic description (much reduced in later editions) of his grandmother and her solitary cabin. Both passages, despite their fitness for other purposes, sound out of pitch with other parts of the *Narrative* written to more telling emotional effect in Douglass's quieter style. Yet the modern reader must be careful about over-nice judgments of tone and language which miss the emotional depths. Chapter 11 contains, for instance, the last of the purple passages, but this one, because it is backed by the accumulated weight of experience of the whole book, rings truer than earlier outbursts. Here deep and genuine feelings roll irresistibly over the reader. "Let him be a fugitive slave in a strange land—" Douglass exclaims,

> a land given up to be the hunting-ground for slaveholders—whose inhabitants are legalized kidnappers—where he is every moment subjected to the terrible liability of being seized upon by his fellow-men, as the hideous crocodile seizes upon his prey!—I say, let him place himself in my situation—without home or friends—without money or credit—wanting shelter, and no one to give it—wanting bread, and no money to buy it,—and at the same time let him feel that he is pursued by merciless menhunters, and in total darkness as to what to do, where to go, where to stay,—perfectly helpless both as to the means of defence and means of escape,—in the midst of plenty, yet suffering the terrible gnawings of hunger,—in the midst of houses, yet having no home,—among

fellowmen, yet feeling as if in the midst of wild beasts, whose greediness to swallow up the trembling and half-famished fugitive is only equalled by that with which the monsters of the deep swallow up the helpless fish upon which they subsist,—I say, let him be placed in this most trying situation,—the situation in which I was placed,—then, and not till then, will he fully appreciate the hardships of, and know how to sympathize with, the toil-worn and whipscarred fugitive slave. (144)

Here, as it seems to me, one experiences what Leo Marx has called the "literary power" of a genuine work of art.[21] The modern reader is prepared to agree with the hopeful editor of the abolitionist *Chronotype* who in 1853 confidently predicated: "This fugitive slave literature is destined to be a powerful lever. We have the most profound conviction of its potency. We see in it the easy and infallible means of abolitionizing the free states. Argument provokes argument, reason is met by sophistry; but the narratives of slaves go right to the hearts of men."[22] Unfortunately, as Charles Nichols pointed out in 1948, the testimony of history does not bear out the editor's belief in the power of these books. Though hearts were indeed moved, minds disabused of much misinformation, and imaginations fired by vivid pictures of slavery and of the black man's actual and potential achievements in coping with slavery, nevertheless American political behavior was not fundamentally altered. Nichols's judgment chastens the enthusiasm of those who believe literary power is readily translated into political action; he points out that only those already predisposed by social, economic, and religious outlook to be openminded were much affected by personal histories like Douglass's. "One is forced to the conclusion that, though widely read, the narratives effected no vital change in American attitudes," Nichols concludes.[23]

When American hearts were moved, Nichols adds, it was chiefly in a sentimental fashion. Settled convictions about the inferiority of the Negro— beliefs one might expect to be upset by reading so powerful and artful a book as the *Narrative*—were, it appears, seldom changed. If this is true—and questions of the impact of propaganda art on public opinion and behavior are exceedingly difficult to measure—a small but significant factor may be the development towards sentimentality and extreme bathos in the slave narratives published after 1849. The later autobiographies of Douglass himself are, if not representative, as least indicative of a general loss of emotional force and economy. *My Bondage and My Freedom* and the *Life and Times* are not only greatly expanded accounts of a long, distinguished career but are also much looser in style, structure, and imaginative power. Jean Yellin, not the first to note this loss of unity, provides a succinct example by contrasting the key sentence of the 1845 *Narrative* with its 1855 revision: "You have, dear reader, seen me humbled, degraded, broken down, enslaved, and brutalized, and you understand how it was done; now let us see the converse of all this, and how it was brought about; and this will take us through the year 1834.[24] Similarly, what was originally an organic pattern of meaningful events and images evoking ships and the sea as metaphors of Douglass's self becomes in later versions mere literary allusions, as in the following: "My poor weather-beaten bark now reached smoother water and gentler breezes. My stormy life at Covey's had been of service to me. The things that would have seemed very hard had I gone directly to Mr. Freeland's from the home of Master Thomas, were now 'trifles light as air.' "[25]

On the other hand, Douglass never fitted himself to popular stereotypes of the ex-slave as did Josiah Henson, nor did the later autobiographies always lapse into chatty, meandering memoirs. During the darkest times of Reconstruction, as his accounts attest, Douglass bore the banner of black independence, insisting on the freedman's rights to "the ballot-box, the jury-box, and the cartridgebox."[26] When temporarily barred from the White House at Lincoln's second inaugural reception, he commented wryly but gently of the servants: "They were simply complying with an old custom, the outgrowth of slavery, as dogs will sometimes rub their necks, long after their collars are removed, thinking they are still there."[27] In general, however, he was unable to sustain a sharp sense of his own voice and identity through a long historical narrative. After reading the *Narrative* and then turning to *Life and Times,* one has difficulty agreeing with Rayford Logan in calling the later autobiography a "classic."[28] This reader records a different impression—of the imaginative unity and superior force of the young man's self and story. Reading all three versions of this remarkable life makes one recognize afresh the difficulties of dealing with the long sweep of a public and private history. Douglass is no more to be criticized for writing more than one (and more than one kind of) personal history than are W. E. B. Du Bois or Mark Twain or Gertrude Stein. But if *Life and Times of Frederick Douglass* shows some of the strains of multiple autobiography, the *Narrative* should remind us how hard it is to repeat an early success. But then many of the most compelling black autobiographies have been the work of the young—*Black Boy, The Autobiography of Malcolm X, Manchild in the Promised Land, I Know Why the Caged Bird Sings.* Their precursor is the *Narrative of the Life of Frederick Douglass, an American Slave, Written by Himself.* It is the first native American autobiography to create a black identity in a style and form adequate to the pressures of historic black experience.

Notes

1. Ephraim Peabody, "Narratives of Fugitive Slaves," *Christian Examiner and Religious Miscellany* 47 (July 1849), 61–62.
2. William Wells Brown, *The Black Man: His Antecedents, His Genius, and His Achievements* (New York, 1863), 180–81.

3. Benjamin Quarles, introduction, John Harvard Library edition of the *Narrative of the Life of Frederick Douglass, an American Slave* (Cambridge, 1960), xiii. Subsequent references will be to this edition.

4. Charles H. Nichols, *Many Thousand Gone: The Ex-Slaves' Account of their Bondage and Freedom* (Bloomington, Ind., 1969), xii–xiii.

5. Douglass, *My Bondage and My Freedom* (New York and Auburn, 1855), v.

6. J. H. Hexter, "The Rhetoric of History," *International Encyclopedia of the Social Sciences* 6 (1968), 368–93.

7. F. R. Hart, "Notes for an Anatomy of Modern Autobiography," *New Literary History* 1 (Spring 1970), 488.

8. See Vernon Loggins, *The Negro Author: His Development in America* (Washington, D.C., 1964); Benjamin Brawley, *Early Negro American Writers* (Freeport, N.Y., 1968); Arna Bontemps, introduction, *Great Slave Narratives* (Boston, 1969); Charles H. Nichols, *Many Thousand Gone;* Charles H. Nichols, introduction, *Black Men in Chains: Narratives by Escaped Slaves* (New York, 1972); Benjamin Quarles, introduction, *Narrative;* Benjamin Quarles, "Narrative of the Life of Frederick Douglass," in *Landmarks of American Writing,* ed. Hennig Cohen (New York, 1969), 90–100; Jean F. Yellin, *The Intricate Knot: Black Figures in American Literature, 1776–1863* (New York, 1972); Houston A. Baker, Jr., *Long Black Song: Essays in Black American Literature and Culture* (Charlottesville, 1972).

9. Yellin, *The Intricate Knot,* 161, 164.

10. Baker, *Long Black Song,* 78–79.

11. See Nichols, *Many Thousand Gone,* xi.

12. Douglass, *Narrative,* Third English Edition (Wortley near Leeds, 1846), 124, 126.

13. See Alain Locke, foreword, *Life and Times of Frederick Douglass* (New York, 1941), as reprinted in *Frederick Douglass,* ed. Benjamin Quarles (Englewood Cliffs, N.J., 1968), 172.

14. An earlier version was published in Boston in 1799, but the edition I am citing appeared in Hartford, 1807; a copy is in the Library of Congress.

15. *Ibid.,* 243–48.

16. *Ibid.,* 102–8; 269–72.

17. *Ibid.,* 240–42.

18. See James Olney, *Metaphors of Self: The Meaning of Autobiography* (Princeton, 1972), 30–31.

19. *Speak, Memory: An Autobiography Revisited* (New York, 1967), 19.

20. Quoted in *Frederick Douglass,* B. Quarles, ed., 172–73.

21. See Leo Marx, "American Studies—A Defense of an Unscientific Method," *New Literary History* 1 (October 1969), 80. But for a critique of Marx, see Bruce Kuklick, "Myth and Symbol in American Studies," *American Quarterly* 24 (October 1972), 435–50, especially 448.

22. Leeds Antislavery Series 34 (1853), 12, as quoted in Nichols, *Many Thousand Gone,* 178.

23. See Nichols, "A Study of the Slave Narrative," (Brown University Thesis, 1948), 149.

24. Yellin, *The Intricate Knot,* 179.

25. *Life and Times of Frederick Douglass* (New York, 1962), 149.

26. *Ibid.,* 378.

27. *Ibid.,* 366.

28. *Ibid.,* 15.

Binary Oppositions in Chapter One of
Narrative of the Life of Frederick Douglass
an American Slave Written by Himself

HENRY LOUIS GATES, JR.

I was not hunting for my liberty, but also hunting for my name.
> —William Wells Brown, 1849

Whatever may be the ill or favored condition of the slave in the matter of mere personal treatment, it is the chattel relation that robs him of his manhood.
> —James Pennington, 1849

When at last in a race a new principle appears, an idea,—that conserves it; ideas only save races. If the black man is feeble and not important to the existing races, not on a parity with the best race, the black man must serve, and be exterminated. But if the black man carries in his bosom an indispensable element of a new and coming civilization; for the sake of that element, no wrong nor strength nor circumstance can hurt him: he will survive and play his part. . . . I esteem the occasion of this jubilee to be the proud discovery that the black race can contend with the white: that in the great anthem which we call history, a piece of many parts and vast compass, after playing a long time a very low and subdued accompaniment, they perceive the time arrived when they can strike in with effect and take a master's part in the music.
> —Emerson, 1844

The white race will only respect those who oppose their usurpation, and acknowledge as equals those who will not submit to their rule . . . We must make an issue, create an event and establish for ourselves a position. This is essentially necessary for our effective elevation as a people, directing our destiny and redeeming ourselves as a race.
> —Martin R. Delany, 1854

Autobiographical forms in English and in French assumed narrative priority toward the end of the eighteenth century; they shaped themselves principally

From Dexter Fisher and Robert B. Stepto, ed. *Afro-American Literature* (New York: MLA, 1979), 212–32. Reprinted by permission of the Modern Language Association and Henry Louis Gates, Jr.

79

around military exploits, court intrigues, and spiritual quests. As Stephen Butterfield has outlined, "Elizabethan sea dogs and generals of the War of the Spanish Succession wrote of strenuous campaigns, grand strategy, and gory battles. The memoirs of Louis XIV's great commander, the Prince of Condé, for example, thrilled thousands in Europe and America, as did the 'inside stories' of the nefarious, clandestine doings of the great European courts. The memoirs of the Cardinal De Retz, which told the Machiavellian intrigues of French government during Louis XIV's minority and of the cabal behind the election of a Pope, captivated a large audience. Even more titillating were personal accounts of the boudoir escapades of noblemen and their mistresses. Nell Gwyn, Madame Pompadour, and even the fictitious Fanny Hill were legends if not idols in their day. More edifying but no less marvelous were the autobiographies of spiritual pilgrimage—such as the graphic accounts of Loyola, John Bunyan, and the Quaker George Fox. Their mystical experiences and miraculous deliverances filled readers with awe and wonder." It is no surprise, then, that the narratives of the escaped slave became, during the three decades before the Civil War, the most popular form of written discourse in the country. Its audience was built to order. And the expectations created by this peculiar autobiographical convention, as well as by two other literary traditions, had a profound effect on the shape of discourse in the slave narrative. I am thinking here of the marked (but generally unheralded) tradition of the sentimental novel and, more especially, of the particularly American transmutation of the European picaresque. The slave narrative, I suggest, is a "countergenre," a mediation between the novel of sentiment and the picaresque, oscillating somewhere between the two in a bipolar moment, set in motion by the mode of the Confession. (Indeed, as we shall see, the slave narrative spawned its formal negation, the plantation novel.)

Claudio Guillén's seminal typology of the picaresque,[1] outlined as seven "characteristics" of that form and derived from numerous examples in Spanish and French literature, provides a curious counterpoint to the morphology of the slave narratives and aids remarkably in delineating what has proved to be an elusive, but recurring, narrative structure.

The picaro, who is after all a type of character, only becomes one at a certain point in his career, just as a man or woman "becomes" a slave only at a certain (and structurally crucial) point of perception in his or her "career." Both the picaro and the slave narrators are orphans; both, in fact, are outsiders. The picaresque is a pseudo-autobiography, whereas the slave narratives often tend toward quasi-autobiography. Yet in both, "life is at the same time revived and judged, presented and remembered." In both forms, the narrator's point of view is partial and prejudiced, although the total view "of both is reflective, philosophical, and critical on moral or religious grounds."[2] In both, there is a general stress on the material level of existence or indeed of *subsistence,* such as sordid facts, hunger, and money. There is in the narration of both a profusion of objects and detail. Both the picaro and the slave, as outsiders, comment on if not parody collective social institutions. Moreover, both, in their odysseys, move horizontally through space and vertically through society.

If we combine these resemblances with certain characteristics of the sentimental novel, such as florid asides, stilted rhetoric, severe piety, melodramatic conversation, destruction of the family unit, violation of womanhood, abuse of innocence, punishment of assertion, and the rags-to-riches success story, we can see that the slave narrative grafted together the conventions of two separate literary traditions and became its own form, utilizing popular conventions to affect its reader in much the same way as did cheap, popular fiction. Lydia Child, we recall, was not only the amanuensis for the escaped slave Harriet Jacobs, but also a successful author in the sentimental tradition. (That the plantation novel was the antithesis or negation of the slave narrative becomes apparent when we consider its conventions. From 1824, when George Tucker published *The Valley of the Shenandoah,* the plantation novel concerned itself with aristocratic, virtuous masters; beast-like, docile slaves; great manor houses; squalid field quarters; and idealized, alabaster womanhood—all obvious negations of themes common to the slave narratives. Indeed, within two years of the publication in 1852 of Harriet Beecher Stowe's *Uncle Tom's Cabin,* at least fourteen plantation novels appeared.)

It should not surprise us, then, that the narratives were popular, since the use of well-established and well-received narrative conventions was meant to ensure commercial and hence political success. By at least one account, the sale of the slave narratives reached such profound proportions that a critic was moved to complain that the "shelves of booksellers groan under the weight of Sambo's woes, done up in covers! . . . We hate this niggerism, and hope it may be done away with . . . If we are threatened with any more negro stories—here goes." These "literary nigritudes" [sic], as he calls them, were "stories" whose "editions run to hundreds of thousands."[3] Marion Wilson Starling recalls Gladstone's belief that not more than about five percent of the books published in England had a sale of more than five hundred copies; between 1835 and 1863, no fewer than ten of these were slave narratives.[4] So popular were they in England that a considerable number were published at London or Manchester before they were published in America, if at all. Nor should it surprise us that of these, the more popular were those that defined the genre structurally. It was Frederick Douglass' *Narrative* of 1845 that exploited the potential of and came to determine the shape of language in the slave narrative.

Douglass' *Narrative,* in its initial edition of five thousand copies, was sold out in four months. Within a year, four more editions of two thousand copies each were published. In the British Isles, five editions appeared, two in Ireland in 1846 and three in England in 1846 and 1847. Within the five years after its appearance, a total of some thirty thousand copies of the *Narrative* had been published in the English-speaking world. By 1848, a French edition, a paperback, was being sold in the stalls. *Littell's Living Age,* an American periodical, gave an estimate of its sweep in the British Isles after one year's circulation: "Taking all together, not less than one million persons in Great Britain and Ireland have been excited by the book and its commentators."[5]

Of the scores of reviews of the *Narrative,* two, especially, discuss the work in terms of its literary merits. One review, published initially in the *New York Tribune* and reprinted in *The Liberator,* attempts to place the work in the larger tradition of the narrative tale as a literary form.

> Considered merely as a narrative, we have never read one more simple, true, coherent, and warm with genuine feeling. It is an excellent piece of writing, and on that score to be prized as a specimen of the powers of the black race, which prejudice persists in disputing. We prize highly all evidence of this kind, and it is becoming more abundant.[6]

Even more telling is the review from the *Lynn Pioneer* reprinted in the same issue of *The Liberator;* this review was perhaps the first to attempt to attach a priority to the *Narrative*'s form and thereby place Douglass directly in a major literary tradition.

> It is evidently drawn with a nice eye, and the coloring is chaste and subdued, rather than extravagant or overwrought. Thrilling as it is, and full of the most burning eloquence, it is yet simple and unimpassioned.

Although its "eloquence is the eloquence of truth," and so "is as simple and touching as the impulses of childhood," yet its "message" transcends even its superior moral content: "There are passages in it which would brighten the reputation of any author,—while the book, as a whole, judged as a mere work of art, would widen the fame of Bunyan or De Foe."[7] Leaving the matter of "truth" to the historians,[8] these reviews argue correctly that despite the intention of the author for his autobiography to be a major document in the abolitionist struggle and regardless of Douglass' meticulous attempt at documentation, the *Narrative* falls into the larger class of the heroic fugitive with some important modifications that are related to the confession and the picaresque forms (hence, Bunyan and Defoe), a peculiar blend that would mark Afro-American fiction at least from the publication of James Weldon Johnson's *Autobiography of an Ex-Coloured Man.*

These resemblances between confession and picaresque informed the narrative shape of Afro-American fiction in much the same way as they did in the English and American novel. As Robert Scholes and Robert Kellogg maintain

> The similarity in narrative stance between picaresque and confession enables the two to blend easily, making possible an entirely fictional narrative which is more in the spirit of the confession than the picaresque, such as *Moll Flanders* and *Great Expectations.*

But this same blend makes possible a different sort of sublime narrative, "one that is *picaresque* in spirit but which employs actual materials from the author's life, such as [Wells's] *Tono-Bungay*." Into this class fall slave narratives, the polemical Afro-American first-person form the influence of which would shape the development of point of view in black fiction for the next one hundred years, precisely because

> By turning the direction of the narrative inward the author almost inevitably presents a central character who is an example of something. By turning the direction of the narrative outward the author almost inevitably exposes weaknesses in society. First-person narrative is thus a ready vehicle for ideas.[9]

It is this first-person narration, utilized precisely in this manner, that is the first great shaping characteristic of the slave narratives. But there is another formal influence on the slave narratives the effect of which is telling: this is the American romance.

Like Herman Melville's marvelous romance, *Pierre*, the slave narratives utilize as a structural principle the irony of seeming innocence. Here in American society, both say, is to be found as much that is contrary to moral order as could be found in pre-revolutionary Europe. The novelty of American innocence is, however, the refusal or failure to recognize evil while participating in that evil. As with other American romantic modes of narration, the language of the slave narratives remains primarily an expression of the self, a conduit for particularly personal emotion. In this sort of narrative, language was meant to be a necessary but unfortunate instrument merely. In the slave narratives, this structuring of the self couples with the minute explication of gross evil and human depravity, and does so with such sheer intent as to make for a tyranny of point. If the matter of the shaping of the self can come only after the slave is free, in the context of an autobiographical narrative where he first posits that full self, then slavery indeed dehumanizes and must in no uncertain terms be abolished, by violence if necessary, since it is by nature a violent institution. The irony here is tyranically romantic: Illusion and substance are patterned antitheses.

As with other examples of romance, the narratives turn on an unconsummated love: The slave and the ex-slave are the dark ladies of the new country destined to expire for unrequited love. Yet the leitmotif of the journey north and the concomitant evolution of consciousness within the slave—from an identity as property and object to a sublime identity as a human being and subject—display in the first person the selfsame spirit of the New World's personal experience with Titanic nature that Franklin's *Autobiography* has come to symbolize. The author of the slave narrative, in his flight through the wilderness (re-created in vivid detailed descriptions of the relation between man and land on the plantation and off), seems to be arguing strongly that man can "study nature" to know himself. The two great precepts—the former

Emersonian and the latter Cartesian—in the American adventure become one. Further, as with the American symbolists, the odyssey is a process of *becoming:* Whitman, for instance, is less concerned with explorations of emotion than with exploration as a mode of consciousness. Slave narratives not only describe the voyage but also enact the voyage so that their content is primarily a reflection of their literary method. Theirs is a structure in which the writer and his subject merge into the stream of language. Language indeed is primarily a perception of reality. Yet, unlike the American symbolists, these writers of slave narratives want not so much to adopt a novel stance from which the world assumes new shapes as to impose a new form onto the world. There can be no qualification as to the nature of slavery; there can be no equivocation.

Stephen Butterfield explicates[10] this idea rather well by contrasting the levels of diction in the slave narrative *The Life of John Thompson*[11] with a remarkably similar passage from Herman Melville's *Moby-Dick.*

The first is from Thompson:

> The harpoon is sharp, and barbed at one end, so that when it has once entered the animal, it is difficult to draw it out again, and has attached to its other end a pole, two inches thick and five feet long. Attached to this is a line 75 to 100 fathoms in length, which is coiled into the bow of the boat.

Melville follows:

> Thus the whale-line folds the whole boat in its complicated coils, twisting and writhing about it in almost every direction. All the oarsmen are involved in its perilous contortions; so that to the timid eye of the landsman they seem as festooning their limbs.

There is a difference here of rhetorical strategies that distinguishes the two. Melville's language is symbolic and weighted with ambiguous moral meanings: The serpentine rope allows for no innocence; "all the oarsmen" are involved, even those who have nothing to do with coiling it in the tub; the crew lives with the serpent and by the serpent, necessarily for their livelihood, unaware of the nature of the coil yet contaminated and imperiled by its inherent danger. Melville thus depicts the metaphysical necessity of evil.

John Thompson's language is distinguished formally from the concrete and symbolistic devices in Melville. Thompson allows the imagery of a whaling voyage to carry moral and allegorical meanings, yet he means his narration to be descriptive and realistic; his concern is with verisimilitude. There can be nothing morally ambiguous about the need to abolish slavery, and there can be little ambiguity about the reason for the suffering of the slave. "The slave narrative," Butterfield concludes, "does not see oppression in terms of a symbol-structure that transforms evil into a metaphysical necessity. For to do so would have been to locate the source of evil outside the master-slave relationship, and thus would have cut the ideological ground from under the entire thrust of the abolitionist movement."[12] Thompson means not so much to narrate as to convey a message, a value system; as with the black sermon, the slave's narrative functions as a single sign. And the nature of Frederick Douglass' rhetorical strategy directly reflects this sentiment through the use of what rhetoricians have called antitheses and of what the structuralists have come to call the binary opposition.

In the act of interpretation, we establish a sign relationship between the description and a meaning. The relations most crucial to structural analysis are functional binary oppositions. Roman Jakobson and Morris Halle argue in *Fundamentals of Language* that binary oppositions are inherent in all languages, that they are, indeed, a fundamental principle of language formation itself.[13] Many structuralists, seizing on Jakobson's formulation, hold the binary opposition to be a fundamental operation of the human mind, basic to the production of meaning. Levi-Strauss, who turned topsy-turvy the way we examine mythological discourse, describes the binary opposition as "this elementary logic which is the smallest common denominator of all thought."[14] Levi-Strauss' model of opposition and mediation, which sees the binary opposition as an underlying structural pattern as well as a method for revealing that pattern, has in its many variants become a most satisfying mechanism for retrieving almost primal social contradictions, long ago "resolved" in the mediated structure itself.[15] Perhaps it is not irresponsible or premature to call Levi-Strauss' contribution to human understanding a classic one.

Frederic Jameson, in *The Prison-House of Language,* maintains that

> the binary opposition is . . . at the outset a heuristic principle, that instrument of analysis on which the mythological hermeneutic is founded. We would ourselves be tempted to describe it as a technique for stimulating perception, when faced with a mass of apparently homogeneous data to which the mind and the eyes are numb: a way of forcing ourselves to perceive difference and identity in a wholly new language the very sounds of which we cannot yet distinguish from each other. It is a decoding or deciphering device, or alternately a technique of language learning.

How does this "decoding device" work as a tool to practical criticism? When any two terms are set in opposition to each other the reader is forced to explore qualitative similarities and differences, to make some connection, and, therefore, to derive some meaning from points of disjunction. If one opposes A to B, for instance, and X to Y, the two cases become similar as long as each involves the presence and absence of a given feature. In short, two terms are brought together by some quality that they share and are then opposed and made to signify the absence and presence of that quality. The relation between presence and absence, positive and negative signs, is the simplest form of the binary opposition. These relations, Jameson concludes, "embody a tension 'in which one of the two terms of the binary opposition is apprehended as positively having a certain feature while the other is apprehended as deprived of the feature in question.' "[16]

Frederick Douglass' *Narrative* attempts with painstaking verisimilitude to reproduce a system of signs that we have come to call plantation culture, from the initial paragraph of Chapter i:

> I was born in Tuckahoe, near Hillsborough, and about twelve miles from Easton, in Talbot County, Maryland. I have no accurate knowledge of my age, never having seen any authentic record containing it. By far the larger part of the slaves know as little of their ages as horses know of theirs, and it is the wish of most masters within my knowledge to keep their slaves thus ignorant. I do not remember to have ever met a slave who could tell of his birthday, they seldom come nearer to it than planting-time, harvest-time, cherry-time, spring-time, or fall-time. A want of information concerning my own was a source of unhappiness to me even during childhood. The white children could tell their ages. I could not tell why I ought to be deprived of the same privilege. I was not allowed to make any inquiries of my master concerning it. He deemed such inquiries on the part of a slave improper and impertinent, and evidence of a restless spirit. The nearest estimate I can give makes me now between twenty-seven and twenty-eight years of age. I come to this, from hearing my master say, some time during 1835, I was about seventeen years old.[17]

We see an ordering of the world based on a profoundly relational type of thinking, in which a strict barrier of difference or opposition forms the basis of a class rather than, as in other classification schemes, an ordering based on resemblances or the identity of two or more elements. In the text, we can say that these binary oppositions produce through separation the most inflexible of barriers: that of meaning. We, the readers, must exploit the oppositions and give them a place in a larger symbolic structure. Douglass' narrative strategy seems to be this: He brings together two terms in special relationships suggested by some quality that they share; then, by opposing two seemingly unrelated elements, such as the sheep, cattle, or horses on the plantation and the specimen of life known as slave, Douglass' language is made to signify the presence and absence of some quality—in this case, humanity.[18] Douglass uses this device to explicate the slave's understanding of himself and of his relation to the world through the system of the perceptions that defined the world the planters made. Not only does his *Narrative* come to concern itself with two diametrically opposed notions of genesis, origins, and meaning itself, but its structure actually turns on an opposition between nature and culture as well. Finally and, for our purposes, crucially, Douglass' method of complex mediation—and the ironic reversals so peculiar to his text—suggests overwhelmingly the completely arbitrary relation between description and meaning, between signifier and signified, between sign and referent.

Douglass uses these oppositions to create a unity on a symbolic level, not only through physical opposition but also through an opposition of space and time. The *Narrative* begins "I was born in Tuckahoe, near Hillsborough, and about twelve miles from Easton, in Talbot County, Maryland." Douglass knows the physical circumstances of his birth: Tuckahoe, we know, is near Hillsborough and is twelve miles from Easton. Though his place of birth is fairly definite, his date of birth is not for him to know: "I have no accurate knowledge of my age," he admits, because "any authentic record containing it" would be in the possession of others. Indeed, this opposition, or counterpoint, between that which is *knowable* in the world of the slave and that which is *not,* abounds throughout this chapter. Already we know that the world of the master and the world of the slave are separated by an inflexible barrier of meaning. The knowledge the slave has of his circumstances he must deduce from the *earth;* a quantity such as time, our understanding of which is *cultural* and not *natural,* derives from a nonmaterial source, let us say the *heavens:* "The white children could tell their ages. I could not."

The deprivation of the means to tell the time is the very structural center of this initial paragraph: "A want of information concerning my own [birthday] was a source of unhappiness to me even during childhood." This state of disequilibrium motivates the slave's search for his humanity as well as Douglass' search for his text. This deprivation has created that gap in the slave's imagination between self and other, between black and white. What is more, it has apparently created a relation of likeness between the slave and the animals. "By far," Douglass confesses, "the large part of slaves know as little of their ages as horses know of theirs." This deprivation is not accidental; it is systematic: "it is the wish of most masters within my knowledge to keep their slaves thus ignorant." Douglass, in his subtle juxtaposition here of "masters" and "knowledge" and of "slaves" and "ignorance," again introduces homologous terms. "I do not remember to have ever met a slave," Douglass emphasizes, "who could tell of his birthday." Slaves, he seems to conclude, are they who cannot plot their course by the linear progression of the calendar. Here, Douglass summarizes the symbolic code of this world, which makes the slave's closest blood relations the horses and which makes his very notion of time a cyclical one, diametrically opposed to the master's linear conception: "They [the slaves] seldom come nearer to [the notion of time] than planting-time, harvest-time, cherry-time, spring-time, or fall-time." The slave had arrived, but not *in time* to partake at the welcome table of human culture.

For Douglass, the bonds of blood kinship are the primary metaphors of human culture.[19] As an animal would know its mother, so Douglass knows his. "My mother was named Harriet Bailey. She was the daughter of Isaac and Betsey Bailey." Both of whom were "colored," Douglass notes, "and quite dark." His mother "was of a darker complexion" even than either grandparent. His father, on the other hand, is some indefinite "white man," suggested through innuendo to be his master: "The opinion was also whispered," he says, "that my master was my father." His master was his father; his father his master: "of the correctness of this opinion," Douglass concludes, "I know nothing," only and precisely because "the means of knowing was withheld from me." Two paragraphs below, having reflected on the death of his mother, Douglass repeats this peculiar unity twice again. "Called thus suddenly away," he commences, "she left me without the slightest intimation of who my father was." Yet Douglass repeats "the whisper that my father was my master" as he launches into a description of the rank odiousness of a system "that slaveholders have ordained, and by law established," in which the patrilinear succession of the planter has been forcibly replaced by a matrilinear succession for the slave: "the children of slave women shall in all cases follow the condition of their mothers." The planters therefore make of the "gratification of their wicked desires," spits Douglass, a thing "profitable as well as pleasurable." Further, the end result of "this cunning arrangement" is that "the slaveholder, in cases not a few, sustains to his slaves the double relation of master and father." "I know of such cases," he opens his sixth paragraph, using a declaration of verisimilitude as a transition to introduce another opposition, this one between the fertile slave-lover-mother and the planter's barren wife.

The profound ambiguity of this relationship between father and son and master and slave persists, if only because the two terms "father" and "master" are here embodied in one, with no mediation between them. It is a rather grotesque bond that links Douglass to his parent, a bond that embodies "the distorted and unnatural relationship endemic to slavery."[20] It is as if the usually implied primal tension between father and son is rendered apparent in the daily contact between father-master-human and son-slave-animal, a contact that occurs, significantly, only during the light of day.

Douglass' contact with his mother ("to know her as such," he qualifies) never occurred "more than four or five times in my life." Each of these visits, he recalls, "was of short duration," and each, he repeats over and over, took place "at night." Douglass continues: "[My mother] made her journey to see me in the night, travelling the whole distance," he mentions as if an afterthought, "on foot." "I do not recollect of ever seeing my mother," he repeats one sentence later, "by the light of day. She was with me in the *night*" (emphasis added). Always she returned to a Mr. Stewart's plantation, some twelve miles away, "long before I waked" so as to be at the plantation before dawn, since she "was a field hand, and a whipping is the penalty of not being in the field at sunrise." The slaves, metaphorically, "owned" the night, while the master owned the day. By the fourth paragraph of the narrative, the terms of our homology—the symbolic code of this world—are developed further to include relations of the animal, the mother, the slave, the night, the earth, matrilinear succession, and nature opposed to relations of the human being, the father, the master, the daylight, the heavens, patrilinear succession, and culture. Douglass, in short, opposes the absolute and the eternal to the mortal and the finite. Our list, certainly, could be expanded to include oppositions between spiritual/material, aristocratic/base, civilized/barbaric, sterile/fertile, enterprise/sloth, force/

principle, fact/imagination, linear/cyclical, thinking/feeling, rational/ irrational, chivalry/cowardice, grace/brutishness, pure/cursed, and human/ beastly.

Yet the code, Douglass proceeds to show, stands in defiance of the natural *and* moral order. Here Douglass commences as mediator and as trickster to reverse the relations of the opposition. That the relation between the slave-son and his master-father was an unnatural one and even grotesque, as are the results of any defilement of Order, is reflected in the nature of the relation between the plantation mistress and the planter's illegitimate offspring. "She is ever disposed to find fault with them," laments Douglass; "she is never better pleased than when she sees them under the lash." Indeed, it is the white mistress who often compels her husband, the master, to sell "this class of his slaves, out of deference to the feelings of his white wife." But it is the priority of the economic relation over the kinship tie that is the true perversion of nature in this world: "It is often the dictate of humanity for a man to sell his own children to human flesh-mongers," Douglass observes tellingly. Here we see the ultimate reversal: For it is now the mistress, the proverbial carrier of culture, who demands that the master's son be delivered up to the "human flesh-mongers" and traded for consumption. Douglass has here defined American cannibalism, a consumption of human flesh dictated by a system that could only be demonic.

Douglass' narrative demonstrates not only how the deprivation of the hallmarks of identity can affect the slave but also how the slaveowner's world negates and even perverts those very values on which it is built. Deprivation of a birth date, a name, a family structure, and legal rights makes of the deprived a brute, a subhuman, says Douglass, until he comes to a consciousness of these relations; yet, it is the human depriver who is the actual barbarian, structuring his existence on the consumption of human flesh. Just as the mulatto son is a mediation between two opposed terms, man and animal, so too has Douglass' text become the complex mediator between the world as the master would have it and the world as the slave knows it really is. Douglass has subverted the terms of the code he was meant to mediate: He has been a trickster. As with all mediations the trickster is a mediator and his mediation is a trick—only a trick; for there can be no mediation in this world. Douglass' narrative has aimed to destroy that symbolic code that created the false oppositions themselves. The oppositions, all along, were only arbitrary, not fixed.

Douglass first suggests that the symbolic code created in this text is arbitrary and not fixed, human-imposed not divinely ordained in an ironic aside on the myth of the curse of Ham, which comes in the very center of the seventh paragraph of the narrative and which is meant to be an elaboration on the ramifications of "this class of slaves" who are the fruit of the unnatural liaison between animal and man. If the justification of this order is the curse on Ham and his tribe, if Ham's tribe signifies the black African, and if this prescription for enslavement is scriptural, then, Douglass argues, "it is certain that slavery at the south must soon become unscriptural; for thousands are ushered into the world, annually, who, like myself, owe their existence to white fathers, and those fathers," he repeats for the fourth time, are "most frequently their own masters."

As if to underscore the falsity of this notion of an imposed, inflexibly divine order, Douglass inverts a standard Christian symbol, that of the straight and narrow gate to Paradise. The severe beating of his Aunt Hester, who "happened," Douglass advises us parenthetically, "to be absent when my master desired her presence," is the occasion of this inversion. "It struck me with awful force," he remembers. "It was the blood-stained gate," he writes, "the entrance to the hell of slavery, through which I was about to pass. It was," he concludes, "a most terrible spectacle." This startling image suggests that of the archetypal necromancer, Faustus, in whose final vision the usual serene presence of the Cross is stained with warm and dripping blood.

Douglass has posited the completely arbitrary nature of the sign. The master's actions belie the metaphysical suppositions on which is based the order of his world: It is an order ostensibly imposed by the Father of Adam, yet one in fact exposed by the sons of Ham. It is a world the oppositions of which have generated their own mediator, Douglass himself. This mulatto son, half-animal, half-man, writes a text (which is itself another mediation) in which he can expose the arbitrary nature of the signs found in this world, the very process necessary to the destruction of this world. "You have seen how a man was made a slave," Douglass writes at the structural center of his *Narrative,* "you shall see how a slave was made a man."[21] As with all mediation, Douglass has constructed a system of perception that becomes the plot development in the text but that results in an inversion of the initial state of the oppositions through the operations of the mediator himself, as indicated in this diagram:

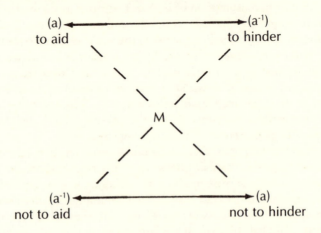

$$
\begin{array}{ccc}
\text{(a)} & \longleftrightarrow & \text{(a}^{-1}\text{)} \\
\text{to aid} & & \text{to hinder} \\
& M & \\
\text{(a}^{-1}\text{)} & \longleftrightarrow & \text{(a)} \\
\text{not to aid} & & \text{not to hinder}
\end{array}
$$

With this narrative gesture alone, slave has become master, creature has become man, object has become subject. What more telling embodiment of

Emersonian idealism and its "capacity" to transubstantiate a material reality! Not only has an *idea* made subject of object, but creature has assumed self and the assumption of self has created a race. For, as with all myths of origins, the relation of self to race is a relation of synecdoche. As Michael Cooke maintains concerning the characteristics of black autobiography:

> The self is the source of the system of which it is a part, creates what it discovers, and although (as Coleridge realized) it is nothing unto itself, it is the possibility of everything for itself. Autobiography is the coordination of the self as content—everything available in memory, perception, understanding, imagination, desire—and the self as shaped, formed in terms of a perspective and pattern of interpretation.[22]

If we step outside the self-imposed confines of Chapter i to seek textual evidence, the case becomes even stronger. The opposition between culture and nature is clearly contained in a description of a slave meal, found in Chapter v.[23] "We were not regularly allowanced. Our food was coarse corn meal boiled. This was called *mush*. It was put into a large wooden tray or trough, and set down upon the ground. The children were then called, like so many pigs, and like so many pigs they would come and devour the mush; some with oyster-shells, others with pieces of shingle, some with naked hands, and none with spoons. He that ate fastest got most; he that was strongest secured the best place; and few left the trough satisfied." The slave, we read, did not eat food; he ate mush. He did not eat with a spoon; he ate with pieces of shingle, or on oyster shells, or with his naked hands. Again we see the obvious culture-nature opposition at play. When the slave, in another place, accepts the comparison with and identity of a "bad sheep," he again has inverted the terms, supplied as always by the master, so that the unfavorable meaning that this has for the master is supplanted by the favorable meaning it has for the slave. There is in this world the planter has made, Douglass maintains, an ironic relation between appearance and reality. "Slaves sing most," he writes at the end of Chapter ii, "when they are most unhappy. . . . The singing of a man cast away upon a desolate island might be as appropriately considered as evidence of contentment and happiness, as the singing of a slave; the songs of the one and of the other are prompted by the same emotion."

Finally, Douglass concludes his second chapter with a discourse on the nature of interpretation, which we could perhaps call the first charting of the black hermeneutical circle and which we could take again as a declaration of the arbitrary relation between a sign and its referent, between the signifier and the signified. The slaves, he writes, "would compose and sing as they went along, consulting neither time nor tune. The thought that came up, came out—if not in the word, [then] in the sound;—and as frequently in the one as in the other."[24] Douglass describes here a certain convergence of perception peculiar only to members of a very specific culture: The thought could very well be embodied nonverbally, in the sound if not in the word. What is more, sound and sense could very well operate at odds to create through tension a dialectical relation. Douglass remarks: "They would sometimes sing the most pathetic sentiment in the most rapturous tone, and the most rapturous sentiment in the most pathetic tone. . . . They would thus sing as a chorus to words which to many would seem unmeaning jargon, but which, nevertheless, were full of meaning to themselves." Yet the decoding of these cryptic messages did not, as some of us have postulated, depend on some sort of mystical union with their texts. "I did not, when a slave," Douglass admits, "understand the deep meaning of those rude and apparently incoherent songs." "Meaning," on the contrary, came only with a certain aesthetic distance and an acceptance of the critical imperative. "I was myself within the circle," he concludes, "so that I neither saw nor heard as those without might see and hear." There exists always the danger, Douglass seems to say, that the meanings of nonlinguistic signs will seem "natural"; one must view them with a certain detachment to see that their meanings are in fact merely the "products" of a certain culture, the result of shared assumptions and conventions. Not only is meaning culture-bound and the referents of all signs an assigned relation, Douglass tells us, but *how* we read determines *what* we read, in the truest sense of the hermeneutical circle.

Notes

1. Claudio Guillén, *Literature as System: Essays toward the Theory of Literary History* (Princeton Univ. Press, 1971), pp. 71–106 and esp. pp. 135–58.

2. Guillén, p. 81.

3. George R. Graham, "Black Letters; or Uncle Tom-Foolery in Literature," *Graham's Illustrated Magazine of Literature, Romance, Art, and Fashion*, 42 Feb. 1853, p. 209.

4. Starling, *The Slave Narrative: Its Place in American Literary History*, Diss. New York Univ. 1946, pp. 47–48.

5. "Narrative of Frederick Douglass," *Littell's Living Age*, 1 April 1846, p. 47.

6. *New York Tribune*, 10 June 1845, p. 1, col. 1; rpt. in *Liberator*, 30 May 1845, p. 97.

7. *Lynn Pioneer;* rpt. in *Liberator*, 30 May 1845, p. 86.

8. See esp. John Blassingame, "Black Autobiography as History and Literature," *Black Scholar*, 5:4 (Dec. 1973–Jan. 1974), 2–9; and his *Slave Testimony: Two Centuries of Letters, Speeches, Interviews, and Autobiographies* (Baton Rouge: Louisiana State Univ. Press, 1977).

9. Scholes and Kellogg, *The Nature of Narrative* (New York: Oxford Univ. Press, 1966), p. 76.

10. Stephen Butterfield, *Black Autobiography in America* (Amherst: Univ. of Massachusetts Press, 1974), p. 36.

11. Thompson, *The Life of John Thompson, a Fugitive Slave, Containing His History of Twenty-Five Years in Bondage and His Providential Escape* (Worcester: n.p., 1856), p. 113.

12. Butterfield, p. 37.

13. Jakobson and Halle, *Fundamentals of Language* (The Hague: Mouton, 1971), pp. 4, 47–49.

14. *Totemism* (New York: Penguin, 1969), p. 130.

15. What has this rather "obvious" model of human thought to do with the study of mundane literature generally and with the study of Afro-American literature specifically? It has

forced us to alter irrevocably certain long-held assumptions about the relation between sign and referent, between signifier and signified. It has forced us to remember that we must not always mean what we say; or to remember what queries we intended to resolve when we first organized a discourse in a particular way. What's more, this rather simple formulation has taught us to recognize texts where we find them and to read these texts as they demand to be read. Yet, we keepers of the black critical activity have yet to graft fifty years of systematic thinking about literature onto the consideration of our own. The study of Afro-American folklore, for instance, remains preoccupied with unresolvable matters of genesis or with limitless catalogs and motif indices. Afraid that Brer Rabbit is "merely" a trickster or that Anansi spiders merely spin webs, we reduce these myths to their simplest thematic terms—the perennial relation between the wily, persecuted black and the not-too-clever, persecuting white. This reduction belies our own belief in the philosophical value of these mental constructs. We admit, albeit inadvertently, a nagging suspicion that these are the primitive artifacts of childish minds, grappling with a complex Western world and its languages, three thousand years and a world removed. These myths, as the slave narratives would, did not so much "narrate" as they did convey a value system; they functioned, much like a black sermon, as a single sign. The use of binary opposition, for instance, allows us to perceive much deeper "meanings" than a simplistic racial symbolism allows. Refusal to use sophisticated analysis on our own literature smacks of a symbolic inferiority complex as blatant as were treatments of skin lightener and hair straightener.

16. Frederic Jameson, *The Prison-House of Language: A Critical Account of Structuralism and Russian Formalism* (Princeton: Princeton Univ. Press, 1972), pp. 113; 35, citing Troubetskoy's *Principes de phonologie*. See also Jonathan Culler, *Structuralist Poetics: Structuralism, Linguistics, and the Study of Literature* (Ithaca: Cornell Univ. Press, 1975), pp. 93, 225–27; Roland Barthes, *S/Z, An Essay,* trans. Richard Miller (New York: Hill and Wang, 1975), p. 24.

17. Frederick Douglass, *Narrative* (Boston: Anti-Slavery Office, 1845), p. 1. All subsequent quotes, unless indicated, are from pp. 1–7.

18. There is overwhelming textual evidence that Douglass was a consummate stylist who, contrary to popular myth, learned the craft of the essayist self-consciously. The importance of Caleb Bingham's *The Columbian Orator* (Boston: Manning and Loring, 1797) to Douglass' art is well established. John Blassingame is convinced of Douglass' use of Bingham's rhetorical advice in his writing, especially of antitheses. (Personal interview with John Blassingame, 7 May 1976.) For an estimation of the role of language in the political struggle of antebellum blacks see Alexander Crummell, "The English Language in Liberia," in his *The Future of Africa* (New York: Scribners, 1862), pp. 9–57.

19. See also Nancy T. Clasby, "Frederick Douglass's *Narrative:* A Content Analysis," *CLA Journal,* 14 (1971), 244.

20. Clasby, p. 245.

21. Douglass, p. 77.

22. Michael Cooke, "Modern Black Autobiography in the Tradition," in *Romanticism, Vistas, Instances, and Continuities,* ed. David Thorburn and Geoffrey Hartman (Ithaca: Cornell Univ. Press, 1973), p. 258.

23. Douglass, pp. 13–15.

24. Douglass, p. 30.

Autobiographical Acts
and the Voice of the
Southern Slave

HOUSTON A. BAKER, JR.

The southern slave's struggle for terms for order is recorded by the single, existential voice engaged in what Elizabeth Bruss calls "autobiographical acts."[1] How reliable are such acts? Benedetto Croce called autobiography "a by-product of an egotism and a self-consciousness which achieve nothing but to render obvious their own futility and should be left to die of it." And a recent scholar of black autobiography expresses essentially the same reservations: "Admittedly, the autobiography has limitations as a vehicle of truth. Although so long an accepted technique towards understanding, the self-portrait often tends to be formal and posed, idealized or purposely exaggerated. The author is bound by his organized self. Even if he wishes, he is unable to remember the whole story or to interpret the complete experience."[2] A number of eighteenth- and nineteenth-century American thinkers would have taken issue with these observations. Egotism, self-consciousness, and a deep and abiding concern with the individual are at the forefront of American intellectual traditions, and the formal limitations of autobiography were not of great concern to those white authors who felt all existent literary forms were inadequate for representing their unique experiences. The question of the autobiography's adequacy, therefore, entails questions directed not only toward the black voice in the South, but also toward the larger context of the American experiment as a whole.

Envisioning themselves as God's elect and imbued with a sense of purpose, the Puritans braved the Atlantic on a mission into the wilderness. The emptiness of the New World, the absence of established institutions and traditions, reinforced their inclination to follow the example of their European forebears and brothers in God. They turned inward for reassurance and

From Houston A. Baker, Jr., *The Journey Back: Issues in Black Literature and Criticism* (Chicago: University of Chicago Press, 1980), 27–46.©1980 by the University of Chicago. All rights reserved.

guidance. Self-examination became the sine qua non in a world where some were predestined for temporal leadership and eventual heavenly reward and others for a wretched earthly existence followed by the fires of hell. The diary, the journal, the meditation, the book of evidences drawn from personal experiences were the literary results of this preoccupation with self, and even documents motivated by religious controversy often took the form of apology or self-justification. A statement from Jonathan Edwards's *Personal Narrative* offers a view of this tradition: "I spent most of my time in thinking of divine things, year after year: often walking alone in the woods, and solitary places, for meditation, soliloquy, and prayer, and converse with God; and it was always my manner at such time, to sing forth my contemplations."[3]

The man alone, seeking self-definition and salvation, certain that he has a God-given duty to perform, is one image of the white American writer. Commenting on Edwards and the inevitable growth of autobiography in a land without a fully articulated social framework, Robert Sayre writes: "Edwards could and had to seek self-discovery within himself because there were so few avenues to it outside himself. The loneliness and the need for new forms really go together. They are consequences of one another and serve jointly as inducements and as difficulties to autobiography."[4] This judgment must be qualified, since Edwards's form does not differ substantially from John Bunyan's, and his isolated meditations fit neatly into a Calvinistic spectrum, but Sayre is fundamentally correct when he specifies a concern with solitude and a desire for unique literary expression as key facets of the larger American experience.

Despite the impression of loneliness left by Edwards and the sense of a barren and unpromising land for literature left by comments like those of Hawthorne in his preface to *The Marble Faun* or James in *Hawthorne,* there were a number of a priori assumptions available to the white American thinker. They developed over a wide chronological span (the original religious ideals becoming, like those treated in the discussion of black writers above, increasingly secular) and provided a background ready to hand. There was the white writer's sense that he was part of a new cultural experience, that he had gotten away from what D. H. Lawrence calls his old masters and could establish a new and fruitful way of life in America. There was the whole panoply of spiritual sanctions; as one of the chosen people, he was responsible for the construction of a new earthly paradise, one that would serve as a holy paradigm for the rest of the world. There was the white writer's belief, growing out of the liberal, secular thought of Descartes, Locke, and Newton, that the individual was unequivocally responsible for his own actions; a man was endowed with inalienable rights, and one of these was the right to educate himself and strive for commercial success. There was also the feeling that America offered boundless opportunities for creative originality: a unique culture with peculiar sanctions should produce a sui generis art.

Thus, while James's "extraordinary blankness—a curious paleness of colour and paucity of detail" was characteristic for some early white Americans, there were also more substantial aspects or qualities of the American experience that stood in contrast to this "blankness." The writer could look to a Puritan ontology and sense of mission, to conceptions of the self-made man, or to a prevailing American concern for unique aesthetic texts as preshaping influences for his work. The objective world provided both philosophical and ideological justifications for his task. When Emerson wrote, "Dante's praise is that he dared to write his autobiography in colossal cipher, or into universality," he optimistically stated the possibilities immanent in the white author's situation. The writer of comprehensive soul who dared to project his experiences on a broad plane would stand at the head of a great tradition. According to Emerson, the world surrounding such a person—that supposedly void externality—offered all the necessary supports. The permanence and importance of works such as Edwards's *Personal Narrative,* Whitman's *Leaves of Grass,* and Adams's *The Education of Henry Adams* in American literature confirm his insight. As the American autobiographer turned inward to seek "the deepest *whole* self of man" (Lawrence's phrase), he carried with him the preexistent codes of his culture. They aided his definition of self and are fully reflected in the resultant texts—self-conscious literary autobiographies.

This perspective on white American autobiography highlights the distinctions between two cultures. Moved to introspection by the apparent "blankness" that surrounded him, the black, southern field slave had scarcely any a priori assumptions to act as stays in his quest for self-definition. He was a man of the diaspora, a displaced person imprisoned by an inhumane system. He was among alien gods in a strange land. Vassa[5] describes his initial placement in the New World:

> We were landed up a river a good way from the sea, *about Virginia country,* where we saw few or none of our native Africans, and not one soul who could talk to me. I was a few weeks weeding grass and gathering stones in a plantation; and at last all my companions were distributed different ways, and only myself was left. I was now exceedingly miserable, and thought myself worse off than any of the rest of my companions, for they could talk to each other, but I had no person to speak to that I could understand. In this state, I was constantly grieving and pining, and wishing for death rather than anything else. (*Life,* p. 34)

For the black slave, the white externality provided no ontological or ideological certainties; in fact, it explicitly denied slaves the grounds of being. The seventeenth- and eighteenth-century black codes defined blacks as slaves in perpetuity, removing their chance to become free, participating citizens in the American city of God. The Constitution reaffirmed the slave's bondage, and the repressive legislation of the nineteenth century categorized him as "chattel personal." Instead of the ebullient sense of a new land offering limitless opportunities, the slave, staring into the heart of whiteness around him, must have felt as though he had been flung into existence without a human purpose. The white externality must have loomed like the Heideggerian "nothingness," the negative foundation of being. Jean Wahl's characterization of Heidegger's theory of existence captures the point of view a black American slave might justifiably have held: "Man is in this world, a world limited by death and experienced in anguish; is aware of himself as essentially anxious; is burdened by his solitude within the horizon of his temporality."[6]

There were at least two alternatives to this vision. There was the recourse of gazing idealistically back to "Guinea." Sterling Stuckey has shown that a small, but vocal, minority of blacks have always employed this strategy.[7] And we have already considered its employment in the work of a northern spokeswoman like Wheatley or a black abolitionist like Vassa.[8] There was also the possibility of adopting the God of the enslaver as solace. A larger number of blacks chose this option and looked to the apocalyptic day that would bring their release from captivity and vengeance on the oppressors. (Tony McNeill's words, "between Africa and heaven," come to mind.) Finally, though, the picture that emerges from the innumerable accounts of slaves is charged with anguish—an anguish that reveals the black bondsman to himself as cast into the world, forlorn and without refuge.

And unlike white Americans who could assume literacy and familiarity with existing literary models as norms, the slave found himself without a system of written language—"uneducated," in the denotative sense of the word. His task was not simply one of moving toward the requisite largeness of soul and faith in the value of his experiences. He first had to seize the word. His being had to erupt from nothingness. Only by grasping the word could he engage in the speech acts that would ultimately define his selfhood. Further, the slave's task was primarily one of creating a human and liberated self rather than of projecting one that reflected a peculiar landscape and tradition. His problem was not to answer Crèvecoeur's question: "What then is the American, this new man?" It was, rather, the problem of being itself.

The *Narrative of the Life of Frederick Douglass*, one of the finest black American slave narratives, serves to illustrate the black autobiographer's quest for being.[9] The recovered past, the journey back, represented in the work is a sparse existence characterized by brutality and uncertainty:

I have no accurate knowledge of my age. The opinion was . . . whispered about that my master was my father; but of the correctness of this opinion, I know nothing. (Pp. 21–22)

My mother and I were separated when I was but an infant. (P. 22)

I was seldom whipped by my old master, and suffered little from anything else than hunger and cold. (P. 43)

Our food was coarse corn meal boiled. This was called *mush*. It was put into a large wooden trough, and set down upon the ground. The children were then called, like so many pigs, and like so many pigs they would come out and devour the mush. (P. 44)

Unlike David Walker who, in his *Appeal*, attempts to explain why blacks are violently held in bondage, the young Douglass finds no explanation for his condition. And though he does describe the treatment of fellow slaves (including members of his own family), the impression left by the first half of the *Narrative* is one of a lone existence plagued by anxiety. The white world rigorously suppresses all knowledge and action that might lead the narrator to a sense of his humanity.

The total process through which this subjugation is achieved can be seen as an instance of the imposed silence suggested by Forten's address.[10] Mr. Hugh Auld, whom Douglass is sent to serve in Baltimore, finding that his wife—out of an impulse to kindness rare among whites in the *Narrative*—has begun to instruct the slave in the fundamentals of language, vociferously objects that "learning would *spoil* the best nigger in the world." Not only is it illegal to teach slaves, but it is also folly. It makes them aspire to exalted positions. The narrator's reaction to this injunction might be equated with the "dizziness" that, according to Heidegger, accompanies a sudden awareness of possibilities that lie beyond anguish:

These words sank into my heart, stirred up sentiments within that lay slumbering, and called into existence an entirely new train of thought. It was a new and special revelation, explaining dark and mysterious things, with which my youthful understanding had struggled, but struggled in vain. I now understood what had been to me a most perplexing difficulty—to wit, the white man's power to enslave the black man. (*Narrative*, p. 49)

Douglass had come to understand, by the "merest accident," the power of the word. His future is determined by this moment of revelation: he resolves, "at whatever cost of trouble, to learn how to read." He begins to detach himself from the white externality around him, declaring:

What he (Mr. Auld) most dreaded, that I most desired. What he most loved, that I most hated. That which to him was a great evil, to be carefully shunned, was to me a great good to be diligently sought; and the argument which he so warmly urged, against my learning to read, only served to inspire me with a desire and determination to learn. (*Narrative*, p. 50)

The balanced antithesis of the passage is but another example—an explicit and forceful one—of the semantic competition involved in culture contact. Mr. Auld is a representation of those whites who felt that by superimposing the cultural sign *nigger* on vibrant human beings like Douglass, they would be able to control the meanings and possibilities of life in America. One marker for the term *nigger* in Auld's semantic field is «subhuman agency of labor». What terrifies and angers the master, however, is that Douglass's capacities—as revealed by his response to Mrs. Auld's kindness and instructions—are not accurately defined by this marker. For Douglass and others of his group are capable of learning. Hence, the markers in Auld's mapping of *nigger* must also include «agent capable of education». The semantic complexity, indeed the wrenching irony, of Auld's "nigger" is forcefully illustrated by the fact that the representation of Auld and *his* point of view enters the world of the learned by way of a narrative written by a "nigger." Douglass, that is to say, ultimately controls the competition among the various markers of *nigger* because he has employed meanings (e.g., agent having the power of literacy) drawn from his own field of experience to represent the competition in a way that invalidates «subhuman agency of labor». The nature of the autobiographical act, in this instance, is one of self-enfolding ironies. Douglass, the literate narrator, represents a Douglass who is perceived by Auld as a "nigger." Certainly the narrator himself, who is a learned writer, can see this "nigger" only through Auld, who is the "other." And it is the "otherness" of Auld that is both repudiated and controlled by the narrator's balanced antithesis. By converting the otherness of Auld (and, consequently, his "nigger") into discourse, Douglass becomes the master of his own situation. And the white man, who wants a silently laboring brute, is finally (and ironically) visible to himself and a learned reading public only through the discourse of the articulate black spokesman.

Much of the remainder of the *Narrative* counterpoints the assumption of the white world that the slave is a brute[11] against the slave's expanding awareness of language and its capacity to carry him toward new dimensions of experience. Chapter seven (the one following the Auld encounter), for example, is devoted to Douglass's increasing command of the word. He discovers *The Columbian Orator,* with its striking messages of human dignity and freedom and its practical examples of the results of fine speaking. He also learns the significance of that all-important word *abolition.* Against these new perceptions, he juxtaposes the unthinking condition of slaves who have not yet acquired language skills equal to his own. At times he envies them, since they (like the "meanest reptile") are not fully and self-consciously aware of their situation. For the narrator, language brings the possibility of freedom but renders slavery intolerable. It gives rise to his decision to escape as soon as his age and the opportunity are appropriate. Meanwhile, he bides his time and perfects his writing, since (as he says in a telling act of autobiographical conflation) "I might have occasion to write my own pass" (*Narrative,* p. 57).

Douglass's description of his reaction to ships on the Chesapeake illustrates that he did, effectively, write his own pass: "Those beautiful vessels, robed in purest white, so delightful to the eye of freemen, were to me so many shrouded ghosts to terrify and torment me with thoughts of my wretched condition (*Narrative,* p. 76). He continues with a passionate apostrophe that shows how dichotomous are his own condition and that of these white, "swift-winged angels."

> You are loosed from your moorings, and are free: I am fast in my chains, and am a slave! You move merrily before the gentle gale, and I sadly before the bloody whip! You are freedom's swift-winged angels, that fly around the world; I am confined in bands of iron! O that I were free! O, that I were on one of your gallant decks, and under your protecting wing! Alas! betwixt me and you, the turbid waters roll. Go on, go on. O that I could also go! Could I but swim! If I could fly! O, why was I born a man, of whom to make a brute! The glad ship is gone; she hides in the dim distance. I am left in the hottest hell of unending slavery. O God, save me! God, deliver me! Let me be free! Is there any God? Why am I a slave? I will run away. I will not stand it. Get caught, or get clear, I'll try it. (*Narrative,* p. 76)

When clarified and understood through language, the deathly, terrifying nothingness around him reveals the grounds of being. Freedom, the ability to choose one's own direction, makes life beautiful and pure. Only the man free from bondage has a chance to obtain the farthest reaches of humanity. From what appears a blank and awesome backdrop, Douglass wrests significance. His subsequent progression through the roles of educated leader, freeman, abolitionist, and autobiographer marks his firm sense of being.

But while it is the fact that the ships are loosed from their moorings that intrigues the narrator, he also drives home their whiteness and places them in a Christian context. Here certain added difficulties for the black autobiographer reveal themselves. The acquisition of language, which leads to being, has ramifications that have been best stated by the West Indian novelist George Lamming, drawing on the relationship between Prospero and Caliban in *The Tempest:*

> Prospero has given Caliban Language; and with it an unstated history of consequences, an unknown history of future intentions. This gift of language meant not English, in particular, but speech and concept as a way, a method, a necessary avenue towards areas of the self which could not be reached in any other way. It is in this way, entirely Prospero's enterprise, which makes Caliban aware of possibilities. Therefore, all of Caliban's future—for future is the very name for possibilities—must derive from Prospero's experiment, which is also his risk.[12]

Mr. Auld had seen that "learning" could lead to the restiveness of his slave. Neither he nor his representer, however, seem to understand that it might be possible to imprison the slave even more thoroughly in the way described by Lamming. The angelic Mrs. Auld, however, in accord with the evangelical codes of her era, has given Douglass the rudiments of a system that leads to intriguing restrictions. True, the slave can arrive at a sense of being only through language. But it is also true that, in Douglass's case, a conception of the preeminent form of being is conditioned by white, Christian standards.

To say this is not to charge him with treachery. Africa was for the black southern slave an idealized backdrop, which failed to offer the immediate tangible means of his liberation. Moreover, whites continually sought to strip Africans of their distinctive cultural modes. Vassa's isolation and perplexity upon his arrival in the New World, which are recorded in a passage previously cited, give some notion of the results of this white offensive. Unable to transplant the institutions of his homeland in the soil of America—as the Puritans had done—the black slave had to seek means of survival and fulfillment on that middle ground where the European slave trade had deposited him. He had to seize whatever weapons came to hand in his struggle for self-definition. The range of instruments was limited. Evangelical Christians and committed abolitionists were the only discernible groups standing in the path of America's hypocrisy and inhumanity. The dictates of these groups, therefore, suggested a way beyond servitude. And these were the only signs and wonders in an environment where blacks were deemed animals, or "things." Determined to move beyond a subservient status, cut off from the alternatives held out to whites, endowed with the "feeling" that freedom is the natural condition of life, Douglass adopted a system of symbols that seemed to promise him an unbounded freedom. Having acquired language and a set of dictates that specified freedom and equality as norms, Douglass becomes more assured. His certainty is reflected by the roles he projects for himself in the latter part of his *Narrative*. They are all in harmony with a white, Christian, abolitionist framework.

During his year at Mr. Freeland's farm, for example, he spends much of his time "doing something that looked like bettering the condition of my race" (*Narrative*, p. 90). His enterprise is a Sabbath school devoted to teaching his "loved fellow-slaves" so they will be able "to read the will of God" (*Narrative*, p. 89). His efforts combine the philanthropic impulse of the eighteenth-century man of sympathy with a zeal akin to Jupiter Hammon's.[13]

Having returned to Mr. Auld's house after an absence of three years, he undertakes a useful trade and earns the right to hire out his own time. All goes well until he attends a religious camp meeting one Saturday night and fails to pay the allotted weekly portion of his wages to his master. When Auld rebukes him, the demands of the "robber" are set against the natural right of a man to worship God freely. Once again, freedom is placed in a Christian context. Infuriated, Douglass decides that the time and circumstances are now right for his escape. When he arrives in New York, he feels like a man who has "escaped a den of hungry lions" (a kind of New World Daniel), and one of his first acts is to marry Anna Murray in a Christian ceremony presided over by the Reverend James W. C. Pennington. It would not be an overstatement to say that the liberated self portrayed by Douglass is firmly Christian, having adopted cherished values from the white world that held him in bondage. It is not surprising, therefore, to see the narrator moving rapidly into the ranks of the abolitionists—that body of men and women bent on putting America in harmony with its professed ideals. Nor is it striking that the *Narrative* concludes with an appendix in which the narrator justifies himself as a true Christian.

In recovering the details of his past, then, the autobiographer shows a progression from baffled and isolated existent to Christian abolitionist lecturer and writer. The self in the autobiographical moment (the present, the time in which the work is composed), however, seems unaware of the limitations that have accompanied this progress. Even though the writer seems to have been certain (given the cohesiveness of the *Narrative*) how he was going to picture his development and how the emergent self should appear to the reader, he seems to have suppressed the fact that one cannot transcend existence in a universe where there is *only* existence. One can realize one's humanity through "speech and concept," but one cannot distinguish the uniqueness of the self if the "avenue towards areas of the self" excludes rigorously individualizing definitions of a human, black identity.

Douglass grasps language in a Promethean act of will, but he leaves unexamined its potentially devastating effects. One reflection of his uncritical acceptance of the perspective made available by literacy is the *Narrative* itself, which was written at the urging of white abolitionists who had become the fugitive slave's employers. The work was written to prove that the narrator had indeed been a slave. And while autobiographical conventions forced him to portray as accurately as possible the existentiality of his original condition, the light of abolitionism is always implicitly present, guiding the narrator into calm, Christian, and publicly accessible harbors. The issue here is not simply one of intentionality (how the author wished his utterances to be taken). It is, rather, one that combines Douglass's understandable desire to keep his job with more complex considerations governing "privacy" as a philosophical concept.

Language, like other social institutions, is public; it is one of the surest means we have of communicating with the "other," the world outside ourselves. Moreover, since language seems to provide the principal way in which we conceptualize and convey anything (thoughts, feelings, sensations, and so forth), it is possible that no easily describable "private" domain exists. By adopting language as his instrument for extracting meaning from nothingness, being from existence, Douglass becomes a public figure.

He is comforted, but also restricted, by the system he adopts. The results are shown in the hierarchy of preferences that, finally, constitute value in the *Narrative*. The results are additionally demonstrated by those instances in the *Narrative* where the work's style is indistinguishable from that of the sentimental-romantic oratory and creative writing that marked the American nineteenth century. Had there been a separate, written black language available, Douglass might have fared better. What is seminal to this discussion, however, is that the nature of the autobiographer's situation seemed to force him to move to a public version of the self—one molded by the values of white America. Thus Mr. Auld can be contained and controlled within the slave narrator's abolitionist discourse because Auld is a stock figure of such discourse. He is the penurious master corrupted by the soul-killing effects of slavery who appears in poetry, fiction, and polemics devoted to the abolitionist cause.

But the slave narrator must also accomplish the almost unthinkable (since thought and language are inseparable) task of transmuting an authentic, unwritten self—a self that exists outside the conventional literary discourse structures of a white reading public—into a literary representation. The simplest, and perhaps the most effective, way of proceeding is for the narrator to represent his "authentic" self as a figure embodying the public virtues and values esteemed by his intended audience. Once he has seized the public medium, the slave narrator can construct a public message, or massage, calculated to win approval for himself and (provided he has one) his cause. In the white abolitionist William Lloyd Garrison's preface to Douglass's *Narrative,* for example, the slave narrator is elaborately praised for his seemingly godlike movement "into the field of public usefulness" (*Narrative,* pp. v–vi). Garrison writes of his own reaction to Douglass's first abolitionist lecture to a white audience:

> I shall never forget his first speech at the convention—the extraordinary emotion it excited in my own mind—the powerful impression it created upon a crowded auditory, completely taken by surprise—the applause which followed from the beginning to the end of his felicitous remarks. I think I never hated slavery so intensely as at that moment; certainly, my perception of the enormous outrage which is inflicted by it, on the godlike nature of its victims, was rendered far more clear than ever. There stood one, in physical proportion and stature commanding and exact—in intellect richly endowed—in natural eloquence a prodigy—in soul manifestly "created but a little lower than the angels"— trembling for his safety, hardly daring to believe that on the American soil, a single white person could be found who would befriend him at all hazards, for the love of God and humanity. Capable of high attainments as an intellectual and moral being—needing nothing but a comparatively small amount of cultivation to make him an ornament to society and a blessing to his race—by the law of the land, by the voice of the people, by the terms of the slave code, he was only a piece of property, a beast of burden, a chattel personal, nevertheless! (*Narrative,* p. vi)

Obviously, a talented, heroic, and richly endowed figure such as Garrison describes here was of inestimable "public usefulness" to the abolitionist crusade. And the Nantucket Convention of 1841 where Garrison first heard Douglass speak may be compared to a communicative context in which the sender and receiver employ a common channel (i.e., the English language) to arrive at, or to reinforce for each other, an agreed-upon message. Douglass transmits the "heroic fugitive" message to an abolitionist audience that has made such a figure part of its conceptual, linguistic, and rhetorical repertoire.

The issue that such an "autobiographical" act raises for the literary analyst is that of authenticity. Where, for example, in Douglass's *Narrative* does a prototypical black American self reside? What are the distinctive narrative elements that combine to form a representation of this self? In light of the foregoing discussion, it seems that such elements would be located in those episodes and passages of the *Narrative* that chronicle the struggle for literacy. For once literacy has been achieved, the black self, even as represented in the *Narrative*, begins to distance itself from the domain of experience constituted by the oral-aural community of the slave quarters (e.g., the remarks comparing fellow slaves to the meanest reptiles). The voice of the unwritten self, once it is subjected to the linguistic codes, literary conventions, and audience expectations of a literate population, is perhaps never again the authentic voice of black American slavery. It is, rather, the voice of a self transformed by an autobiographical act into a sharer in the general public discourse about slavery.

How much of the lived (as opposed to the represented) slave experience is lost in this transformation depends upon the keenness of the narrator's skill in confronting both the freedom and the limitations resulting from his literacy in Prospero's tongue. By the conclusion of Douglass's *Narrative*, the represented self seems to have left the quarters almost entirely behind. The self that appears in the work's closing moments is that of a public spokesman, talking about slavery to a Nantucket convention of whites:

> while attending an anti-slavery convention at Nantucket, on the 11th of August, 1841, I felt strongly moved to speak, and was at the same time much urged to do so by Mr. William C. Coffin, a gentleman who had heard me speak in the colored people's meeting at New Bedford. It was a severe cross, and I took it up reluctantly. The truth was, I felt myself a slave, and the idea of speaking to white people weighed me down. I spoke but a few moments, when I felt a degree of freedom, and said what I desired with considerable ease. From that time until now, I have been engaged in pleading the cause of my brethren—with what success, and with what devotion, I leave to those acquainted with my labors to decide. (*Narrative*, pp. 118–19)

The Christian imagery ("a severe cross"), strained reluctance to speak before whites, discovered ease of eloquence, and public-spirited devotion to the cause of his brethren that appear in this passage are all in keeping with the image of the publicly useful and ideal fugitive captured in Garrison's preface. Immediately before telling the reader of his address to the Nantucket convention, Douglass notes that "he had not long been a reader of the 'Liberator' [Garrison's abolitionist newspaper]" before he got "a pretty correct idea of the principles, measures and spirit of the anti-slavery reform"; he adds that he "took right hold of the cause . . . and never felt happier than when in an anti-slavery meeting" (*Narrative,* p. 118). This suggests to me that the communication between Douglass and Garrison begins long before their face-to-face encounter at Nantucket, with the fugitive slave's culling from the white publisher's newspaper those virtues and values esteemed by abolitionist readers. The fugitive's voice is further refined by his attendance and speeches at the "colored people's meeting at New Bedford," and it finally achieves its emotionally stirring participation in the white world of public discourse at the 1841 Nantucket convention.

Of course, there are tangible reasons within the historical (as opposed to the autobiographical) domain for the image that Douglass projects. The feeling of larger goals shared with a white majority culture has always been present among blacks. . . . From at least the third decade of the nineteenth century this feeling of a common pursuit was reinforced by men like Garrison and Wendell Phillips, by constitutional amendments, civil rights legislation, and perennial assurances that the white man's dream is the black man's as well. Furthermore, what better support for this assumption of commonality could Douglass find than in his own palpable achievements in American society?

When he revised his original *Narrative* for the third time, therefore, in 1893, the work that resulted represented the conclusion of a process that began for Douglass at the home of Hugh Auld. *The Life and Times of Frederick Douglass Written by Himself* is public, rooted in the language of its time, and considerably less existential in tone than the 1845 *Narrative.* What we have is a verbose and somewhat hackneyed story of a life, written by a man of achievement. The white externality has been transformed into a world where sterling deeds by blacks are possible. Douglass describes his visit to the home of his former master who, forty years after the slave's escape, now rests on his deathbed:

> On reaching the house I was met by Mr. Wm. H. Buff, a son-in-law of Capt. Auld, and Mrs. Louisa Buff, his daughter, and was conducted to the bedroom of Capt. Auld. We addressed each other simultaneously, he called me "Marshal Douglass," and I, as I had always called him, "Captain Auld." Hearing myself called by him "Marshal Douglass," I instantly broke up the formal nature of the meeting by saying, "not *Marshal,* but Frederick to you as formerly." We shook hands cordially and in the act of doing so, he, having been long stricken with palsy, shed tears as men thus afflicted will do when excited by any deep emotion. The sight of him, the changes which time had wrought in him, his tremulous hands constantly in motion, and all the circumstances of his condition affected me deeply, and for a time choked my voice and made me speechless.[14]

A nearly tearful silence by the black "Marshal" (a term repeated three times in very brief space) of the District of Columbia as he gazes with sympathy on the body of his former master—this is a great distance, to be sure, from the aggressive young slave who appropriated language in order to do battle with the masters.

A further instance of Douglass's revised perspective is provided by his return to the home plantation of Colonel Lloyd on the Wye River in Talbot County, Maryland:

> Speaking of this desire of mine [to revisit the Lloyd Plantation] last winter, to Hon. John L. Thomas, the efficient collector at the Port of Baltimore, and a leading Republican of the State of Maryland, he urged me very much to go, and added that he often took a trip to the Eastern Shore in his revenue cutter *Guthrie* (otherwise known in time of war as the *Ewing*), and would be much pleased to have me accompany him on one of these trips. . . . In four hours after leaving Baltimore we were anchored in the river off the Lloyd estate, and from the deck of our vessel I saw once more the stately chimneys of the grand old mansion which I had last seen from the deck of the *Sally Lloyd* when a boy. I left there as a slave, and returned as a freeman; I left there unkown to the outside world, and returned well known; I left there on a freight boat and returned on a revenue cutter; I left on a vessel belonging to Col. Edward Lloyd, and returned on one belonging to the United States.   (*Life and Times,* pp. 445–46)

The "stately chimneys of the grand old mansion" sounds very much like the Plantation Tradition, and how different the purpose of the balanced antithesis is in this passage from that noted in the delineation of the slave's realization of language as a key to freedom ("What he most dreaded, that I most desired . . ."). This passage also stands in marked contrast to the description of ships on the Chesapeake cited earlier ("those beautiful vessels . . . so many shrouded ghosts"). The venerable status of the *Guthrie* is now matched by the eminence of the marshal of the District of Columbia.

Douglass, in his public role, often resembles the courteous and gentlemanly narrator of Vassa's work—a man determined to put readers at ease by assuring them of his accomplishments (and the sterling company he keeps) in language that is careful not to offend readers' various sensibilities. It is strikingly coincidental that *The Life and Times of Frederick Douglass* was reprinted in 1895, the year in which its author died and Booker T. Washington emerged as one of the most influential black public spokesmen America had ever known. . . .

Notes

1. Elizabeth Bruss, *Autobiographical Acts* (Baltimore: Johns Hopkins University Press, 1976). "All reading (or writing) involves us in choice: we choose to pursue a style or subject matter, to struggle with or against a design. We also choose, as passive as it may seem, to take part in an interaction, and it is here that generic labels have their use. The genre does not tell us the style or construction of a text as much as how we should expect to 'take' that style or mode of

construction—what force it should have for us" (p. 4). Professor Bruss is drawing on speech-act theory as delineated by J. L. Austin, Paul Strawson, and John Searle. The nature, or force, of the speech act combines context, conditions, and intentions; it is called by the philosophers of language mentioned above the *illocutionary force* of an utterance. If the illocutionary force of a speech act is one involving certain rules, contexts, and intentions of self-revelation, the act can be called autobiographical. What I shall be investigating in the next few pages is the peculiar illocutionary force of certain black autobiographies produced during the nineteenth century. For an account of black autobiography, see Stephen Butterfield, *Black Autobiography in America* (Amherst: University of Massachusetts Press, 1974).

2. Rebecca Chalmers Barton, *Witnesses for Freedom* (New York: Harper, 1948), p. xii.

3. George McMichael, ed., *Anthology of American Literature* (New York: Macmillan, 1974), 1:228.

4. Robert Sayre, *The Examined Self* (Princeton: Princeton University Press, 1964), p. 39.

5. [*Ed. note:* Gustavus Vassa is the Christian name of Olaudah Equiano (1745?–1797), the African-born author of the most widely read slave narrative of the eighteenth century, *The Interesting Narrative of the Life of Olaudah Equiano, or Gustavus Vassa, the African,* 2 vols. (London: the author, 1789).]

6. Jean Wahl, *A Short History of Existentialism* (New York: Philosophical Library, 1949), p. 31. See also Jean Wahl, *Philosophies of Existence: An Introduction to the Basic Thought of Kierkegaard, Heidegger, Jaspers, Marcel, Sartre* (New York: Schocken, 1959).

7. Sterling Stuckey, *The Ideological Origins of Black Nationalism* (Boston: Beacon, 1972).

8. Baker refers to Phillis Wheatley's idealization of Gambia in her 1775 poem "Philis's Reply to the Answer in Our Last by the Gentleman in the Navy" (see William H. Robinson, ed., *Phillis Wheatley and Her Writings* [New York: Garland, 1984], 286–87) and to Vassa's nostalgic and idyllic image of his African homeland in the first two chapters of his *Interesting Narrative.* [Ed.]

9. Frederick Douglass, *Narrative of the Life of Frederick Douglass an American Slave Written by Himself* (New York: Signet, 1968), p. 21.

10. James Forten (1766–1842) was a freeborn Philadelphia businessman and civil rights leader whose opposition to the enforced colonization of black Americans in Africa was articulated in his "To the Humane and Benevolent Inhabitants of the City and County of Philadelphia, Address Delivered August 10, 1837." [Ed.]

11. In a fine analysis of the *Narrative* ("Animal Farm Unbound," *New Letters* 43 [1977]: 25–48), H. Bruce Franklin explores the significance for American literature of white assumptions that blacks are outside the human family. But cf. my own treatment of animal imagery in Douglass, which appeared in my collection of essays *Long Black Song* (Charlottesville: University Press of Virginia, 1972); and Albert Stone, "Identity and Art in Frederick Douglass' Narrative," *CLA Journal* 17 (1973): 192–213.

12. Quoted from Janheinz Jahn, *Neo-African Literature* (New York: Grove, 1969), p. 240.

13. Jupiter Hammon (1711–1806) was an early black American poet known especially for his Christian piety and evangelical preoccupations. [Ed.]

14. Frederick Douglass, *The Life and Times of Frederick Douglass Written by Himself* (New York: Collier, 1973), p. 442.

Storytelling in Early Afro-American Fiction:
Frederick Douglass's "The Heroic Slave"

ROBERT B. STEPTO

In 1847 Frederick Douglass finally decided to close the chapter of his "semi-exile" in England and Ireland and to return to the United States. Upon his return, he soon discovered that many of his old friends and supporters were skeptical about and even hostile toward his plans for the creation of an anti-slavery newspaper. Instead of contributing to the funds freely given in England for the purchase of a press and printing materials, they offered advice of a most discouraging sort. According to the account Douglass provides in *My Bondage and My Freedom,* they opposed his venture not only because they thought "the paper was not needed" and could not succeed but also because Douglass himself was, in their estimation, more useful as a lecturer and "better fitted to speak than to write."[1] One notices in these arguments—especially the latter two—a distinct echo of the dispiriting admonition Douglass had heard time and again during the years just after he was "discovered" by William Lloyd Garrison and other Massachusetts abolitionists in the fall of 1841. In those days, whenever Douglass strayed from narrating wrongs to denouncing them, Garrison would gently correct him by whispering, "Tell your story Frederick," and John Collins would remark more directly, "Give us the facts . . . we will take care of the philosophy" (*Bondage,* p. 361).

After two years abroad, Douglass returned to America only to discover that the arguments often used to limit his speech at anti-slavery meetings would be revived—indeed, they were ready and waiting—for the purpose of shutting down his newspaper before it began. Years later, well after the tumultuous split with Garrison, Douglass would write that he had decided to go ahead with his newspaper and to publish it in Rochester, New York, not Boston, "from motives of peace": hundreds of miles away from "New England friends" and "among strangers," the circulation of the *North Star* (for so the newspaper would be named) "could not interfere with the local circulation of the Liberator and the Standard" (*Bondage,* p. 395). Douglass's preference to be among

From *Georgia Review* 36 (Summer 1982): 355–68. ©1982 by The University of Georgia. Reprinted by permission of The Georgia Review and Robert Stepto.

"strangers" in "Western New York" rather than with "New England friends" tells us in no uncertain terms that, when faced with opposition to his newspaper *and* his full development not just as an anti-slavery agent but also as a human being, he chose to embark upon another "semi-exile." In a special sense, it can thus be said that Douglass's move to Rochester was at least a third expatriation in a persistent quest for greater freedom and literacy.

By 1852 Douglass's newspaper was five years old and generally on its way to attaining the circulation figure of 3000 that he reports in *Bondage*. However, it is also true that the newspaper was going through a bit of a crisis. In May of the previous year, at the annual convention of the American Anti-Slavery Society, Douglass had formally proclaimed his dissociation from the cardinal tenets of Garrisonian abolitionism, and Garrison had responded by removing the *North Star* from the list (in truth, Garrison's list) of approved abolitionist publications. Of course, Garrison's move had great effect: supporters of the cause were no longer directed to the pages of the *North Star,* and Garrisonians who had subscribed to the *North Star* in the past were not likely to do so again. Part of Douglass's counter-response was to rename the newspaper *Frederick Douglass' Paper,* and more than a few of his detractors would suggest that such a name was the inevitable issue of an arrogance they had seen and deplored before. It can be said, however, that the newspaper's new name was an expression not so much of his arrogance as of his exile and solitude: while not alone in his opposition to Garrison, Douglass was nevertheless in the relatively unique and harrowing position of being the editor of a newspaper that was more dependent than ever upon its editor's resources.

In a sense, Douglass's chief resource was his name, but of course he knew that to keep his newspaper alive his bank checks would have to be worth more than his signature. Various fund-raising activities were pursued, among these being the publication in 1853 of *Autographs for Freedom,* a collection of anti-slavery writings edited for the Rochester Ladies' Anti-Slavery Society so that they might assist in raising funds for *Frederick Douglass' Paper.* While not often cited, *Autographs for Freedom* is worthy of the attention of scholars of Afro-American literature for at least three reasons. First, as a fund-raising mechanism for Douglass's paper, commissioned by women abolitionists, it stands as remarkable evidence of the alliance Douglass was able to strike with various women's organizations, especially after he had been the "only man to take a prominent part in the proceedings of the Equal Rights for Women Convention" in July of 1848.[2] Second, the list of contributors to *Autographs for Freedom* provides us with a roster of those individuals, black and white, who presumably were willing—or at least not afraid—to align themselves with Douglass and his newspaper even after both had been in some sense "blacklisted" by the Garrisonians. The contributors included William H. Seward, Harriet Beecher Stowe, Horace Mann, Richard Hildreth, John Greenleaf Whittier, James M. Whitfield, James McClure Smith, Lewis

Tappan, Horace Greeley and James G. Birney. Finally, the volume is worthy of
interest because Douglass's own contribution to it is not an extract from a
famous speech (such as "What to the Slave is the Fourth of July?" or "The
Nature of Slavery"—both of which were written and available for inclusion at
the time) but a novella entitled "The Heroic Slave,"[3] a new work in what was
for Douglass a new form. Why and how Douglass wrote this novella are
questions well worth pursuing, for the answers tell us much about the
beginnings of Afro-American fiction.

One reason why Douglass wrote "The Heroic Slave" is easy to come by. In
1845, in response to the taunting cries that he had never been a slave, Douglass
was "induced," as he put it, "to write out the leading facts connected with [his]
experience in slavery, giving names of persons, places, and dates—thus putting
it in the power of any who doubted, to ascertain the truth or falsehood of [his]
story of being a fugitive slave" (*Bondage*, p. 363). Thus the *Narrative of the Life
of Frederick Douglass, An American Slave, Written by Himself* came to life. And in
1847, while harassed by suggestions that his *place* was to speak, not write,
Douglass began the *North Star*, his mission being to demonstrate that a
"tolerably well conducted press, in the hands of persons of the despised race,"
could prove to be a "most powerful means of removing prejudice, and of
awakening an interest in them" (*Bondage*, p. 389). Then, in 1852, Douglass
took a logical next step: he wrote a historical fiction about a heroic slave named
Madison Washington who had led a slave revolt aboard a slave ship in 1841. All
these *writing* activities, as opposed to speaking duties, are of a piece, each one
bolder than the one preceding it, each a measure of Douglass's remove from acts
of literacy involving merely spoken renditions of what Garrison and company
alternately called Douglass's "facts" or "story" or "simple narrative." This
suggests something of why Douglass would attempt a novella at this time, but
we must also ask why he chose Madison Washington's story for his subject
matter.

The ship upon which Washington and his fellow slaves revolted was
known as the *Creole*. The revolt occurred while the *Creole* was en route from
Hampton, Virginia (in "The Heroic Slave" it is Richmond, not Hampton), to
New Orleans. After the takeover, the *Creole's* course was altered for Nassau,
where the British set the former slaves free. A revealing feature of the American
response to the episode was that some of the prominent individuals who had
argued so strenuously in favor of freedom for the Spanish slaves (who had
revolted aboard the *Amistad* in 1839) soon became outraged by what they saw
to be British interference. Daniel Webster, for example, cried out, "The British
Government cannot but see that their case is one calling loudly for redress . . .
What duty or power, according to the principles of national intercourse, had
they to inquire at all [into the status of the slaves]?"[4] Webster's "double
talk"—and that of many others—regarding the *Amistad* case on the one hand
and the *Creole* case on the other undoubtedly had much to do with Douglass's
interest in the literary possibilities of Madison Washington's story. The Word

and the contradiction of the Word, to paraphrase Ralph Ellison, is, to a substantial degree, Douglass's primary theme and, quite understandably, his obsession.

To be sure, Douglass was also attracted to other features of the *Creole* affair, one such feature being the heroic role played by the British government in Nassau when it freed *American* slaves who had revolted. This was of use to Douglass in at least three ways, for here was an example of a government upholding the Word rather than contradicting it; here was an example as well of successful anti-slavery agitation on the part of British abolitionists; and here, on a more personal level, was an opportunity for Douglass to salute those same British abolitionists, many of whom had hosted him in England and given generously to the creation and support of his newspaper when "New England friends" had not.

Another attractive feature of the episode for Douglass was the militancy of the slaves as a group and the militant heroism of Madison Washington as the group's stalwart leader. The opportunity to retell Washington's story was also one for making clear to all that he had indeed broken from the Garrisonian policies condemning agitation and armed force, and that he believed more than ever that "the sable arms which had been engaged in beautifying and adorning the South" should not shrink from the increasingly necessary chore of "spreading death and devastation there."[5] Moreover, Douglass might very possibly have been attracted to Washington's story because it in some measure revises his *own* story. Both Washington and Douglass began their escape attempts in 1835, and both gained public attention as free men in the fall of 1841. However, while Douglass caulked ships in Baltimore (including, perhaps a slaver or two such as the *Creole*), Washington led black slaves in a ship's revolt. Similarly, while Douglass escaped from slavery wearing a sailor's suit, Washington was, in both a literal and a figurative sense, a truer and more heroic sailor. Douglass was a good man, and it would be wrong to suggest that he thought that Washington was a better man than himself, or that Washington's story was altogether better than his own. Nevertheless Douglass was embattled and open to self-doubt, and he was more than willing to review his own history and present circumstances by way of writing a novella about a personal hero.

"The Heroic Slave" is not an altogether extraordinary piece of work. I'm not about to argue that it should take a place beside, say, *Benito Cereno* as a major short fiction of the day. Still, after dismissing the florid soliloquies which unfortunately besmirch this and too many other anti-slavery writings, we find that the novella is full of craft, especially of the sort that combines artfulness with a certain fabulistic usefulness. Appropriately enough, evidence of Douglass's craft is available in the novella's attention to both theme and character. In Part I of "The Heroic Slave" we are told of the "double state" of Virginia and introduced not only to Madison Washington but also to Mr. Listwell, who figures as the model abolitionist in the story. The meticulous development of the Virginia theme and of the portrait of Mr. Listwell, much more than the portrayal of Washington as a hero, is the stuff of useful art-making in Douglass's novella.

The theme of the duality or "doubleness" of Virginia begins in the novella's very first sentence: "The State of Virginia is famous in American annals for the multitudinous array of her statesmen and heroes." The rest of the paragraph continues as follows:

> She has been dignified by some the mother of statesmen. History has not been sparing in recording their names, or in blazoning their deeds. Her high position in this respect, has given her an enviable distinction among her sister States. With Virginia for his birth-place, even a man of ordinary parts, on account of the general partiality for her sons, easily rises to eminent stations. Men, not great enough to attract special attention in their native States, have, like a certain distinguished citizen in the State of New York, sighed and repined that they were not born in Virginia. Yet not all the great ones of the Old Dominion have, by the fact of their birthplace, escaped undeserved obscurity. By some strange neglect, *one* of the truest, manliest, and bravest of her children—one who, in after years, will, I think, command the pen of genius to set his merits forth—holds now no higher place in the records of that grand old Commonwealth than is held by a horse or an ox. Let those account for it who can, but there stands the fact, that a man who loved liberty as well as did Patrick Henry—who deserved it as much as Thomas Jefferson—and who fought for it with a valor as high, an arm as strong, and against odds as great as he who led all the armies of the American colonies through the great war for freedom and independence, lives now only in the chattel records of his native state.[6]

At least two features here are worthy of note. The paragraph as a whole, but especially its initial sentences, can be seen as a significant revoicing of the conventional opening of a slave narrative. Slave narratives usually begin with the phrase "I was born"; this is true of Douglass's 1845 *Narrative* and true also, as James Olney reminds us, of the narratives of Henry Bibb, Henry "Box" Brown, William Wells Brown, John Thompson, Samuel Ringgold Ward, James W. C. Pennington, Austin Steward, James Roberts, and many, many other former slaves.[7] In "The Heroic Slave," however, Douglass transforms "I was born" into the broader assertion that in Virginia many heroes have been born. After that, he then works his way to the central point that a certain *one*—an unknown hero who lives now only in the chattel records and not the history books—has been born. Douglass knows the slave-narrative convention, partly because he has used it himself; but, more to the point, he seems to have an understanding of how to exploit its rhetorical usefulness in terms of proclaiming the existence and identity of an individual without merely employing it verbatim. This is clear evidence, I think, of a first step, albeit a small one, toward the creation of an Afro-American fiction based upon the conventions of the slave narratives. That Douglass himself was quite possibly thinking in these terms while writing is suggested by his persistent reference to the "chattel records" which must, in effect, be transformed by "the pen of genius" so that his hero's merits may be set forth—indeed, set free. If by this Douglass means that his hero's story must be liberated from the realm—the text—of brutal fact and, more, that texts must be created to compete with other texts, then it's safe to say that he brought to the creation of "The Heroic Slave" all the intentions, if not all the skills, of the self-conscious *writer*.

The other key feature of the paragraph pertains more directly to the novella's Virginia theme. I refer here to the small yet delightfully artful riddle which permits a certain ingenious closure of the paragraph. After declaring that his hero loved liberty as much as did Patrick Henry, and deserved it as much as Thomas Jefferson, Douglass refuses to name the third famous son of Virginia with whom his hero is to be compared. He speaks only of "he who led all the armies of the American colonies through the great war for freedom and independence." Of course, as any schoolboy or schoolgirl knows, the mystery man is Washington. And that is the answer—and point—to Douglass's funny-sad joke about the "double state" of Virginia as well: *his* mystery man is also a hero named Washington. Thus Douglass advances his comparison of heroic statesmen and heroic chattel, and does so quite ingeniously by both naming and *not* naming them in such a way that we are led to discover that statesmen and slaves may share the same name and be heroes and Virginians alike. Rhetoric and meaning conjoin in a very sophisticated way in this passage, thus providing us with an indication of how seriously and ambitiously Douglass will take the task of composing the rest of the novella.

"The Heroic Slave" is divided into four parts, and in each Virginia becomes less and less of a setting (especially of a demographic or even historical sort) and more of a ritual ground—a "charged field," as Victor Turner would say—for symbolic encounters between slaves and abolitionists or Virginians and Virginians. For example, in Part I, the encounter between Mr. Listwell, our soon-to-be abolitionist, and Madison Washington, our soon-to-be fugitive slave, takes place in a magnificent Virginia forest. In accord with many familiar notions regarding the transformational powers of nature in its purest state, both men leave the sylvan glen determined and resolved to become an abolitionist and a free man respectively. Thus the Virginia forest is established as a very particular space within the figurative geography of the novella, one which will receive further definition as we encounter other spaces which necessarily involve very different rituals for slave and abolitionist alike, and one to which we'll return precisely because, as the point of departure, it is the only known point of return.

Part II of "The Heroic Slave" takes place in Ohio. Listwell lives there and has the opportunity to aid an escaping slave who turns out to be none other than Madison Washington. This change in setting from Virginia to Ohio assists in the development of the Virginia theme chiefly because it gives Douglass the opportunity to stress the point that something truly happened to each man in that "sacred" forest, one happy result being that their paths did cross once again in the cause of freedom. As Listwell and Washington converse with each other before Listwell's hearth, and each man tells his story of self-transformation in the forest and what happened thereafter, we are transported back to the forest, however briefly and indirectly. By the end of Part II, it becomes clear in the context of the emerging novella that Ohio, as a free state, is an increasingly symbolic state to be achieved through acts of fellowship initiated however indirectly before. Ohio and that part of Virginia which we know only as "the forest" become separate but one, much as our heroic slave and model abolitionist become separate but one as they talk and truly hear each other.[8]

In Part III the return to Virginia and the forest is far more direct and in keeping with the brutal realities of life in the ante-bellum south. Listwell is back in Virginia on business, and so is Washington, who has come surreptitiously in quest of his wife still in slavery. Having portrayed Virginia's heaven—the forest replete with pathways to freedom—Douglass now offers Virginia's hell. As one might imagine, given Douglass's zeal for temperance and the abolition of slavery, hell is a tavern full of drunkards, knaves and traders of human flesh. Hell's first circle is the yard adjacent to the tavern where slaves on their way to market are "stabled" while the soul-driver drinks a dram. Its second circle is the remaining fifteen miles to Richmond where a slave auction awaits. The third circle may be sale to a new Virginia master and a long walk to a new plantation, or it may be a horrific re-encounter with Middle Passage, in the form of a "cruise" aboard a Baltimore-built slaver bound for New Orleans. If the latter, many other circles of hell await, for there will be another auction, another sale, another master, another long walk, and perhaps yet another auction.

The point to Part III is that, while Washington has returned to Virginia, lost his wife in their escape attempt and been re-enslaved, Listwell is also there and able to provide the means by which Washington may free himself—*and others*. The suggestion is that it is quite one thing to aid an escaping slave in Ohio and quite another to assist one in deepest, darkest Virginia. Listwell rises to the occasion and, immediately after the slave auction in Richmond, slips Washington several files for the chains binding him. What Washington and the rest do once on board the *Creole* is, of course, a matter of historical record.

One might think that the fourth and last part of "The Heroic Slave" would be totally devoted to a vivid narration of swashbuckling valor aboard the high seas. This is not the case. The scene is once again Virginia; the time is set some time after the revolt on the *Creole;* the place is a "Marine Coffee-house" in Richmond; and the conversation is quite provocatively between two white Virginia sailors, obviously neither statesmen nor slaves.[9] One of the sailors had shipped on the *Creole,* the other had not. The conversation takes a sharp turn when the latter sailor, Jack Williams, makes it clear that "For my part I feel ashamed to have the idea go abroad, that a ship load of slaves can't be safely taken from Richmond to New Orleans. I should like, merely to redeem the character of Virginia sailors, to take charge of a ship load of 'em to-morrow" (p. 186). Tom Grant, who had been on the *Creole,* soon replies, "I dare say *here* what many men *feel,* but *dare not speak,* that this whole slave-trading business is a disgrace and scandal to Old Virginia" (pp. 186–7). The conversation goes on and, before it's done, Tom Grant has indeed told the story of the revolt led by Madison Washington.[10] The point is, however, that Tom Grant, not the narrator, tells this story, and he does so in such a way that it is clear that he has become a transformed man as a result of living through the episode.

Thus Douglass ends his novella by creating the dialogue between Virginians about the "state" of Virginia which was effectively prefigured in the novella's first paragraph. The duality or doubleness of Virginia (and indeed of America) first offered as an assertion and then in the form of a riddle now assumes a full-blown literary form. More to the point, perhaps, is the fact that Tom Grant—the sailor who was forced to listen, if you will, to both the speech *and* action of Madison Washington—has become something of an abolitionist (though he bristles at the suggestion) and, most certainly, something of a white southern storyteller of a tale of black freedom. This particular aspect of Grant's transformation is in keeping with what happens to our white northerner, Mr. Listwell. What we see here, then, is an expression within Douglass's narrative design of the signal idea that freedom for slaves can transform the south and the north and hence the nation.

This brings us to Mr. Listwell, whose creation is possibly the most important polemical and literary achievement of the novella. In many ways, his name is his story and his story his name. He is indeed a "Listwell" in that he *enlists* as an abolitionist and does *well* by the cause—in fact, he does magnificently. He is also a "Listwell" in that he *listens* well; he is, in the context of his relations with Madison Washington and in accord with the aesthetics of storytelling, a model story-listener and hence an agent, in many senses of the term, for the continuing performance of the story he and Washington increasingly share and "tell" together. Of course, Douglass's point is that both features of Listwell's "listing" are connected and, ideally, inextricably bound: one cannot be a good abolitionist without being a good listener, with the reverse often being true as well.

Douglass's elaborate presentation of these ideas begins in Part I of "The Heroic Slave" when Washington apostrophizes in the Virginia forest on his plight as an abject slave and unknowingly is *overheard* by Listwell. At the end of his speech, the storyteller slave vows to gain freedom and the story-listener white northerner vows to become an abolitionist so that he might aid slaves such as the one he has just overheard. This is storytelling of a sort conducted at a distance. Both storyteller and story-listener are present, and closure of a kind occurs in that both performers resolve to embark on new journeys or careers. But, of course, the teller (slave) doesn't know yet that he has a listener (abolitionist, brother in the cause), and the listener doesn't know yet what role he will play in telling the story that has just begun. In this way, Douglass spins three primary narrative threads: one is the storyteller/slave's journey to freedom; another is the story-listener/abolitionist's journey to service; the third is the resolution or consummation of purposeful human brotherhood between slave and abolitionist, as it may be most particularly achieved through the communal aesthetic of storytelling.

In Part II the three primary threads reappear in an advanced state. Washington has escaped and is indeed journeying to freedom; Listwell is now a confirmed abolitionist whose references to conversations with other abolitionists suggest that he is actively involved; and Washington and Listwell are indeed in the process of becoming brothers in the struggle, both because they befriend each other on a cold night and because, once settled before Listwell's fire, they engage for long hours in storytelling. Several features of their storytelling are worth remarking upon. One is that Washington, as the storyteller, actually tells two stories about his adventures in the Virginia forest, one about a thwarted escape attempt and the resulting limbo he enters while neither slave nor free, and the other about how he finally breaks out of limbo, reasserting his desire for freedom.[11] The importance of this feature is that it occasions a repetition of the novella's "primary" forest episode which creates in turn a narrative rhythm that we commonly associate with oral storytelling. While it would be stretching things to say that this is an African residual in the novella, we are on safe ground, however, in suggesting that in creating this particular episode Douglass is drawing deeply on his knowledge of storytelling among slaves.

Another pertinent feature is that Listwell, as the story-listener, is both a good listener and, increasingly, a good prompter of Washington's stories. Early on, Listwell says, "But this was five years ago; where have you been since?" Washington replies, "I will try to tell you," and to be sure storytelling ensues. Other examples of this abound. In one notable instance, in response to Washington's explanation of why he stole food while in flight, Listwell asserts: "And just there you were right . . . I once had doubts on this point myself, but a conversation with Gerrit Smith, (a man, by the way, that I wish you could see, for he is a devoted friend of your race, and I know he would receive you gladly,) put an end to all my doubts on this point. But do not let me interrupt you" (p. 160). Listwell interrupts, but his is what we might call a good interruption, for he *authenticates* the slave's rationale for stealing instead of questioning it. In this way, Listwell's remarks advance both story *and* cause, which is exactly what he's supposed to do now that he's an abolitionist.[12]

Resolution of this episode takes the form of a letter from Washington to Listwell, written in Canada a few days after both men have told stories into the night. It begins, "My dear Friend—for such you truly are:— . . . Madison is out of the woods at last." The language here takes us back to the initial encounter in the Virginia forest between Washington and Listwell, back to a time when they weren't acquaintances, let alone friends—nor on their respective journeys to freedom and service. In examining the essential differences between Washington's apostrophe to no apparent listener and his warm letter to a dear friend, we are drawn to the fact that in each case a simple voice cries out, but in the second instance a listener is not only addressed but remembered and hence re-created. The great effect is that a former slave's conventional token of freedom and literacy bound and found in Canada takes on certain indelible storytelling properties.

From this point on in "The Heroic Slave" little more needs to be established between Washington and Listwell, either as fugitive slave and abolitionist or as storyteller and listener, except the all-important point that their bond is true and that Listwell will indeed come to Washington's aid in Virginia just as promptly as he did before in the north. In a sense their story is over, but in another respect it isn't: there remains the issue, endemic to both oral and written art, of how their story will live on with full flavor and purpose. On one hand, the story told by Washington and Listwell lives on in a direct, apparent way in the rebellion aboard the *Creole,* the resulting dialogue between the two Virginia sailors who debate the state of their state, and the transformation of one of the sailors, Tom Grant, into a teller of the story. On the other, the story lives on in another way which draws the seemingly distant narrator into the communal bonds of storytelling and the cause.

Late in the novella, in Part III, the narrator employs the phrase "Mr. Listwell says" and soon thereafter refers to Listwell as "our informant." These phrases suggest rather clearly that Listwell has told his shared tale to the narrator and that he has thus been a storyteller as well as a story-listener all along. The other point to be made is, of course, that the narrator has been at some earlier point a good story-listener, meaning in part that he can now tell a slave's tale well because he was willing to *hear* it before making it his own tale to tell. What's remarkable about this narrative strategy is how it serves Douglass's needs both as a novelist and as a black public figure under pressure. Here was a theory of narrative distilled from the relations between tellers and listeners in the black and white worlds Douglass knew best; here was an answer to all who cried, "Frederick, tell your story"—and then couldn't or wouldn't hear him.

Notes

1. Frederick Douglass, *My Bondage and My Freedom* (1855; repr. New York: Dover, 1969), p. 393. Hereafter cited as *Bondage.*

2. Benjamin Quarles, "Chronology of Frederick Douglass, 1817?–1895," in Quarles (ed.), *Narrative of the Life of Frederick Douglass, An American Slave, Written by Himself* (Cambridge, Mass.: Harvard University Press, 1960), pp. xxv–xxvi.

3. Frederick Douglass, "The Heroic Slave," in *Autographs for Freedom* (Boston, Mass.: John P. Jewett, 1853), pp. 174–239. The novella is more readily available to the contemporary reader as a volume in the Mnemosyne Press reprint series (Miami, Fla., 1969) and as a selection in Abraham Chapman (ed.), *Steal Away: Stories of the Runaway Slaves* (New York: Praeger, 1971), pp. 145–93.

4. Cited in Mary Cable, *Black Odyssey: The Case of the Slave Ship "Amistad"* (New York: Penguin, 1977), p. 151. For further discussion of comparisons made between the *Amistad* and *Creole* affairs, see Howard Jones, "The Peculiar Institution and National Honor: The Case of the *Creole* Slave Revolt," *Civil War History,* 21 (March 1975), pp. 34 ff.

5. Frederick Douglass in the *North Star,* 15 June 1849; cited in Leon F. Litwack, *North of Slavery: The Negro in the Free States, 1790–1860* (Chicago, Ill.: University of Chicago Press, 1961), p. 246. The same language may be found in Douglass's "Slavery, The Slumbering Volcano," an address delivered in New York City on 23 April 1849. Texts of the address appear in the *National Anti-Slavery Standard* (3 May 1849), the *Liberator* (11 May 1849) and the *North Star* (11 May 1849). The address pertains to this discussion in that it concludes with a spirited telling of the story of Madison Washington and the *Creole* revolt. I am indebted to John W. Blassingame and the staff of the Frederick Douglass Papers Project for providing me with a copy of their annotated text of this address.

6. Douglass, "The Heroic Slave," in Chapman (ed.), op. cit., p. 146. All future page references are to this republication of the novella.

7. James Olney, "I Was Born: Slave Narratives, Their Status as Autobiography and as Literature." An unpublished manuscript.

8. Listwell's role as host and story-listener in Part II suggests that he may be, at least in this section of the novella, a fictive portrait of abolitionist Joseph Gurney. Douglass himself plants this idea when he remarks in "Slavery, The Slumbering Volcano" that Washington debated with Gurney how advisable it would be to attempt to rescue his wife from slavery.

9. Placing the sailors in a "Marine Coffee-house" is possibly both an awkward and a revealing touch. To be sure, such establishments existed, but one cannot help but feel that a tavern would be a more "natural" setting. The braggadocio and general belligerence of Jack Williams, for example, suggest the behavior of a man whose cup contains a headier brew than coffee or tea. Of course, the problem for Douglass was that, given his advocacy of temperance, he could not easily situate Tom Grant, the reformed sailor and a voice of reason, in one of the Devil's haunts. This is quite likely an instance where Douglass's politics and penchant for realism conflicted in a way he had not encountered before he attempted prose fiction.

10. Early in Part IV, Tom Grant is referred to as "our first mate" (p. 185). This suggests that Grant is loosely modeled upon Zephaniah Gifford, the actual first mate of the *Creole*. Gifford gave many depositions on the revolt and hence told Washington's story many times. See Jones, op. cit., pp. 29–33.

11. These two stories of immersion in and ascent from a kind of limbo are central to the history of Afro-American letters, chiefly because they so conspicuously prefigure the trope of hibernation most accessible to the modern reader in Ralph Ellison's *Invisible Man,* published almost exactly one hundred years later. Madison Washington's cave in the realm between the plantation and the world beyond—"In the dismal swamps I lived, sir, five long years—a cave for my home during the day. I wandered at night with the wolf and the bear—sustained by the promise that my good Susan would meet me in the pine woods, at least once a week"—anticipates the Invisible Man's hole in the region between black and white Manhattan. Once Washington's wolf and bear become, in the mind's eye, Brer Wolf and Brer Bear, this particular contour in Afro-American literary history is visible and complete.

12. This brief and seemingly utilitarian passage in the novella becomes remarkable when one realizes that Douglass is also about the task of composing a salute or "praise song" for a new but fast friend in the cause, Gerrit Smith. "The Heroic Slave," we must recall, was Douglass's contribution to an anthology collected for the purpose of raising funds for the newly established *Frederick Douglass' Paper*. The *Paper* was created when Douglass's *North Star* merged with Gerrit Smith's *Liberty Party Paper* and Smith committed himself to subsidizing the new publication. Listwell's praise of Smith in the novella is, in effect, both a tribute and a "thank-you note" from Douglass to his new business partner. And it is something else as well: praise for Smith and not, say, Garrison is a clear signal from Douglass that he has broken with the Garrisonian abolitionists

and aligned himself with new friends. His praise for Smith took an even grander form when Douglass dedicated *My Bondage and My Freedom:* "To Honorable Gerrit Smith, as a slight token of esteem for his character, admiration for his genius and benevolence, affection for his person, and gratitude for his friendship, and as a small but most sincere acknowledgement of his pre-eminent services in behalf of the rights and liberties of an afflicted, despised and deeply outraged people, by ranking slavery with piracy and murder, and by denying it either a legal or constitutional existence, this volume is respectfully dedicated, by his faithful and firmly attached friend, Frederick Douglass." The doffing of the cap in "The Heroic Slave" became, within two years, a full and reverent bow.

Frederick Douglass: Literacy and Paternalism

Eric J. Sundquist

The chronological point at which Frederick Douglass's second autobiography, *My Bondage and My Freedom* (1855), surpasses his first, *Narrative of the Life of Frederick Douglass* (1845), reveals an important discrepancy that goes to the heart of his controversial career. The *Narrative* concludes with a brief description of Douglass's first significant public speech in Nantucket on 11 August 1841. "I spoke but a few moments," Douglass writes, "when I felt a degree of freedom, and said what I desired with considerable ease. From that time until now, I have been engaged in pleading the cause of my brethren— with what success, and with what devotion, I leave those acquainted with my labors to decide." In *My Bondage and My Freedom,* on the other hand, Douglass reports, "It was with the utmost difficulty that I could stand erect, or that I could command and articulate two words without hesitating and stammering. I trembled in every limb."

These different recollections of the occasion may both be relatively accurate; but the later version is more significant because it introduces the rest of Douglass's account of his life to date—his successful oratorical career, his widely acclaimed tour of Britain, his founding of the *North Star,* his battle against discrimination in the North, and the event against which his most important achievements must be judged: his break with the radical abolitionist William Lloyd Garrison. "But excited and convulsed as I was," Douglass continues in the second version of his initiation at Nantucket, "the audience, though remarkably quiet before, became as much excited as myself. Mr. Garrison followed me, taking me as his text; and now, whether I had made an eloquent speech or not, his was one never to be forgotten by those who heard it."

To be presented as Garrison's "text" was for Douglass the primary role of his early career: "I was generally introduced as a *'chattel'*—a *'thing'*—a piece of southern *'property'*—the chairman assuring the audience that *it* could speak." Or, "I was a 'graduate from the peculiar institution . . . *with my diploma written on my back!'*" His eventual disgust with being told to look and act like a slave, to keep "a *little* of the plantation" in his speech, is well known, and the

Reprinted by permission from *Raritan* 6, no. 2 (Fall 1986): 108–24. ©1986 by Raritan.

writing career that began with the *Narrative* has been rightly seen as an attempt both to refute accusations that his story was not authentic and to seize personal power over it at the same time. In transfiguring the text of his scarred slave's body into the combative written narrative that forced him to flee to England, Douglass took the first step in a lifelong series of autobiographical revisions that would culminate in the *Life and Times of Frederick Douglass* in 1881 and its extended version in 1892. Both the contents and the serial development of his autobiographical writings make evident the subversive lesson young Frederick first learned in reading the alphabet—that literacy is power.

Even if one prefers the fresh, stark text of the *Narrative*, it must be recognized that it too is no simple recitation of Douglass's slave and fugitive life. As Houston Baker has remarked, the *Narrative* itself represents a public version of Douglass's self already molded by white America, for "the voice of the unwritten self, once it is subjected to the linguistic codes, literary conventions, and audience expectations of a literate population, is perhaps never again the authentic voice of black American slavery." Because this is doubly true of *My Bondage and My Freedom,* part of the interest of the revised text lies in the fact that it is written against the grain both of recent historiography on slavery, which has been preoccupied with recovering the lost facts of Afro-American life, and also most recent work on slave narratives as a distinctive Afro-American genre.

Douglass's language in his second autobiography is thoroughly "American," in political as well as in literary terms, as is the versatile language of the self-made man which dominates the later chapters of *Life and Times*. One might argue that *My Bondage and My Freedom* therefore anticipates what some consider the pompous style and accommodating posture of Douglass's mature career. But a preference for the *Narrative* could also be seen as a later version of the condescending instructions Douglass himself despised: 'Let us have the facts,' . . . said Friend George Foster, who always wished to pin me down to my simple narrative. 'Give us the facts,' said [John] Collins, 'we will take care of the philosophy.' '. . . Tell your story, Frederick,' would whisper my then revered friend, William Lloyd Garrison, as I stepped upon the platform." As Douglass notes, he was by this time "reading and thinking," and it "did not entirely satisfy me to *narrate* wrongs; I felt like *denouncing* them." In its spirit of individualism and rebellion, *My Bondage and My Freedom* "is an American book, for Americans, in the fullest sense of the idea," as the black abolitionist James McCune Smith wrote in a preface that replaced the authenticating introductory letters of Garrison and Wendell Phillips which had opened the *Narrative*. It is precisely in his adopted American language that Douglass rehearses his own "adoption" by America and acquires the power that was to make him the leading black figure in America for nearly half a century. How could it fail to be the disturbing language of that "double-consciousness"— "American" and "Negro"—which W. E. B. DuBois would identify in the Afro-American tradition at the turn of the century: "two souls, two thoughts, two unreconciled strivings; two warring ideals in one dark body, whose dogged strength alone keeps it from being torn asunder."

DuBois's famous description of the black American dilemma is all the more relevant because Douglass's late career and legend have been subject to as much problematic appropriation and counter-claim as Lincoln's. This is no surprise, for the two figures have at times been mythologically fused, and both were exposed to abuse by the collapse of black civil rights in the last decades of the century. For example, Booker T. Washington's 1906 biography of Douglass is praising but overtly conciliatory in tone; whereas DuBois, whatever his doubts about Douglass on other occasions, argues in the Washington chapter of *The Souls of Black Folk* (1903) that Douglass, throughout his life, "bravely stood for the ideals of his early manhood,—ultimate assimilation *through* self-assertion, and on no other terms." Washington's spirit of compromise in the three crucial areas of suffrage, civil rights, and higher education, DuBois goes on to imply, is an utter betrayal of Douglass.

The argument between Washington and DuBois over Douglass, like the more extreme arguments that found Lincoln alternately a white supremacist and a martyred champion of immediate black rights, brings into focus two aspects of the same doubled character. *My Bondage and My Freedom* makes that doubling a powerful and explicit theme. It reconceives rebellion in terms of an embracing ideology of liberation rooted in the rhetoric of the American Revolution. But it would be a mistake to read the Douglass of 1855 as an embarrassing sentimentalist and "white" patriot, an incipient Booker T. Washington; he would better be likened to Madison Washington, the black hero of the revolt aboard the slave ship *Creole* in 1841 and the subject of Douglass's only work of fiction, "The Heroic Slave."

Quite apart from the content of "The Heroic Slave," the very fact of its publication, in Julia Griffiths's giftbook, *Autographs for Freedom* (1853), alerts us to its autobiographical implications: the story represents, in effect, Douglass's own "autograph for freedom," his declaration of liberty through acts of increasingly rebellious literacy. Proceeds from the collection were intended to mitigate the financial difficulties of the *North Star,* and Douglass offered *Autographs* free to new subscribers to his paper. His own contribution to the collection placed him in the mainstream of intellectual antislavery. It invites us to identify him with his quasi-fictional rebel-hero, who appears throughout his speeches of the period as a model of black achievement. In "The Heroic Slave," Douglass invokes the domestic cult surrounding the legend of George Washington but subverts its inherent conservatism by making Madison Washington, the *black* Virginian rebel, articulate his ideal of liberty: "We have done that which you applaud your fathers for doing, and if we are murderers, *so were they.*" These same sentiments pervade *My Bondage and My Freedom* and echo Douglass's endorsement of violent slave rebellion. Dramatized in the fictional setting, however, they suggest as well that Douglass's persona in the new autobiography is also part of a rhetorical masquerade, a deliberate augmentation of his power at a new level of literacy. The Douglass who wrote the *Narrative,* had a successful tour of Britain, moved to Rochester and founded his own paper (against the wishes of Phillips and Garrison), endorsed the Constitution, entered on a struggle against the narrow fanaticism of the Massachusetts abolitionists who would make him their puppet, changed the name of the *North Star* to *Frederick Douglass' Paper* after Garrison blacklisted it in response to Douglass's disavowal of Garrisonian positions—this Douglass is the patriotic rebel-slave, the hero of his own fictionalized story based on fact.

"The Heroic Slave" thus links the two autobiographies, and by implicitly dramatizing his own rebellion portrays Douglass's escape from a new enslavement to the Boston abolitionists' ethnocentric paternalism. Its narrative form, in which a fugitive slave, through the power of his character and his story, converts a white man to antislavery, anticipates the unlikely role in which Douglass—punning on his recent status as chattel, as a *thing*—cast himself first as a speaker and then as a young editor in *My Bondage and My Freedom:* "A slave, brought up in the very depths of ignorance, assuming to instruct the highly civilized people of the north in the principles of liberty, justice, and humanity! The thing looked absurd." By itself, the lecture platform possibly seemed too much like the auction block. The newspaper, like the autobiography or the short story, offered Douglass, as it had Benjamin Franklin, the opportunity to "edit" his own American identity and thus reach a wider audience, white and black. It leads directly into *My Bondage and My Freedom,* defining the public self as a newly revised and more vitally marketed "thing"—a man with property in himself.

In the *Life and Times,* Douglass's longer account of his newspaper career supports Robert Stepto's observation that, when he renamed his paper *Frederick Douglass' Paper* in 1851, Douglass was expressing less his supposed arrogance than his sense of exile and solitude. As he conceived of it, the change is a signal instance of American self-reliance. "I have come to think," he writes in 1881, "that, under the circumstances, it was the best school possible for me," making it "necessary for me to lean upon myself, and not upon the heads of our antislavery church . . . There is nothing like the lash and sting of necessity to make a man work, and my paper furnished the motive power." Like the title of his always popular lecture on "Self-Made Men," this striking metaphorical appropriation of slavery's whip by the work ethic of American success clarifies the doubleness entailed in Douglass's career as a writer and editor. "My feet have been so cracked with frost, that the pen with which I am writing might be laid in the gashes," Douglass writes in a famous passage that appears in all the autobiographies. Not only the voice, but the pen was the key to liberty, no less for black Americans than it had been for the pamphleteers of the Revolutionary period.

During the late 1840s and 1850s, however, Douglass continually chastised free blacks for their comparative lack of interest in abolitionism, and in antislavery papers like his own (eighty percent of his subscribers were white). If blacks were active in the underground railroad or the freeing of fugitive slaves, they were, Douglass argued, unsupportive of freedom's most crucial instruments—public protest and the written word. "They reason thus: Our fathers got along pretty well through the world without learning and without meddling with abolitionism, and we can do the same." But their fathers were not Douglass's father; his father—probably his first master, Aaron Anthony— was almost certainly white. The intricate attitude toward fathers and family in *My Bondage and My Freedom* is directly related to Douglass's growing literacy, his sense of self-reliance, and his imagined role as another Madison Washington. In a typically American gesture, he makes himself his own father. This fictional self is composed at once of the absent father who so absorbs his attention in *My Bondage and My Freedom,* of the black rebel-slave who leads others to freedom and converts a white audience to antislavery, and of the Founding Fathers, whose rhetoric of democratic liberty punctuates Douglass's writing after 1848 and begins fully to flower in the break with Garrison over the proper reading of the Constitution of the United States. The white father-figure who took Douglass as his "text" is replaced by a self-fathered figure combining black and white ideals. The doctrine of self-reliance that will become conspicuous in Douglass's later speeches and autobiography is thus at the center of this creative process insofar as it partakes of the Emersonian impulse to liberate the ego from inherited constraints, to seize and aggrandize the power of domineering ancestors, or their surrogates, in order to fashion one's own paternity.

Because Douglass's act of self-fathering is embedded in the rhetoric and ideals of the Revolutionary fathers, the literacy he says he acquired from reading speeches on the meaning of liberty in *The Columbian Orator,* his first secret textbook, takes on a special tone in *My Bondage and My Freedom.* His characterization of the Irish orator Richard Sheridan's "bold denunciation of slavery and . . . vindication of human rights," as the *Narrative* phrases it, becomes his "powerful denunciation of oppression, and . . . most brilliant vindication of the rights of man." Not the "silver trump of freedom," but "Liberty! the inestimable birthright of every man," now rouses Douglass; and the much extended passage becomes a virtual oration itself, attacking religion as the opiate of the slaves and indulging in rhetoric at once revolutionary and sentimentally gothic: "Knowledge had come; light had penetrated the moral dungeon where I dwelt; and, behold! there lay the bloody whip, for my back, and here was the iron chain; and my good, *kind master,* he was the author of my situation." Modern readers have tended to disparage such language in *My Bondage and My Freedom.* Yet the text reminds us that the revolutionary language of liberation and the abolitionist language of sentiment are virtually synonymous, not just in the best antislavery writing but in many of the era's literary and political treatments of the problem of bondage. Douglass transplants the language of oppression and liberation from the Romantic and Gothic traditions (where it had been a particular spur to Britain's successful antislavery movement), and binds it to the language of American Revolutionary sentiment. In doing so he reimagines the escape from bondage into a world of natural rights as a new confrontation with the paradox of the Founding Fathers' belief that American freedom was compatible with black slavery.

The "author of my situation" in this case is his Baltimore master Hugh Auld, who forbade his wife to continue teaching young Frederick to read. The meaning of Auld's "authority"—his suppression of Douglass's rebellious literate self—is clarified by other revisions Douglass makes in his second version of his life. In teaching Frederick his "A,B,C," "as if I had been her own child," Sophia Auld makes him, as he now recalls it, "master of the alphabet." In his remonstrance Auld predicts not only that a literate slave would quickly become discontent, but that literacy would produce in the slave a dangerous sequence leading him to seize control of his own self: " 'If you learn him how to read, he'll want to know how to write; and, this accomplished, he'll be running away with himself." This "true philosophy of training a human chattel," Douglass adds in the revised version, was "the first decidedly antislavery lecture to which it had been my lot to listen." Douglass's conception of himself as an object to be stolen, his mastery of the alphabet, Auld's "iron sentences," which stir up his feelings "into a sort of rebellion" and take their place alongside the many references to the "iron rule" of slavery that echo through *My Bondage and My Freedom*—these revisions suggest that Douglass attributes his literacy as much to the "opposition of my master" as to Sophia Auld's initial kindness, and they predict a more vivid struggle that unfolds along paternal, or more accurately, paternalistic, lines. Literacy is linked to the power to enslave and, alternatively, to the power to liberate and hence father oneself. In *My Bondage and My Freedom* Hugh Auld stands emphatically in a sequence of fathers that now includes the abolitionists and the Revolutionary fathers themselves, against all of whom Douglass must work to define himself as though in "opposition to my master."

This autobiographical portrait of the Romantic mind awakened to the Enlightenment language of liberation is duplicated in the scene in "The Heroic Slave" in which Listwell, the white protagonist and soon-to-be antislavery convert, overhears Madison Washington's plaintive soliloquy in the woods:

A giant's strength, but not a giant's heart was in him. His broad mouth and nose spoke only of good nature and kindness. But his voice, that unfailing index of his soul, though full and melodious, had that in it which could terrify as well as charm. . . . There came another gush from the same full fountain; now bitter, and now sweet. Scathing denunciations of the cruelty and injustice of slavery; heart-touching narrations of his own personal suffering, intermingled with prayers to the God of the oppressed for help and deliverance, were followed by presentations of the dangers and difficulties of escape, and formed the burden of his eloquent utterances; but his high resolution clung to him,—for he ended each speech by an emphatic declaration of his purpose to be free.

The self-consciousness revealed here, along with the subtle sense of a predominantly sentimental audience, is played upon throughout *My Bondage and My Freedom*. The heroic figure of Madison Washington, like the heroic figure of Frederick Douglass, speaks to an audience open to the double rhetoric of benevolence and liberty, a language both feminine and masculine. In the figure of Madison Washington the hybrid feminine or maternal image of George Washington—inspired by the popular archetype of mothers instructing their children about the nation's father—is joined to the masculine specter of rebellion and terror, the Nat Turner rebel. The double character of sentiment and rebellion that appears in Douglass's short story and in his autobiography, as in other popular antislavery texts like *Uncle Tom's Cabin*, was reflected in different form in the split slave personality—the docile "Sambo" that concealed the rebellious "Nat"—that John Blassingame has identified in accounts of plantation life following the Turner cataclysm in 1831. Douglass's fictional hero and his created autobiographical self combine these two forms of doubleness. In embracing violent slave rebellion Douglass tapped the energy of Romantic liberation and rescued the unfinished task of American freedom, imposing the mask of subversive uprising upon the face of the nation's archetypal father.

◆ ◆ ◆

The contradictory laws of the southern slaveholding fathers and the northern democratic fathers—agonizingly fused in the Fugitive Slave Law—required of Douglass a complex response that is evident in his treatment of slaveholding paternalism and the problem of his own paternity. The figure of Douglass's lost or unknown father underlies the combined problems of paternalism and self-fathering rebellion that animate Douglass's revised text. The instrument of such self-fathering was language, through which Douglass reshaped his life into the most effective and powerful form in his autobiographies and other public documents. The famous 1848 public letter to Thomas Auld, which first appeared in Garrison's *Liberator* and was then appended to *My Bondage and My Freedom*, falsely charged Auld with a number of brutalities (Douglass later apologized): but Douglass revealed his hand in saying, "I intend to make use of you as a weapon with which to assail the system of slavery—as a means of concentrating public attention on the system, and deepening their horror of trafficking in the souls and bodies of men."

If Douglass seems somewhat less certain about his true paternity in the 1855 text, it is in part because the ambiguity of his origins has itself become a part of his rhetorical strategy: fathers had become a weapon in Douglass's arsenal of literacy. "Genealogical trees do not flourish among slaves," Douglass writes. "A person of some consequence here in the north, sometimes designated *father*, is literally abolished in slave law and practice." The whimsical punning is less overt in a later passage: "I say nothing of *father*, for he is shrouded in a mystery I have never been able to penetrate. Slavery does away with fathers as it does away with families . . . When they *do* exist, they are not the outgrowths of slavery, but are antagonistic to that system." These revisions indicate more than just new uncertainty about his paternity, for his attack on the slaveholder's breeding of new property and on the tragedy of miscegenation and broken families is expanded throughout the volume into a meditation on the corruption of the family by paternalistic power. In the *Narrative,* for example, he had written of the separation of children and mothers, "for what [reason] this separation is done, I do not know, unless it be to hinder the development of the child's affection toward its mother, and to blunt and destroy the natural affection of the mother for the child. This is the inevitable result." But in *My Bondage and My Freedom,* he contends that the practice of separation "is a marked feature of the cruelty and barbarity of the slave system. But it is in harmony with the grand aim of slavery, which, always and everywhere, is to reduce man to a level with the brute. It is a successful method of obliterating from the mind and heart of the slave, all just ideas of the sacredness of *the family,* as an institution." Like the father, the family, its sacred symbolism claimed by North and South alike, takes its place in an ideological conflict that Douglass the public figure can now more accurately judge and use to advantage.

Accordingly, mothers are now carefully juxtaposed to fathers in Douglass's rendering. The extended description of his mother's death in *My Bondage and My Freedom* may reflect his intervening reading of *Uncle Tom's Cabin,* but it does so with full irony: "Scenes of sacred tenderness, around the deathbed, never forgotten, and which often arrest the vicious and confirm the virtuous during life, must be looked for among the free, though they may sometimes occur among the slaves." Because he has "no striking words of hers treasured up," Douglass has to "learn the value of my mother long after her death, and by witnessing the devotion of other mothers to their children." He recollects her image by looking at a picture in *Pritchard's Natural History of Man* (the Egyptian picture of Ramses the Great, which as James McCune Smith notes is markedly European as well). While he learns after her death that his mother could read and thus can attribute his "love of letters . . . *not* to my admitted Anglo-Saxon paternity, but to the native genius of my sable, unprotected, and uncultivated *mother,*" he must still get her teaching from a series of white "mothers"—the kind Lucretia Auld, Sophia Auld, the abolitionist Julia Griffiths, and now perhaps Harriet Beecher Stowe herself. Douglass deliberately situates his childhood in the domestic tradition of moral instruction, ironically renders it forbidden and subversive, then reconceives of it as part of the antislavery assault on the law of the proslavery fathers. That is to say, Douglass's maternity, whatever priority it takes over his obscure paternity, is nonetheless ambiguous, bordering on the fictional and participating in the literary construction of an ideological family that mediates between Douglass's slaveholding fathers and the flawed tradition of the Revolutionary fathers he sought to redeem.

In his lectures, Douglass often burlesqued the purported paternalism of slavery and held up the slave codes themselves, along with abundant fugitive testimony to the institution's brutality, in counterpoint. He could do so all the more effectively because he saw, as his farewell speech in England had put it, that "the whip, the chain, the gag, the thumb-screw, the bloodhound, the stocks, and all the other bloody paraphernalia of the slave system are indispensably necessary to the relations of master and slave. The slave must be subjected to these, or he ceases to be a slave." Torture or its threat defines the slave's subjection: but for Douglass, as his spiritually liberating fight with the slave breaker Covey suggests, it also comes to define his subjectivity, his liberation from the status of object, of property, of thing. In *My Bondage and My Freedom* the greater attention given to incidents of whipping is therefore not simply a matter of gothic ornamentation, but as in the newly added story of Doctor Isaac Copper, the old slave who teaches slave children the "Our Father" of the Lord's Prayer with whip in hand, demonstrates the infectious power of power, the fact that "everybody, in the South, wants the privilege of whipping somebody else." The whip defines the paternalism of slaveholding and becomes the primary symbol of Douglass's now much more precisely characterized "total institution" of slavery.

One need not accept the much debated thesis that, in its brutal dehumanization of slaves and its power to induce in them an imitative behavioral bondage, the plantation resembled the concentration camp, the prison, or other total institutions, in order to be struck by Douglass's new account of Colonel Lloyd's immense plantation in *My Bondage and My Freedom*. He not only gives a much fuller picture of slave life, but the greater detail and the emphasis on the plantation's self-sufficient, dark seclusion, maintained by diverse labor and trade with Baltimore on Lloyd's own vessels, turn this deceptively abundant, "Eden-like" garden world into a veritable heart of darkness. Both the unusual size of Lloyd's estate and his prominent public place as Maryland's three-time Governor and two-time Senator allow Douglass to expand his own story into an archetype of life under southern slavery's total institution. In this era of reform movements and utopian communal projects, the plantation posed as a pastoral asylum in which state control and paternal coercion in fact imprisoned the slave in a corrupt "family"—one he might belong to by blood but not by law—and fused the theory of chattel slavery with the sexuality of power. The apotheosis of the total institution of slavery lay for Douglass in this "double relation of master and father," as he called it in the *Narrative* before making it the defining figure of *My Bondage and My Freedom*.

Only outside the peculiar institution could Douglass see its totality and its paternalistic power at full play; similarly, only in the 1850s could he see himself as a self-fathered subject, subject now to the equally contradictory paternal institutions of radical antislavery and Revolutionary America. The range of paternal figures whom Douglass contrasts to the master-father figure of the plantation is striking. The new invocations of Nat Turner in *My Bondage and My Freedom* suggest, as do a number of Douglass's speeches, that his new heroes would not simply be white patriots but, like Joseph Cinque and Madison Washington, black patriots as well. In his greatest instance of ironic oratory, the Fourth of July address of 1852, Douglass places himself outside the American dream but within the circle of the post-Revolutionary generation's principal rhetoric: "It is the birthday of your National Independence, and of your political freedom . . . Your fathers have lived, died, and have done their work, and have done much of it well. You live and must die, and you must do your work. You have no right to enjoy a child's share in the labor of your fathers, unless your children are to be blessed by your labors." As George Forgie has argued, the entrapments of perpetual union and perpetual youth induced in the post-Revolutionary generation a paralysis on the issue of slavery that was not broken until Lincoln, a figure equal to the Fathers' heroic stature, embraced and overcame the Fathers at the same time, saving the union and abolishing slavery. As Douglass spoke, however, Lincoln was still following the moderate proslavery course of Henry Clay's Compromise of 1850, as he would for nearly another decade. Douglass, who derided Clay upon his death in 1852 as a man-stealer who did "more than any man in this country to make slavery perpetual," was at that time—perhaps always—a truer son of the Revolutionary generation than Lincoln. While proslavery ideologues like Thomas Dew and James Henry Hammond warned that abolitionist propaganda would tear down the slave "family" and its paternal structure of protection, making slaves *"parricides* instead of *patriots"*—as Dew warned after Turner's revolt— Douglass said it could make them both. For the slave in particular, the post-Revolutionary anxiety over the intent of the Founding Fathers could not be separated from personal fatherhood and, more to the point, from the impulse to self-fathering freedom.

The tendency for *My Bondage and My Freedom* to become an oration does not destroy its coherence, for the moments in which oratory is most evident are often those in which Douglass's new paternal ideology is most strongly espoused. The passage on the ethics of stealing now leads to the assertion that if the slave steals, "he takes his own; if he kills his master, he imitates only the heroes of the revolution." In the most dramatic event of Douglass's life story, his fight with the brutal slave-breaker Covey, the tone of the expanded exclamation of freedom is altered by certain phrases—"embers of liberty," "the unjust and cruel aggressions of a tyrant," and "manly independence"— which appeal to international democratic ideals and differentiate the incident from the then widely popular capitulation of Uncle Tom to the murderous whip of Simon Legree. Most strikingly, Douglass accuses the slaveholder of violating "the just and inalienable rights of man" and thereby "silently whetting the knife of vengeance for his own throat. He never lisps a syllable in commendation of the fathers of this republic, nor denounces any attempted oppression of himself, without inviting the knife to his own throat, and asserting the rights of rebellion for his own slaves." Replacing the lost slaveholding father with the rebel-fathers who authorize parricide in the name of freedom, and replacing his lost literate mother with the tradition of antislavery rhetoric, at once fiery and sentimental, *My Bondage and My Freedom* portrays the rebel-patriot Frederick Douglass as a figure who merges the urgency of eloquent personal facts and the heroic text of a national ideal.

◆ ◆ ◆

Douglass continually declared himself a man, not a thing, a man, not a child. Freedom and the new powers of literacy it offered countered the fear he experienced on his second arrival at Hugh Auld's in Baltimore when he saw how little Tommy Auld, whose copybooks Douglass had imitated in learning to write, had begun to acquire the habits of adult slaveholding, aware of his place and his power: "He could grow, and become a MAN; I could grow, though I could *not* become a man, but must remain, all my life, a minor—a mere boy." It is not surprising that this passage should be added to *My Bondage and My Freedom,* for Douglass's own growth between 1845 and 1855 must have seemed to him a new phase of maturation that left behind the boy orator of Nantucket. Still, Douglass's life would entail a continued fight for the manhood of his race against the paternalism that prevailed in American custom.

The rhetorical form of that fight was predicted in Douglass's response in 1859 to the voters' rejection of a New York state amendment granting blacks nondiscriminatory voting rights, even as they cast ballots in favor of Lincoln's presidency. "We were overshadowed and smothered by the presidential struggle—overlaid by Abraham Lincoln and Hannibal Hamlin," Douglass wrote. "The black baby of Negro Suffrage was thought too ugly to exhibit on so grand an occasion. The Negro was stowed away like some people put out of sight their deformed children when company comes." It was Douglass's fate, of course, to remain overshadowed by Lincoln, despite his frequent criticism of the president for failing to act more resolutely on the issue of black troops, colonization, emancipation, and civil rights. Douglass's struggle to effect the Negro's "full and complete adoption into the national family of America," as he put it in 1863, employed familial rhetoric in the only logical way, in which the Negro "child" confronted the white "father." Whatever his awareness of the doubleness of his own meanings, perhaps Douglass himself could not have said whether such language was a compromise with racism or instead acted ironically to subvert it. Neither Lincoln's open and generous manner on the two occasions he sought Douglass's advice nor Douglass's appointment to prominent positions by later Republican presidents could make that adoption completely meaningful.

Douglass's own ambivalence can best be seen in the terms by which he memorialized Lincoln at the dedication of the Freedman's Lincoln Monument in 1876. The monument, paid for primarily by the contributions of black veterans, was unveiled on 14 April, the anniversary both of Lincoln's assassination and of the emancipation of slaves in the District of Columbia. Grant and his cabinet, the Supreme Court justices, and other dignitaries listened as Douglass declared that "when the foul reproach of ingratitude is hurled at us, and it is attempted to scourge us beyond the range of human brotherhood, we may calmly point to the monument we have this day erected to the memory of Abraham Lincoln." But this moderate and gracious conclusion suspends a more critical tone in the body of the address, a tone in which Douglass seems to be measuring his own relationship with Lincoln. Was Lincoln "tardy, cold, dull, and indifferent," or "swift, zealous, radical, and determined?" Douglass posed a question historians have not yet answered to satisfaction, and a similar one would later be asked about Douglass himself. Douglass no doubt identified with Lincoln the self-made man, who studied his "English Grammar by the uncertain flare and glare of the light made by a pine-knot," the "son of toil himself [who] was linked in brotherly sympathy with the sons of toil in every loyal part of the Republic." But he stood apart from Lincoln even so: "It must be admitted, truth compels me to admit, even here in the presence of the monument we have erected to his memory, Abraham Lincoln was not, in the fullest sense of the word, either our man or our model. In his interests, in his associations, in his habits of thought, and in his prejudices, he was a white man." "You," Douglass said, returning to the divisive rhetoric he had employed in such powerful forms as the Fourth of July address, "You are the children of Abraham Lincoln. We are at best only his step-children; children by adoption, children by forces of circumstance and necessity."

Freedom's step-children, even Lincoln's step-children: Douglass probes the limits of paternalistic rhetoric even as he accepts a familiar role. Conceivably, Lincoln had become a new weapon in Douglass's arsenal; and yet the subversive power of his literacy was in this case circumscribed and contained by the ritual necessities of the occasion. Douglass later confessed that he did not like Thomas Ball's design for the monument, which may itself have inspired his metaphor of the step-child. The statue, in Benjamin Quarles's words, "revealed Lincoln in a standing position, holding in his right hand the Emancipation Proclamation, while his left hand was poised above a slave whom he gazed upon. The slave was represented in a rising position with one knee still on the ground. The shackles on his wrists were broken. At the base of the monument the word 'EMANCIPATION' was carved." What, then, are we to make of the fact that Douglass appended the speech to his third autobiography, the 1881 *Life and Times?* The matter might seem inconsequential were it not that Douglass's appendices reveal an interesting pattern. In his early oratorical mode, the notorious appendix to the *Narrative* attacks the relations between American church and American slavery with vicious irony; the appendices to *My Bondage and My Freedom* consist of extracts from Douglass's public letter to

Thomas Auld, the Fourth of July address, and other documents from the phase of Revolutionary fervor in his thought from 1848 through the war; and the Lincoln Monument speech shows Douglass at his most formal and public, ambiguously embracing America's martyred hero even while resisting him, just as Lincoln himself had both embraced and overthrown the Founding Fathers. Lincoln became for Douglass the last father with whom he would have to struggle, conscious all the while of the continued "double consciousness" that defined him, perhaps now more than ever, as both a Negro and an American, two souls—two bloods—at war in one body.

The spirit of "self-reliance, self-respect, industry, perseverance, and economy" that Douglass urges on his black audience at the end of the *Life and Times* has led commentators to dub him a "Negro edition of Ben Franklin" or a "black Horatio Alger." Rightly seen, Douglass's acceptance of the American enterprise of self-making begins at least as early as the *North Star;* and Smith's preface to *My Bondage and My Freedom* praises Douglass's "self-elevation" from the barbarism of slavery and calls him "a Representative American man—a type of his countrymen," bearing "upon his person and upon his soul every thing that is American." Douglass's American odyssey surely reaches a climax when he inserts into the 1881 version of his life a copy of a Rochester newspaper's description of a commemorative bust of Douglass placed in the University of Rochester. The notice praises Douglass as one who has seized the opportunities the Republic "offers to self-made men," despite his severe trials as a fugitive, and celebrates him as the eloquent redeemer and deliverer of his race. It makes him, one might say, comparable to—justly equal to—Lincoln, his brother, not his step-child. Douglass is now able to look upon himself as a public figure, even a public monument about which public opinion and encomium, no doubt coincidental with his own, can be quoted. Having created a final public self out of the overcome texts of the past, Douglass has become no mere boy but one of the fathers he had worked at such cost to be.

My Bondage and My Freedom and the American Literary Renaissance of the 1850s

WILLIAM L. ANDREWS

At the beginning of the 1850s, when American literature was to undergo its extraordinary renaissance of thought and expression, Ralph Waldo Emerson wrote in *Representative Men* (1850): "The search after the great is the dream of youth, and the most serious occupation of manhood."[1] As the decade progressed, inquiries into the nature of greatness in individuals pervaded American letters. Ishmael, the narrator of Herman Melville's *Moby-Dick* (1851), is fascinated by the "grand, ungodly, god-like man," Captain Ahab, though he concludes from the results of Ahab's "fatal pride" that "all mortal greatness is but disease." The example of Margaret Fuller's "great soul" led three New England transcendentalists to edit two volumes of her *Memoirs* in 1852, so that, in the words of James Freeman Clarke, tribute could be paid to her "power of exerting profoundest influence on individual souls."[2] From a standpoint of lofty disdain for "the commonest sense," Henry David Thoreau condemned the leveling tendency of custom and conformity. In *Walden* (1854) he urged his readers to advance, however audaciously, in the direction of their dreams so as to "live with the license of a higher order of beings." In a similar spirit Walt Whitman proclaimed in 1855, "Nothing, not God, is greater to one than one's self is." The persona of "Song of Myself" would not praise greatness without allying it to representativeness. Thus Whitman recalled Emerson's "search after the great" to its starting point in the individual self freely speaking "without check with original energy."

Shortly after the publication of Whitman's *Leaves of Grass* in the summer of 1855, Frederick Douglass took his place among the great "I-narrators" of the American renaissance with *My Bondage and My Freedom,* his second autobiography. Introducing Douglass's book, James McCune Smith, a black physician and abolitionist, hailed Douglass as "a Representative American man—a type of his countrymen," whose record of "self-elevation" from the lowest to the

From Frederick Douglass, *My Bondage and My Freedom,* ed. William L. Andrews (Urbana: University of Illinois Press, 1987), xi–xxviii. © 1987 by the Board of Trustees of the University of Illinois. Reprinted by permission of the University of Illinois Press.

highest condition in society marked him as a "noble example" for all Americans to emulate. In ascribing to Douglass both greatness and representativeness, Smith identified the hero of *My Bondage and My Freedom* with some of the ideals most cherished by American Romantic writers like Emerson, Fuller, Thoreau, and Whitman. Douglass knew that the literary climate of the American 1850s was open to what Thoreau would call "a simple, sincere account" of a representative life, provided it transcended the merely personal to offer insight into universal Nature.[3] Consequently, in the preface to his autobiography Douglass emphasized that his story ought not to be read as an illustration of the "heroic achievements" of a particular man. It should be seen as a vindication of "a just and beneficent principle, in its application to the whole human family." *My Bondage and My Freedom* thus became the first Afro-American autobiography publicly designed to argue that a black man's life story had a wider significance than was usually accorded to the narratives of former slaves.

Most slave narratives, including Douglass's own written ten years earlier, were composed and read in a spirit of extreme sectionalism. Northerners studied them for information about the horrors of the South's "peculiar institution" and the sufferings of enslaved blacks. Southerners analyzed them to refute the calumnies of Yankee abolitionists and to expose the untrustworthiness of fugitive slaves celebrated in the North. *My Bondage and My Freedom,* however, would treat the life of Frederick Douglass as *nationally* significant, revelatory of the complex meaning of slavery and freedom in the North as well as the South for a black man who, for better or worse (in Smith's words), bore "upon his person and upon his soul every thing that is American."

In speaking of Douglass as representative, Smith asked his readers to think of this quality in a distinctly Emersonian sense, as denoting a kind of epitome or standard by which others might measure themselves. To Emerson, "representative men" served as examples *to,* not of, the general run of humankind because such men revealed "moral truths" to "the general mind." Their "genius" and their example, Emerson believed, could stimulate an "irresistible upward force into our own thought," enlightening us as to the powers of perception held universally by all people. The great social service of the "representative man," therefore, was to liberate and inspire the democracy in which, not above which, he lived.[4] In keeping with this ideal, the personae of works like *Walden,* "Song of Myself," and Fuller's *Woman in the Nineteenth Century* (1845) all adopt a stance of representativeness before the readership they hope to awaken and free. In a similar stance, though in a less oracular manner, the narrator of *My Bondage and My Freedom* addresses his readers. Douglass designed his second autobiography to delineate through his own triumphs and reversals the making of a black socioliterary leader for the unprecedented crises and challenges of the 1850s. The book's frankness about its protagonist's frailties as well as his strengths levels an implicit critique of individualism at a time of rampant romantic egoism in American letters. This is but one way in which the book confirms Douglass's special contribution to the chorus of representative voices that distinguished the American literary renaissance.

When Douglass took the rostrum at the Corinthian Hall in Rochester, New York, to deliver a Fourth of July speech in 1852, his audience, numbering more than 500 persons, hushed to hear the words of the most famous black American of the era. From his birth in 1818 on an obscure farm on Maryland's Eastern Shore, the one-time slave had become an international celebrity in the English-speaking world. An antislavery lecturer since 1841, Douglass had traveled throughout the northern United States and the British Isles, making a name for himself as perhaps the most effective agent of William Lloyd Garrison's American Anti-Slavery Society. Many of his early speeches recounted the story of his life as a slave: his growing up on the plantation of one of the richest men in Maryland, his self-education on the streets of Baltimore, his fight to maintain his manhood against a cruel slave-breaker—the whole process by which he prepared himself for his triumphant seizing of freedom in 1838. By 1845, the publication of his *Narrative of the Life of Frederick Douglass, An American Slave* had made him a best-selling author, the leader of what one of his biographers has termed "the heroic fugitive school of American literature" in the antebellum period.[5] Yet as he addressed his Rochester audience in 1852, Douglass made it clear that his personal success story gave him little solace in the face of the ironies besetting him in his role as Independence Day orator.

"Fellow-citizens, pardon me," Douglass asked in tones of mock innocence, "why am I called upon to speak here to-day? What have I, or those I represent, to do with your national independence? Are the great principles of political freedom and of natural justice, embodied in that Declaration of Independence, extended to us?" The black man answered his own rhetorical questions by punning ironically, "I am not included within the pale of this glorious anniversary!" Recent events had forced every black person in the so-called free states of the North to realize the fact of their increasing alienation from the promise of America. "By an act of American Congress, not yet two years old, slavery has been nationalized in its most horrible and revolting form." As a result of the Fugitive Slave Act of 1850, the crucial difference between the northern and southern sections of the nation had been obliterated. "New York has become as Virginia" insofar as the safety of a slave seeking freedom was concerned. Anyone in the North or the South could take possession of a black person simply by convincing a federal magistrate that he or she owned that person. Blacks charged as runaways had no recourse to judicial hearings or jury trials. All citizens were required to cooperate with slave-catchers, and anyone who impeded the disposition of the law could be fined or imprisoned. Under the threat of this "kidnapping law," as many blacks termed it, could a person in Douglass's position be content with arguing "the equal manhood of the negro race" or "the wrongfulness of slavery"? "The time for such argument is past,"

Douglass pronounced. "For it is not light that is needed, but fire; it is not the gentle shower, but thunder" that America required if the country were to recognize what was happening to its ideals.[6]

This was Douglass's version of the "NO! in thunder" for which Melville had so extravagantly praised Nathaniel Hawthorne's "power of blackness" a year earlier. Hawthorne's imagination was fired, Melville surmised, by a "Calvinistic sense of Innate Depravity and Original Sin." Douglass's literary naysaying, on the other hand, evolved from a less cosmic and intellectual, a more social and experiential, vision of the depravity of America's particular national sins. Melville saw Hawthorne (and himself) seeking answers to "the Problem of the Universe" by breaking through the boundaries of American intellectual orthodoxy and literary decorum to plumb "the blackness of darkness beyond." Black writers like Douglass in the 1850s sought answers to the Problem of America by undertaking similar critiques of mainstream thinking as viewed from the shadowy borders of other-consciousness. Yet it was Douglass's wisdom to realize that he could not play the role of alienated critic of America without acknowledging that as a Negro he had also been, in Richard Wright's phrase, a metaphor of America. The narrator he fashioned for *My Bondage and My Freedom* brilliantly exemplifies Melville's contention that only "through the mouths of the dark characters" of great writers do we find that which is "so terrifically true, that it were all but madness for any good man, in his own proper character, to utter, or even hint of them."[7]

For many black leaders of the 1850s, the outrage of the fugitive slave law demanded that free blacks in the North face the fact that their new legal status was in no essential sense different from that of slaves. As Martin R. Delany wrote in 1852, the "true condition" of black people, slave or free, in the United States was "as mere nonentities among the citizens, and excrescences on the body politic." Since whites denied blacks an American identity, a number of black writers, including Delany and Samuel Ringgold Ward, argued that free blacks should embrace exile from America as a badge of honor.[8] Alienation would become a sign of black freedom from the contamination of the corrupt American Dream. Douglass, however, distrusted any form of black cooperation with white racist efforts to marginalize the free black population out of the country. He wanted to believe there was still a way to reclaim the promise of America, and in even so strident an attack as his 1852 speech in Rochester, he would still conclude by expressing his faith in "the genius of American Institutions," though it had been much perverted by compromises with slavery.[9] Nevertheless, as he approached the writing of his second autobiography, Douglass could not have ignored the fact that, during the previous decade, events had left him much more marginal to, if not alienated from, many of the authorities and ideals with which he had strongly identified when he wrote his *Narrative*.

The *Narrative of the Life of Frederick Douglass* is one of the most remarkable success stories in the history of American autobiography. Without sounding self-congratulatory, the former slave made himself into an exemplar of Romantic individualism, to which transcendentalists like Theodore Parker and Margaret Fuller paid tribute in their reviews of his book.[10] In many respects Douglass's slave narrative represents the culmination of a major tradition in antebellum black autobiography that celebrated the lives of those who had fled the alien status of slave and had made a place for themselves in freedom as "a man and a brother," in the words of a famous antislavery motto. As he wrote his narrative, Douglass was determined to show not just that he had raised himself out of slavery but that he had rapidly been assimilated into the white world of the North, where he had attained a position of respect and influence in the antislavery movement. Among the Garrisonian abolitionists he had come into his own, had "found himself" in a crucial sense, for it was they who had shown him the way to the freedom that climaxes the *Narrative,* the liberation of his voice and with it the discovery of his vocation as an antislavery orator. Thus, when Douglass concluded his first autobiography in 1845, he pictured himself as a man secure in his life's mission. The pattern of his life story assumes the tripartite structure of the classic rites of passage that inform the process by which an individual negotiates crises in life in order to move from one status to another. Douglass's resistance to his status as a slave and his flight from it constitute a rite of separation; his experience as a lonely, displaced fugitive in the North corresponds to a rite of transition; as he achieves status and recognition in the North within the abolitionist movement, he undergoes a rite of incorporation.[11] Nothing at the end of the *Narrative* prepares us to see Douglass as a man who still had a great lesson in irony to learn, namely, as he observed in *My Bondage and My Freedom,* that for him "the settling of one difficulty only opened the way for another."

During the decade between his two autobiographies, Douglass was forced by a series of unexpected reversals in his life to take fresh stock intellectually, to rethink the significance of key concepts like bondage and freedom in light of his widening experience as a freeman. This process began in Great Britain during a twenty-one-month speaking tour on which Douglass had embarked after publication of the *Narrative* forced him to flee America for his safety. England's hearty welcome to the fugitive slave caused him in a letter to Garrison on New Year's Day, 1846, to question seriously all his "prejudices in favor of America." The "outcast" perspective that he had been forced to assume convinced him that throughout the United States, "all is cursed with the infernal spirit of slaveholding." Douglass's *Narrative* had been notably quiet on the topic of racism in the North, but his letter to Garrison exploded in a series of humiliating episodes in Massachusetts when he was refused admission to popular entertainments, public conveyances, a worship service, and an eating establishment, in each case because, in language Douglass attributed to his antagonists, " '*We don't allow niggers in here!*' " When he wrote *My Bondage and My Freedom,* Douglass made sure that this scathing denunciation of American bigotry was reprinted prominently and in full.

After his return from England in the spring of 1847, Douglass's decisions placed him increasingly at odds with Garrison and the ideology of the American Anti-Slavery Society. Against Garrison's counsel his black protégé undertook a new career as an independent antislavery journalist, launching the weekly *North Star* in Rochester, New York, on December 3, 1847.[12] Writing editorial defenses of his antislavery positions required Douglass to reexamine the principles of Garrisonianism, the effect of which was Douglass's growing realization that he could no longer subscribe fully to Garrison's intellectual leadership. By 1851 the relationship between the two men openly and acrimoniously ruptured when Douglass publicly declared the U.S. Constitution (which Garrison had termed a proslavery document) to be an instrument of emancipation and further committed his newspaper to political activism, which the Garrisonians had long disavowed. After Garrison successfully prohibited further funding of the *North Star* by the American Anti-Slavery Society, Douglass turned to Liberty party leader Gerrit Smith for financial aid. This decision to ally himself with a rival faction of abolitionists regarded by the Garrisonians as mischievous temporizers gained for Douglass the reputation among his former associates as "the most malignant" of "all the seceders and apostates from our ranks."[13]

One lesson Douglass learned from his falling-out with the Garrisonians was the necessity of solidarity and self-sufficiency among northern blacks as a bulwark against white paternalism. On the eve of the publication of *My Bondage and My Freedom,* he insisted that blacks realize that "OUR ELEVA-TION AS A RACE, IS ALMOST WHOLLY DEPENDENT UPON OUR OWN EXERTIONS." He justified this contention by noting that "we have called down upon our devoted head, the holy (?) horror of a certain class of Abolitionists, because we have dared to maintain our Individuality, and have opened our own eyes, and looked out of them, through another telescope." Douglass charged that, despite their reputation as the champions of the Negro, Garrison and his adherents were only theoretically, not practically, committed to "the Idea of our Equality with the whites." It was high time, therefore, for northern blacks to desert the false "self-appointed generals of the Anti-Slavery host" and become more communally self-reliant. It was equally incumbent on Afro-American writers to set aside their loyalties to everything but "the truth, and the whole truth." "The redemption of our whole race"—in the North as well as the South—"from every species of oppression" was at stake as never before.[14] Out of a deeper awareness of the guises of oppression in his past, and with a new standard of candor and sense of literary mission, Douglass wrote *My Bondage and My Freedom.*

From its opening pages, where James McCune Smith, known for his vehement criticism of Garrison, supplants Douglass's former mentor as prefacer of his memoir, one can see that *My Bondage and My Freedom* was not designed to serve as merely an updated, second installment of the *Narrative.* In its tone, structure, and dominant metaphors, the new book represents a thoughtful revised reading of the meaning of Douglass's life. A cursory comparison of the *Narrative* and *My Bondage and My Freedom* indicates that the latter is bigger, roomier, more detailed, and more expository, befitting the more reflective mood of its author in 1855. The few paragraphs allotted in the *Narrative* to the seven years he had spent in freedom are expanded to seventy pages in the second autobiography so that Douglass could integrate his additional ten years as a freeman into the scheme of his life story. As he reflected on the significance of his rites of passage through Garrisonianism during his seventeen years in freedom, Douglass found himself rethinking his previous understanding of the pattern of his life in slavery. In 1855 he could no longer see his life reaching its climax in his incorporation into the Garrisonian sphere. What the *Narrative* treats as the denouement of Douglass's struggle for freedom is pictured in *My Bondage and My Freedom* as just another stage of ironic disillusionment in the former slave's quest for liberation. Why, Douglass seems to have asked himself as he wrote his second autobiography, had he not recognized much earlier the kind of bondage that his attachment to the Garrisonians had held in store for him? To answer this question Douglass probed the dynamics of love, authority, and power in almost all of the major relationships in his life, particularly those involving father figures.

The 1845 *Narrative* pictures Douglass's consuming goals in life as freedom and independence, the attainment of which is symbolized in the transformation of the former slave into a spokesman for abolitionism. In *My Bondage and My Freedom,* however, Douglass suggests that before the ideal of freedom had infused his consciousness, his heart had been profoundly touched by hunger for a home. The first two chapters of Douglass's 1855 autobiography nostalgically reminisce at length about "MY HOME—the only home I ever had," the "joyous circle" under the care of his grandmother Betsey Baily, with whom the slave boy lived until he was about seven years old. The *Narrative* says virtually nothing about the home that Betsey Baily provided young Frederick, but in 1855 it is described as a place of "the veriest freedom" and "sweet content" where the "authority of grandmamma" sealed the child in a protective ignorance that insulated him from all but a vague awareness of his actual unfree condition. It was only when he left home with his grandmother to walk the twelve miles from her Tuckahoe cabin to "Old Master's" plantation on the Wye River that Frederick received his "first introduction to the realities of slavery." His initiation came in a moment of powerful disillusionment. His trusted grandmother, having hidden from him the reason why she had taken him away from home, left him without warning or explanation "almost heart-broken" among the strangers of "old master's domicile." Douglass brings out the significance of this crucial early episode in his life in the simple statement, "I had never been deceived before." He had believed implicitly in Betsey Baily, but she, the first authority figure in his life, had deceived him. In whom, then, could he place his trust, other than in himself? Under his grandmother's benign authority he had enjoyed an ideal blend of freedom from restraint and the security of a protective parent's nurture. Would it ever be possible to discover or recreate in a personal or communal relationship this kind of home, where individuality and authority could be reconciled?

In the 1845 version of his life Douglass portrays himself in slavery as an incipient rebel-individualist who learned early the necessity of defiance of authority. By 1855, however, he had come to recognize and admit that he had often been a seeker of authority, even "something of a hero worshiper, by nature," to use the autobiographer's own phrase, who had been all too ready to attach himself to paternal figures whom he identified unconsciously with all that home signified. The structure of Douglass's life in his second autobiography shows us an evolving dialectic between two sides of the man's personality: one side jealously guarding its private temple of the free self, the other zealously devoted to idealized authorities outside the self. The narrator of *My Bondage and My Freedom* identifies ultimately with neither of these alter egos, for each one's limitations necessitate its displacement by the other as Douglass moved through youth and young manhood in the South and the North. The goal of the writing of Douglass's second autobiography was freedom from the prisons of both individualism and authoritarianism in a truly communal Afro-American home.

In this introductory discussion of *My Bondage and My Freedom,* I can only outline the pattern of Douglass's psychological struggles after leaving his first home. Douglass's discussion of his childhood on Colonel Lloyd's plantation shows how early he became acquainted with whites as paternalistic authorities. Captain Aaron Anthony, young Frederick's "Old Master," whom he had learned to fear from his days with his grandmother, embodies the contradictions inherent in slavery as a paternalistic system. The 1845 *Narrative* depicts Anthony simply and briefly as "a cruel man," but ten years later Douglass gave this figure a more complex character. He could be gentle, affectionate, "almost fatherly" to the winsome child he called "his 'little Indian boy.'" Yet when provoked by an affront to his patriarchal pride and prerogative, as in Esther Baily's defiance of his commandment against her love for Ned Roberts, Anthony's pretense of familial regard for his "servants" exploded in naked passion and sadistic revenge. "A wretched man, at war with his own soul," Anthony, like his slave Esther, was a victim of the grotesque intimacies that arose from the perverse paternalism of the South's peculiar institution. Many masters like Aaron Anthony subscribed to a patriarchal interpretation of their relationship to their black "families," so that slaveowners might be justified in demanding obedience and loyalty in exchange for providing and caring for their slaves. However, by implicitly endorsing the mutual obligations of patron and servant, Anthony could not help but inspire in the minds of strong-willed slaves like Esther (and later her nephew Frederick) the idea that obligations gave rise to rights for *both* sides in the paternalistic arrangement.[15] Beneath the paternalistic pretensions of Thomas and Hugh Auld lay their assumed right to decide what their slave Frederick owed them and what he could rightfully expect of them in return. But because of the paternalistic relationship that these men and their kindly wives, Lucretia and Sophia, established with Frederick in his boyhood, the conviction that he always deserved not the "inch" that his masters would allot him but the "ell" he desired for himself fired within the slave the rebellious individualism that eventually freed him from bondage.

The reader of *My Bondage and My Freedom* cannot ignore, however, the genuine sense of loss that accompanied Douglass's repeated separation from or rejection of paternal (and sometimes maternal) authorities, from Betsey Baily to William Lloyd Garrison. By 1855 Douglass could see that the most threatening oppression in his life had been the most insidiously beguiling. In some ways it had been harder to break the emotional and intellectual bonds that had held him to messianic leaders like Garrison than it had been to resist the whip of "the snake" Edward Covey. Outright tyrants Douglass would fight implacably; when the issue was the elevation of another's individual authority via the expunction of his own, Douglass felt free to insist on his own will. On the other hand, when paternal authorities offered him the chance to transcend his isolate individuality in the name of a new identification with a higher principle or a larger community, Douglass often proved a willing true believer.

As a young slave whose reading had alienated him emotionally from the Baltimore home of Sophia and Hugh Auld, Frederick felt keenly his loneliness. His white master and later his white mistress treated him with suspicion, while the "stupid contentment" of his fellow slaves made them seem equally unreachable to the black boy who had become "too thoughtful to be happy." Disillusioned by the earthly fathers and mothers who had deceived him, Frederick concluded that he was in "need of God, as a father and protector." He soon attached himself to Charles Lawson, a black drayman who became his "spiritual father" and inspired in him a sense of his destiny and calling as a preacher and a freeman. As a result of the encouragement of "Father Lawson," the black teenager became confident that "my life was under the guidance of a wisdom higher than my own" and that "in His own good time" his heavenly Father would "deliver [him] from bondage." Lawson's ministrations, in other words, saved Frederick from an increasingly desperate sense of alienation and gave a larger purpose to his efforts at self-education. On the other hand, by convincing the youth that he should "trust in the Lord" for the future, Lawson inhibited the growth of Douglass's self-reliance, in which he would have to place profound trust later when he was hired out to Covey. The challenge of the slave-breaker to Douglass's sense of personhood forced the slave to set aside the faith of Lawson in "the authority of God" and see to it that his hands "were no longer tied by my religion." Survival and progress as a self thus required that Douglass violently "backslide" from the religion of his black, as well as white, fathers. We are moved to see in this what might be termed a slave's "fortunate fall" into dignity, just as we are similarly invited to interpret Douglass's "apostasy" from Garrison's "holy cause" as his liberation from "something like a slavish adoration" of his Boston leaders. Yet it is important to remember that for Douglass the immediate result of such dissenting was usually alienation from the sense of community, larger purpose, or transcendent identity that had lured him into discipleship in the first place.

As we approach the end of *My Bondage and My Freedom,* Douglass's renunciations, one after another, of all the false authorities that in the past had betrayed his faith as well as his freedom become one of the major themes of his book. What is not so apparent, however, is the alternative he poses for psychologically and spiritually homeless Afro-Americans who could find no lasting fulfillment in antiauthoritarian individualism. This alternative emerges from several incidents in Douglass's past and again at the conclusion of his autobiography. Consider the aftermath of his battle with Covey. At first the narrator stresses the tonic effect his victory had on his personal sense of "self-respect" and "manly independence." But what was perhaps of greater significance to the development of Douglass's ultimate mission as an orator and agitator for freedom were the Sabbath schools he undertook in 1835, the year after he left Covey's farm. After his disillusionment with the false godliness of his various Maryland masters, Douglass found a spiritual home in sub-rosa socioreligious communities that he created and led among his fellow slaves. What began as a gesture of largess from the comparatively well-educated teenager to his ignorant companions in bondage became the most mutually beneficial and egalitarian community that Douglass would ever experience in the South. "I never loved, esteemed, or confided in men, more than I did in these," Douglass says of his students in the Sabbath school that he conducted on William Freeland's plantation. "No band of brothers could have been more loving. There were no mean advantages taken of each other . . . and no elevating one at the expense of the other. We never undertook to do any thing, of any importance, which was likely to affect each other, without mutual consultation. We were generally a unit, and moved together."

This fraternal instead of paternal relationship between leader and followers stuck in Douglass's mind as an unprecedented model of home. Paternalism tended to fragment the slaves' faith in their peers in favor of the cultivation of their immediate superiors and inferiors. But the fraternalism of Douglass's Freeland band distributed power laterally, not vertically, so that authority could not abuse community. The mutual self-reliance of these black men cemented them into a unity of identity and purpose that liberated Douglass from mere individualism. "I could have died with and for them," he wrote of his closest friends in the school; with them, therefore, he made his first break for freedom.

After his successful escape to the North, Douglass joined the Garrisonians, "young, ardent, and hopeful" of having finally found the kind of community of freedom, brotherhood, and benevolent authority that he had long associated with home. Initially the abolitionist fraternity seemed remarkably color-blind, causing their new associate to "forget that my skin was dark and my hair crisped." Gradually, however, it became clear to the former slave that racial prejudice often governed the ideas that his new "friends" had about how to use him in their cause. Douglass probably was aware that his relationship to Garrison had become "something like that of a child to a parent," as the black man characterized it in a letter to Senator Charles Sumner in 1852.[16] But not until the publication of *My Bondage and My Freedom* did the full cost of Douglass's attachment to his white abolitionist patrons become evident.

In his introduction to the book, James McCune Smith points out that when Douglass launched his newspaper, the *North Star,* over the opposition of Garrison, he could not have expected northern blacks to rally automatically to him because "the wide gulf which separated the free colored people from the Garrisonians, also separated them from their brother, Frederick Douglass." The actual distance that existed between Douglass the Garrisonian and the free blacks of the North cannot be easily determined now. A number of important black pundits (such as Smith) did intensely criticize the American Anti-Slavery Society and those blacks (like Douglass) who continued to adhere to it in the 1840s and 1850s. On the other hand, after the full Douglass-Garrison split, most northern blacks defended Douglass against the harsh attacks on his integrity and leadership mounted by the many Garrison loyalists.[17] Regardless of the extent to which Douglass felt alienated from the free blacks of the North as a consequence of his involvement with the Garrisonians, the conclusion of *My Bondage and My Freedom* testifies to the author's determination to reidentify himself as a leader and spokesman of a nationwide Afro-American community. Separation from the Garrisonians had shown him that the best way of accomplishing the antislavery mission he had begun among them was to immerse himself in the cause of the quasi-free black people of the North. In short, the final image of Douglass in his second autobiography is that of a community-builder. Just as he had labored in his Sabbath school on Freeland's plantation to inspire within his companions a unifying spirit of hope, mutual trust, and aspiration toward freedom, so in the North, through his independent journalism and his new autobiography, would he promote similar ideals: "the moral, social, religious, and intellectual elevation of the free colored people."

"Progress is yet possible," Douglass exhorts the black readers of his second autobiography. It was no small part of his aim in 1855 to show black Americans how to progress toward the kind of "elevation" they all sought. The subtle argument of *My Bondage and My Freedom* is that the elevation of Frederick Douglass, whose "example of self-elevation" qualified him as James McCune Smith's "Representative American man," was not to be attributed merely to his individual exertions alone. By the mid-1850s Douglass could see how much his own life proved his maxim: "A man's character greatly takes its hue and shape from the form and color of things about him." The mature Douglass recognized that his character, his needs, and the direction of his life had been profoundly shaped by the maternal, paternal, and fraternal relationships of his past. The repeated ironic reversals in his quest for freedom had taught him the primary necessity of distinguishing between true and false community as the basis on which real as opposed to delusory freedom depended. Thus, the pattern of his life in his second autobiography reflects his realization that any ascendant Afro-American needed a communal anchor before he or she could attain a truly liberating identity as both an individual and a part of a larger social whole. It is not clear that Douglass felt he had realized in his own self that balance of interdependent individuality and communality that had become his ideal at the end of *My Bondage and My Freedom*. But though the example of his own life illustrates how elusive that ideal can be, Douglass's resolution to pursue it, fortified by his hard-won awareness that only through its attainment could he become truly free, brings his autobiography to both its conclusion and its climax. The ultimate assurance of "progress" in *My Bondage and My Freedom* leaves us with a sense of "new possibilities" for both the individual and society, a quality that Emerson felt would always be the lasting legacy of the biographies of "representative men."[18]

The highest achievement of a "representative man" in Emerson's view is to "preach the equality of souls" and "give a constitution to his people," thereby releasing them "from their barbarous homages," even to himself. *My Bondage and My Freedom* serves its readership well in all these respects. As with *Walden* and *Woman in the Nineteenth Century,* Douglass's autobiography analyzes many kinds of bondage to which antebellum America paid homage. Thoreau's fundamental theme is "self-emancipation" from the chains of custom, habit, and all the material superfluities of life—especially those "golden or silver fetters" that most people fasten on themselves. "It is hard to have a southern overseer," writes the narrator of *Walden;* "it is worse to have a northern one; but worst of all when you are the slave-driver of yourself." Throughout Thoreau's critique, chattel slavery is used as a metaphor of a malaise of spirit that tyrannized all Americans into believing that there was no alternative to their "mean and sneaking" lives of "quiet desperation."[19] Fuller's estimate of her era is similar to Thoreau's in deploring the lack of a single "sample of completed being" in "the mass of men" who, "under the slavery of habit," employ "the freedom of their limbs only with wolfish energy." However, the Cambridge feminist brings the metaphor of slavery to bear on a more specific social injustice than her Concord contemporary would consider. Because "there exists in the minds of men a feeling toward women as toward slaves," under such a relationship of the sexes the married "woman *does* belong to the man" in virtually the same practical and political sense as a slave belonged to his or her southern owner. To remedy this situation Fuller calls on men to remove "the arbitrary barriers" that crowded women into social dependency and degrading marriages. But she places an even greater emphasis on the potential of women to become "the best helpers of each other." Thus, Fuller demands that every woman become creatively "self-centred" and "self-reliant" so that no woman would "make an imperfect man her god, and thus sink to idolatry" and the excessive devotion of a servant.[20]

As an exponent of "the equality of souls," Douglass joined with his Romantic literary contemporaries in emphasizing the idea that human beings, individually and collectively, share a potential for evolution toward a higher self-awareness, fulfillment, and ethical discernment. Some may be farther advanced on the path of self-realization than others, but this does not alter the fact that the human condition is perpetually liminal, that is, poised on a threshold, in transit from one level of knowledge to another. When Douglass concludes his autobiography by affirming that "progress is always possible," he underscores his faith in the transcendentalist creed of individual as well as social progress that writers like Thoreau and Fuller echo. His emphasis on black solidarity as an essential factor in the achievement of Afro-American progress is no more radical or less romantic a message to the oppressed than is Fuller's recommendation in favor of American women's banding together to be their own "best helpers."

The "constitution" that Douglass gave to "his people," that is, to black America, is not a finished political document but an open-ended personal history which, in its dual focus on life in slavery and in freedom, incorporates the crucial parameters of every antebellum Afro-American's experience and thus constitutes a truly representative and national work of black expression. Douglass's second autobiography also constitutes the full significance of the themes of slavery and freedom that writers like Fuller and Thoreau explore. *My Bondage and My Freedom* provides a grounding in specific historical and social reality for Fuller's and Thoreau's largely metaphorical applications of slavery and freedom to American society; moreover, Douglass's acknowledgment of the ironies of his own youthful idealism places in a cautionary perspective the transcendent optimism of a Thoreau or Fuller. Thoreau assures his reader that "there can be no very black melancholy to him who lives in the midst of Nature and has his senses still." Douglass insists on the reality of black melancholy, especially among southern blacks, so as to impress upon his reader the real threat of slavery to subvert even the most aspiring mind, such as his own. But he also insists on the creative uses of black melancholy for slave singers and rebels like himself who needed more than a retreat to Nature to free themselves from slavery-imposed despair.

Douglass joins Thoreau and Fuller in emphasizing the many prejudices, particularly those involving race, that Americans in the North as well as the South had allowed to smother their natural love of freedom. The former slave dramatizes in his personal story the efficacy of both Thoreau's appeal to individual self-emancipation and Fuller's call for an alliance of the oppressed in their own behalf to combat slavery in its many guises. To an extent that neither Thoreau nor Fuller would risk, however, Douglass makes himself a negative as well as a positive example of the impact of bondage and freedom on an American consciousness. "Self-criticism," Douglass asserted a few years after the publication of *My Bondage and My Freedom,* is among "the highest attainments of human excellence"; an unsparing objectivity regarding the self provides "the germinating principle of all reform and all progress."[21] The self-criticism of Douglass's second autobiography, along with its warnings against hero-worship, help to release his readers from excessive "homage" to the myth of Frederick Douglass. This makes progress indeed possible, if nowhere else than on the intellectual front of the Afro-American struggle for independence. By contrast, Thoreau and Fuller, despite their use of the personal essay and autobiographical forms, seem to be either not interested in or inhibited about revealing themselves critically, particularly in circumstances of frustration or failure.[22] We do not learn much from *Walden* or *Woman in the Nineteenth Century* about the process by which the narrators of these two classic books attained the enlightened and liberated perspective from which they speak so confidently.

My Bondage and My Freedom is that rare "I-narrative" of the American 1850s that not only preaches the message of the "representative" men and women of the American literary renaissance but also conducts its reader through the stages of the preacher's realization of his own identity, mission, and message. What we discover from Douglass's most compelling self-portrait in autobiography is not a self-made man but a man still in the making, characterized ultimately by what Melville termed "that lasting temper of all true, candid men—a seeker, not a finder yet."[23]

Notes

1. Ralph Waldo Emerson, "Uses of Great Men," *Representative Men* (Boston: Phillips, Sampson, 1850), p. 10.

2. Along with Ralph Waldo Emerson and William Henry Channing, Clarke edited *Memoirs of Margaret Fuller Ossoli,* 2 vols. (Boston: Phillips, Sampson, 1852). Clarke's comment on Fuller appears in vol. 1, p. 66.

3. Henry David Thoreau, *Walden,* ed. J. Lyndon Shanley (Princeton: Princeton University Press, 1971), p. 3. For a discussion of the transcendentalists' reasons for preferring first-person writing of "universal" applicability, see Lawrence Buell, *Literary Transcendentalism* (Ithaca: Cornell University Press, 1973), pp. 265–83.

4. Emerson, "Uses of Great Men," pp. 14, 24, 26.

5. Benjamin Quarles, ed., *Narrative of the Life of Frederick Douglass* (Cambridge: Belknap Press of Harvard University, 1967), p. xvi. By mid-century sales of Douglass's *Narrative* had reached over 30,000 copies, and both French and Dutch translations were available. See Houston A. Baker, Jr., "Introduction," *Narrative of the Life of Frederick Douglass, An American Slave* (New York: Viking Penguin, 1982), pp. 19–21.

6. Frederick Douglass, "What to the Slave Is the Fourth of July?" in John W. Blassingame, ed., *The Frederick Douglass Papers.* Series 1: Speeches, Debates, and Interviews. (New Haven: Yale University Press, 1982), vol. 2, pp. 367–71. The outline of the provisions of the fugitive slave law is taken from Leon Litwack, *North of Slavery: The Negro in the Free States, 1790–1860* (Chicago: University of Chicago Press, 1961), pp. 248–49.

7. See Melville's "Hawthorne and His Mosses" (first published in the *Literary World,* Aug. 17 and 24, 1850) and his letter to Hawthorne, Apr. 16, 1851, as reprinted in *Moby-Dick,* ed. Harrison Hayford and Hershel Parker (New York: Norton, 1967), pp. 540–42, 555.

8. See Martin R. Delany, *The Condition, Elevation, Emigration and Destiny of the Colored People of the United States* (Philadelphia: the author, 1852), p. 14; and Samuel Ringgold Ward, *Autobiography of a Fugitive Negro* (London: John Snow, 1855).

9. Douglass, "What to the Slave Is the Fourth of July?" p. 387.

10. See Parker's speech, "The American Scholar," in George Willis Cooke, ed., *The American Scholar*, vol. 8 of *Centenary Edition of Theodore Parker's Writings* (Boston: American Unitarian Association, 1907), p. 37. Margaret Fuller's review of Douglass's *Narrative* for the *New York Tribune* of June 10, 1845, is reprinted in Bell Gale Chevigny, *The Woman and the Myth: Margaret Fuller's Life and Writings* (Old Westbury, N.Y.: Feminist Press, 1976), pp. 340–42.

11. Arnold van Gennep, *The Rites of Passage*, trans. Monika B. Vizedom and Gabrielle L. Caffee (1909; Chicago: University of Chicago Press, 1960), pp. 11, 21.

12. Benjamin Quarles, *Frederick Douglass* (Washington, D.C.: Associated Publishers, 1948), pp. 80–81.

13. Philip S. Foner, ed., *The Life and Writings of Frederick Douglass* (New York: International Publishers, 1950), vol. 2, p. 59. The first treatment of the Garrison-Douglass split is in Benjamin Quarles, "The Breach between Douglass and Garrison," *Journal of Negro History*, 23 (Apr. 1938), pp. 144–54. For an extensive discussion of Douglass's split with the Garrisonians, see Foner, *The Life and Writings of Frederick Douglass*, vol. 2, pp. 48–66; and Waldo E. Martin, *The Mind of Frederick Douglass* (Chapel Hill: University of North Carolina Press, 1984), pp. 25–48.

14. "Self-Elevation—Rev. S. R. Ward," *Frederick Douglass' Paper*, Apr. 13, 1855, as reprinted in Foner, *The Life and Writings of Frederick Douglass*, vol. 2, pp. 359–62.

15. For a thorough discussion of paternalism and slavery, see Eugene D. Genovese, *Roll, Jordan, Roll: The World the Slaves Made* (New York: Random House, 1974), especially pp. 89–91, 146–47. The role of patriarchal honor in slave-master relationships is treated in Bertram Wyatt-Brown, *Southern Honor* (New York: Oxford University Press, 1982), pp. 362–65. See also Willie Lee Rose, "The Domestication of Domestic Slavery," *Slavery and Freedom*, ed. William W. Freehling (New York: Oxford University Press, 1982), pp. 18–36.

16. Douglass to Sumner, Sept. 2, 1852, in Foner, *The Life and Writings of Frederick Douglass*, vol. 2, p. 210.

17. For a discussion of black criticism of the Garrisonians and of the black response to the rift between Douglass and Garrison, see Jane H. and William H. Pease, *They Who Would Be Free: Blacks' Search for Freedom, 1830–1861* (New York: Atheneum, 1974), pp. 68–93.

18. Emerson, "Uses of Great Men," p. 37.

19. *Walden*, pp. 6, 7, 15–16. A useful selection of Thoreau's writings on slavery appears in Vincent Freimarck and Bernard Rosenthal, eds., *Race and the American Romantics* (New York: Schocken, 1971), pp. 139–98.

20. S. Margaret Fuller, *Woman in the Nineteenth Century* (New York: Greeley and McElrath, 1845), pp. 10, 22, 158, 161–62.

21. Frederick Douglass, "Pictures and Progress," undated MS. in Frederick Douglass Papers, Library of Congress, reel 18, p. 151. Douglass wrote this lecture sometime in 1864 or 1865.

22. Buell, *Literary Transcendentalism*, p. 269.

23. Melville, "Hawthorne and His Mosses," p. 547.

Antitheses: The Dialectic of Violence and Literacy in Frederick Douglass's *Narrative* of 1845

THAD ZIOLKOWSKI

A word to make change
Ezra Pound

MASTER: Is it impossible, then, to hold you by any other ties but those of constraint and severity?

SLAVE: It is impossible to make me, who has felt the value of freedom, acquiesce in being a slave.

MASTER: Suppose I were to restore you to your liberty, would you reckon that a favor?

SLAVE: The greatest; for although it would only be undoing a wrong, I know too well how few among mankind are capable of sacrificing interest to justice, not to prize the exertion when it is made.

MASTER: I do it, then; be free.

—*Columbian Orator*

In the well-known "Lordship and Bondage" section of *Phenomenology of Spirit,* Hegel posits that self-consciousness hinges upon acknowledgment by another self-consciousness and that, in a kind of *lapsus felix* ("fortunate fall"), this reflection entails both loss and gain: "Self-consciousness is faced by another self-consciousness; it has come *out of itself.* This is of twofold significance: first, it has lost itself, for it finds itself as an *other* being; secondly, in so doing it has superceded the other, for it does not see the other as an essential being, but in the other sees its own self."[1] To affirm its own status, self-consciousness must dominate the other; yet insofar as the other is the very locus for its consciousness, this entails self-conquest. And since the other actually matches the first self in achieved self-consciousness, the scenario becomes that of a perfectly symmetrical dual enacted on the field of awareness:

This essay was written especially for this volume and is published here for the first time by permission of the author.

148

They must engage in this struggle, for they must raise their certainty of being *for themselves* to truth, both in the case of the other and in their own case. And it is only through staking one's life that freedom is won; only thus is it proved that for self-consciousness, its essential being is not just being, not the *immediate* form in which it appears, not its submergence in the expanse of life, but rather that there is nothing present in it which could not be regarded as a vanishing moment, that it is only pure *being-for-itself*. The individual who has not risked his life may well be recognized as a *person*, but he has not attained to the truth of this recognition as an independent self-consciousness.[2]

I cite Hegel at such length because the dialectical movement of his thought provides an appropriate rhythm for a reading of Frederick Douglass's *Narrative of the Life of Frederick Douglass, An American Slave, Written by Himself;* because it is not difficult to imagine Douglass, his tradition realigned, writing this passage (as a philosophical gloss on his confrontation with the overseer Covey, for example); and because Hegel's failure to ground his philosophy in historical, social-material relations serves as a still-needed warning against the Enlightenment-inspired tendency for critical readings to operate mainly, if not solely, in this fabulist realm of universalist discourse.

In Hegel this fabulism results in his "timeless" figures of "Lord" and "Bondsman," interactive states of self-consciousness standing for the poles of "being-of-oneself" and "being-for-another."[3] It is against the grain of such unmoored universalist discourse and its reification in material social relations (slavery) which Douglass writes. Or, phrased another way, Douglass *writes the grain* of lived material circumstances. Yet this depiction of slavery's conditions is bound up in the limitations and modal biases of a complex meditation upon its own becoming, its origin—that of Douglass's Promethean seizure of literacy. The *Narrative* offers more than the usual justification for making the fashionable claim that a given text is "about writing"—or rather, it offers a different kind of textual self-reflection, one concerned with the relations of words to social power as well as with the ways in which the very acquisition of the hegemonic means of expression situates the text in a kind of mediatory limbo. It is inscriptive of Douglass's transitional social status and the specific inflection this "unscheduled" transition gives to the jealously guarded signs of a highly stratified society.

Thus while it is tempting to begin simply by asking the Foucauldian question, "How does Douglass represent himself as learning to recognize himself as a subject of slavery?", then answering with a catalogue of examples and discussion, to do so would be premature. Given the dual problem of self-reflexivity and its traces in autobiographical representation, the first movement in a dialectical investigation of the *Narrative* must be between the thesis of the book itself—standing for *post facto* literacy—and its narrativized antithesis in the ground of preliteracy. The first question becomes then, "For a subject whose original community is defined and controlled in part by an enforced preliteracy, what (if anything) is at stake in his use of hegemonic discourse as a mode of representation?"

These at least are the terms of Houston Baker's argument in his interrogation of the *Narrative*. "Douglass transmits the 'heroic fugitive' message to an abolitionist audience that has made such a figure part of its conceptual, linguistic, and rhetorical repertoire. The issue that such an 'autobiographical' act raises for the literary analyst is that of authenticity. Where, for example, in Douglass's *Narrative* does a prototypical black American self reside?"[4] Since, for Baker, the task of the black author is to "preserve and communicate culturally unique meanings,"[5] only those parts of the *Narrative* "that chronicle the struggle for literacy"[6] meet this criterion by depicting the slave's actual position in society. The cultural capital (to use the French sociologist Pierre Bourdieu's term) of Douglass's literacy and his *Narrative* removes him, for the most part, to the echelon of another class, almost completely compromising the antithetical term—representation of the preliterate slave community. Further, according to Baker, Douglass's very means of freedom from slavery—literacy in the hegemonic discourse—*reenslaves* insofar as it "excludes rigorously individualizing definitions of a human, black identity."[7]

> Douglass grasps language in a Promethean act of will but he leaves unexamined its potentially devastating effects. One reflection of his uncritical acceptance of the perspective made available by literacy is the *Narrative* itself, which was written at the urging of white abolitionists who had become the former slave's employers. The work was written to prove that the narrator had indeed been a slave. And while autobiographical conventions forced him to portray as accurately as possible the existentiality of his original condition, the light of abolitionism is always implicitly present, guiding the narrator into calm, Christian, and publicly accessible harbors.[8]

At its extreme, the paradox Baker advances about Douglass's "prison-house"[9] of hegemonic language amounts to asserting the absolute incommensurability of autobiography and slavery: "The voice of the unwritten self, once it is subjected to the linguistic codes, literary conventions, and audience expectations of a literate population, is perhaps never again the authentic voice of black American slavery."[10] Aside from the questionable essentialism inherent in his notions of "authentic voice" and "voice of the unwritten self," the momentum of Baker's argument propels him to the verge of requiring Douglass to write as though he cannot write—to write as an illiterate slave would write. True, "had there been a separate, written black language available, Douglass might have fared better."[11] But then Douglass would not have been "Douglass" (his very name derives from "Lady of the Lake")[12] and the slave community would not have been the slave community as we now define it, of course—that is, *lacking* a separate, written language.

But Baker's paradox is due to an overemphasis on the antinomies of literacy and illiteracy. In the currency of power that "funded" the slave community, literacy and orality are two faces of a bill. Thus it is not immediately apparent why, for instance, passages in the *Narrative* depicting violence to slaves are any less "authentic" representations of slavery than those centering on the acquisition of literacy. Certainly both force and enforced illiteracy were employed against slaves and, as techniques of oppression, bore comparable burdens. Nor could it be maintained that either type depicts itself less figuratively, that is, partakes any less of the dominant discourse whose rhetoricity structures the *Narrative*. Hence neither type would per se seem any closer to attaining Baker's vanishing point of slave-cultural essence: pure orality or preliteracy.

The contradictions emergent with Baker's call for a slave narrative whose author shares all of his community's definitive features derive finally from an underlying conflation of literary representation and political representation. Such a "political unconscious"[13] tends, unfortunately, to reenact the hierarchizing procedures found within canon formation, here in terms of "authenticity." Baker has in effect inverted the usual hierarchy of literacy values in the case of slave narratives, assigning illiteracy to the place of highest standard.

For Baker, then, a good deal—if not the very possibility for "culturally unique meanings"—is at stake in Douglass's use of hegemonic discourse. As indicated above, however, the bases for his claiming as much, and for focusing on the *Narrative*'s narration of its own origins in the acquisition of literacy, are in my view the wrong ones.

The concentration most apt to do justice to Douglass's achievement in the *Narrative* is not one that at some level hungers for access to the identities of Douglass and the slave community apart from representations of them or one that dreams of an ideal "organic intellectual" whose relations to his group or class remain uncomplicated by the special status attained. To the extent that any attempt at linguistic representation involves partiality, a certain topological unmooring and autonomy, as well as ideological dimensions, and to the extent that this condition must be even more vexed for Douglass, it comprises equally as much the possibility for authorial subversion, control and a certain "mastery." What I hope to delineate is neither merely this limited "mastery," nor Douglass's occasional failures to control the terms of the assumed discourse. I will also discuss the ways in which the *Narrative* fuses a reflection on the conditions of its origins in literacy with a depiction of the mutually constitutive roles of language and violence in the context of slavery.

An instance of Douglass's mastery of the dominant discourse, evidence of his mastering of the master in effect, is apparent almost immediately in the *Narrative*.

> I have not accurate knowledge of my age, never having seen any authentic record containing it. By far the larger part of the slaves know as little of their ages as horses know of theirs, and it is the wish of most masters within my knowledge to keep their slaves thus ignorant. I do not remember to have ever met a slave who could tell of his birthday. They seldom come nearer to it than planting-time, harvest-time, cherry-time, spring-time, or fall-time. A want of information concerning my own was a source of unhappiness to me even during childhood. The white children could tell their ages. I could not tell why I ought to be deprived of the same privilege. (1)

In this first paragraph Douglass introduces as familiars the main members of the Enlightenment family of concepts: the privilege of sight and empiricism ("never having seen any," "within my knowledge"), of the system of verification ("authentic record"), and of the notion of innate reasons and its concomitant rights ("The white children could tell their ages. I could not tell why I ought to be deprived of the same privilege.").

This catalog of the dominant discourse's fundamental concepts enmeshes Douglass in the very net that Euro-America employed to justify its subjugation of blacks. But the detached, civilized tone of the prose—its consummate reasonableness—functions to place Douglass on the outside and thus from the first in a position to cast the net himself. That is to say that this Enlightenment discourse, though treacherous, is also demonstrably ductile, capable of being redirected from within.

In his essay "Binary Oppositions in Chapter One" of the *Narrative*, Henry Louis Gates, Jr., tracks the ways in which Douglass's skillful deployment of antitheses (a technique Gates and others quite plausibly attribute to a careful apprenticeship to essayistic rhetoric) collapses the working terms of slavery's discourse of control:

> Douglass uses this device to explicate the slave's understanding of himself and of his relation to the world through the system of the perceptions that defined the world the planters made. Not only does his *Narrative* come to concern itself with two diametrically opposed notions of genesis, origins, and meaning itself, but its structure actually turns on an opposition between nature and culture as well. Finally . . . Douglass's method of complex mediation—and the ironic reversals so peculiar to his text—suggest overwhelmingly the completely arbitrary relation between description and meaning, between signifier and signified, between sign and referent.[14]

According to Gates, then, the most powerful action of the *Narrative* is its destruction, through a controlled deconstruction of the theses of slavery, of "that symbolic code that created the false oppositions themselves."[15] Hence by mastering slavery's discourse of oppositions and binaries, Douglass struggles to disclose that "the oppositions all along were only arbitrary, not fixed."[16]

By "fixed" Gates means "divinely sanctioned," and his most compelling example of Douglass's success in underlining the baselessness of a fixed meaning in slavery discourse is that of the curse of Ham myth: "If the lineal descendants of Ham are alone to be scripturally enslaved, it is certain that slavery at the south must soon become unscriptural; for thousands are ushered into the world, annually, who, like myself, owe their existence to white fathers, and those fathers most frequently their own masters" (4). Turning a cool Enlightenment gaze on the symbolic order of the Biblical as well as on himself as a living subject of its power, Douglass sees into the arbitrary dimension of his culture. Bourdieu defines this dimension as follows: "The selection of meanings which objectively defines a group's or a class's culture as a symbolic system is *arbitrary* insofar as the structure and functions of that culture cannot be deduced from any universal principle, whether physical, biological or spiritual, not being linked by any sort of internal relation to 'the nature of things' or any 'human nature.' "[17] Further, according to Bourdieu, "every power to exert symbolic violence, i.e., every power which manages to impose meanings and to impose them as legitimate by concealing the power relations which are the basis of its force, adds its own specifically symbolic force to those power relations."[18] The *Narrative* is in effect a tracing of Douglass's negotiation between the physical and symbolic violence generated by slavery's power relations. The dialectical movement between theses of violence eventuates in the synthesis that is the *Narrative* itself.

Douglass's representations of physical violence are consistently the most troubled, always indicating for him the limits of language. "I have often been awakened," he writes, "at the dawn of day by the most heart-rending shrieks of an own aunt of mine, whom [the slave owner] used to tie up to a joist, and whip upon her naked back till she was literally covered with blood. No words, no tears, no prayers, from his gory victim, seemed to move his iron heart from its bloody purpose. The louder she screamed, the harder he whipped; and where the blood ran fastest, there he whipped longest. He would whip her to make her scream, and whip her to make her hush; and not until overcome by fatigue, would he cease to swing the blood-clotted cowskin" (5). In the grips of this insane force, the entire range of human communication—from moans and screams to prayers—is powerless, and it is this futility of expression that "rends" the heart of Douglass's narrative. Here the force of the slave owner and, by implication, the ensemble of power relations underlying his force, are brought to bear upon the slave's speech in such a way as to highlight the meaninglessness of speech when unsupported by a network of power relations. The slave owner "would whip her to make her scream and whip her to make her hush" as a means of demonstrating the indifference, the interchangeableness, of speech and silence in a system of almost total domination. In the rest of the passage Douglass narrates his experience in the passive forms of "witness," "beholder," and "auditor," concluding with an outright confession of his incapacity to convey the scene: "It was a most terrible spectacle. I wish I could commit to paper the feelings with which I beheld it" (5).

This last sentence must be read as more than just a formula standing for "the author has done his best here." Douglass's inability to write "the spectacle" of violence, to commit it to paper and thereby master the master, brings his enterprise of composition to its fearful origin. Its shock carries us from the violence that impelled him toward the escape hatch of literacy to the fact of literacy ("paper"), that is, to the fact of its always being, at this level of failure, merely paper. The revivified horror of this particular whipping stuns literary imagination because it points directly to the foundations of the power of language in an unstable system of social relations (the Fugitive-Slave Law). Confronted with this, the potent magic of literary revisionism dissolves in the rematerialization of the paper before Douglass's eyes.

The limits of the literary here are also those of the dominant discourse. To calm the disturbed surface of his narrative, Douglass opens the second chapter with a reasoned, Enlightenment-inflected account of the slave economy. "As I received my first impressions of slavery on this plantation, I will give some description of it, and of slavery as it there existed. The plantation is about twelve miles north of Easton, in Talbot county, and is situated on the border of Miles River. The principal products raised upon it were tobacco, corn, and wheat" (9). Having just been very much implicated by slavery and its contaminating terror in his description of his Aunt Hester's whipping, Douglass echoes the detached tone of the *Narrative*'s initial paragraph, rewriting himself as a Lockean tabula rasa, as prior to slavery's scarring impressions. The cartographic and encyclopedic concreteness of the images reground the *Narrative,* as if bracing it for another examination of Douglass as slave and language power as relational. Note also how his scrupulous use of past tenses ("products raised upon it were") increases the distance, both spatial and temporal, between himself and a context that was in fact neither very distant nor probably very different.

Chapter two proceeds smoothly in this descriptive register, one that Douglass controls throughout and that permits him the distance necessary for flourishes, such as the following, of an irony that encompasses the entire social spectrum.

Few privileges were esteemed higher, by the slaves of the out-farms, than that of being selected to do errands at the Great House Farm. It was associated in their minds with greatness. A representative could not be prouder of his election to a seat in the American Congress, than a slave on one of the out-farms would be of his election to do errands at the Great House Farm. . . . The competitors for this office sought as diligently to please their overseers, as the office-seekers in the political parties seek to please and deceive the people. The same traits of character might be seen in Colonel Lloyd's slaves, as are seen in the slaves of the political parties. (12–13)

But he concludes the chapter with a conspicuously more problematic passage, one that reintroduces the contradictions inherent in the expressive forms of a disenfranchised group and the vexed relation to it of the author. Describing the songs of slaves on their way to the Great House Farm, Douglass writes that "they would compose and sing as they went along, consulting neither time nor tune. The thought that came up, came out—if not in the word, in the sound;—and as frequently in the one as in the other. They would sometimes sing the most pathetic sentiment in the most rapturous tone, and the most rapturous sentiment in the most pathetic tone" (13). For Douglass, the fundamental disconnection between utterance and social power witnessed in the Aunt Hester passage reemerges in the slave songs' improvisational void, the interchangeableness of sound and word, the wrenching recombination of joyful tone and woeful sentiment. On a formal level the songs can be seen to express the contradictions exerted in the social; where one is whipped into meaningless silence and then whipped into futile pleading, both the spontaneity and the jarring syntax make sense. Encoded in "words which to many would seem unmeaning jargon," the songs were nonetheless "full of meaning to themselves" (14).

Exploring the nature of this meaning, Douglass reveals the rift dividing himself from this community.

> I did not, when a slave, understand the deep meaning of those rude and apparently incoherent songs. I was myself within the circle; so that I neither saw nor heard as those without might see and hear. They told a tale of woe which was then altogether beyond my feeble comprehension; they were tones loud, long, and deep; they breathed the prayer and complaint of souls boiling over with the bitterest anguish. Every tone was a testimony against slavery, and a prayer to God for deliverance from chains. The hearing of those wild notes always depressed my spirit, and filled me with ineffable sadness. I have frequently found myself in tears while hearing them. The mere recurrence to those songs, even now; afflicts me; and while I am writing these lines, an expression of feeling has already found its way down my cheek. (14)

For Gates, this division is exemplary, and he reads the above as evidence of Douglass's realization of the need for "a certain aesthetic distance and an acceptance of the critical imperative."[19] "There exists always the danger, Douglass seems to say, that the meanings of nonlinguistic signs will seem 'natural'; one must view them with a certain detachment to see that their meanings are in fact merely the 'products' of a certain culture, the result of shared assumptions and conventions. Not only is meaning culture-bound and the referents of all signs an assigned relation, Douglass tells us, but *how* we read determines *what* we read, in the truest sense of the hermeneutical circle."[20] But if the *how* and *what* of reading are addressed here, the *whether* seems fully as much at issue. When Douglass again turns his attention to the aural/oral culture of the slave community, he recognizes its origin in the arbitrarily arranged formation of the slave economy. But he is also forced to face the vexing role of literacy in his reading: "The mere recurrence to those songs, even now, afflicts me; and while I am writing these lines, an expression of feeling has already found its way down my cheek." Echoing the Aunt Hester passage—"I wish I could commit to paper the feeling with which I beheld it"—this pained self-consciousness takes its rise in part from the gulf created between Douglass and his community by his acquisition of literacy and its class-specific mobility. Douglass is no longer "within the circle," and thus while his interpretation of the songs is shaped by the cognitive and physical distance literacy permits, this shape is neither simple nor simply the somehow liberating one Gates seems to imply it is in his evocation of the "hermeneutical circle." The distance at issue here is not reducible to the "aesthetic," though it inevitably entails "the critical imperative" since the "expression of feeling" Douglass decorously alludes to is testimony to both the now perceptible pathos of slave songs and the autobiographical definition of that pathos: ". . . I am writing these lines. . . ." Hence the slave songs come to stand for the tragedy of slavery as well as for literacy, the vehicle that permits the apprehension of the songs' symbolic thrust, though not without a prejudicial inflection from the medium of expression.

In their formal recasting of the contradictions exhibited by the Aunt Hester passage, as well as in their affiliation with the groans, cries, and screams Douglass also places at the heart of the slave experience, the songs assume on the one hand a position antithetical to that of literacy in the dominant discourse, and on the other life-giving, parental status: "To those songs I trace my first glimmering conception of the dehumanizing character of slavery. I can never get rid of that conception. Those songs still follow me, to deepen my hatred of slavery, and quicken my sympathies for my brethren in bonds" (14). The songs conceive in Douglass his own eventual conception of them in the dominant discourse. They are a slave-cultural form directly respondent to and emergent from the suffering of slavery's symbolic and actual violence, and they embody the most sophisticated articulation of slavery's self-consciousness. As such they confront Douglass's assumption of the dominant discourse in an ambivalent light, filling its autobiographical moment with an *"ineffable* sadness" (my emphasis). It is hardly surprising, then, that Douglass concludes this passage and chapter with the figure of a man isolated by fate and circumstances from his society: "The singing of a man cast away upon a desolate island might be as appropriately considered as evidence of contentment and happiness, as the singing of a slave; the songs of the one and of the other are prompted by the same emotion" (15). The figure enfolds the autobiographer fully as much as the singing slaves, for while "within the circle" Douglass's understanding was but nascent; yet having attained the critical distance requisite for appreciation he is as "cast away," without real community, by virtue of the medium of a distancing discourse.

If the slave songs may be seen as opposing Douglass's expression in the dominant written discourse *after* his achievement of literacy, then the antithesis against which he represents himself as striving *during* enslavement is that of the brutal violence of slave owners. In their syntax—Douglass's first grammar lesson—these moments of violence reveal the limits and foundation of slavery's pervasive symbolic order. In the *Narrative,* overseers inhabit the site where symbolic and physical violence establish slavery per se. Note his attention to the word-force ratio in this description of Mr. Gore. "Mr. Gore was a grave man, and, though a young man, he indulged in no jokes, said no funny words, seldom smiled. His words were in perfect keeping with his looks, and his looks were in perfect keeping with his words. Overseers will sometimes indulge in a witty word, even with the slaves; not so with Mr. Gore. He spoke but to command, and commanded but to be obeyed; he dealt sparingly with his words, and bountifully with his whip, never using the former where the latter would answer as well" (24). The almost allegorical symmetry of Gore's dispensation of power is expressed in his encounter with a resistant slave.

> He had given Demby but few stripes, when to get rid of the scourging, he ran and plunged himself into a creek, and stood there at the depth of his shoulders, refusing to come out. Mr. Gore told him that he would give him three calls, and that, if he did not come out at the third call, he would shoot him. The first call was given. Demby made no response, but stood his ground. The second and third calls were given with the same result. Mr. Gore then, without consultation or deliberation with any one, not even giving Demby an additional call, raised his musket to his face, taking deadly aim at his standing victim, and in an instant poor Demby was no more. (25)

When words fail the overseer in this grim pedagogy of slavery, death ensues for the slave. The basic equation of slavery's power relations is writ small in this face-off of two figures linked by the bar-sign of the rifle. Of course, above the overseer is an invisible exponent, raising him to the power that places the musket's trigger in his hands as well as allowing the murder to be committed with impunity. When asked to explain this nonetheless "extraordinary expedient," Gore in effect maintains that to act otherwise in such a circumstance would culminate in the inversion of the equation of power. "He argued that if one slave refused to be corrected, and escaped with his life, the other slaves would soon copy the example; the result of which would be, the freedom of the slaves, and the enslavement of the whites. Mr. Gore's defense was satisfactory" (25).

Between overseer and slave, then, there exist the spaces of language, of terror and, ultimately, of death. Dependent as they are for definition upon the continual renegotiation of a brutal social enforcement, the borders between the realms remain fluid, unpredictable. But the spaces of language and terror disappear only on the advent of their failure, signified by death. As we have seen, socially empowered language is almost solely the possession of whites. In the *Narrative,* minimal use of speech or its mirror image—pacified silence—by blacks stands for minimalized power. Note, as exemplary of Douglass's sensitivity to this dispensation, his various use of the formula "with a single word" in the subsequent passages. In the first he is describing the sale of slaves at an auction. "After the valuation, then came the division. *I have no language to express* the high excitement and deep anxiety which were felt among us poor slaves during this time. Our fate for life was now to be decided. We had no more voice in that decision than the brutes among whom we were ranked. *A single word from the white men* was enough—against all our wishes, prayers, and entreaties—to sunder forever the dearest friends, dearest kindred, and strongest ties known to human beings" (48, my emphases). From slaves, the most earnest forms of human expression—wishes, prayers, entreaties—are as silence beside the laconic "speech act" ("Sold.") of the white owners. So much is this the case in the *Narrative* that it is as if, here in the description of his grandmother, "a single word" comes to stand for socially empowered language: "She was nevertheless left a slave—a slave for life—a slave in the hands of strangers; and in their hands she saw her children, her grandchildren, and her great-grandchildren, divided, like so many sheep, without being gratified with the small privilege of a single word, as to their or her own destiny" (50). Thus a diaspora of generations is posed against the isolated grandmother and her slavery-defined wordlessness from which the grandchildren issued.

By contrast, Douglass later depicts himself as *withholding* this trump card of power, gained for himself at this juncture of the *Narrative* by literacy and a mature sense of his actual possibilities for escape: "Saturday night, he [Hugh Auld] called upon me as usual for my week's wages. I told him I had no wages; I had done no work that week. Here we were upon the point of coming to blows. He raved, and swore his determination to get hold of me. *I did not allow myself a single word;* but was resolved, if he laid the weight of his hand upon me, it should be blow for blow" (105, my emphasis). Douglass discloses here his recognition that the "right" to that single word of social power derives from a willingness to resort to the Hegelian death struggle. A "blow" is also a single word in this sense.

Douglass's critical vocabulary of Hegelian violence was built not with Auld, however, but on the farm of a "farm renter," Edward Covey, who, despite being "loaned" slaves such as Douglass for the purpose of "breaking" them, was nevertheless a "poor man" (65). He owned only one slave himself and thus existed in a particularly conflictual position vis-à-vis that class of laborers.

Covey's strategy of control involved an internalization of the discipline he imposed on his slave laborers: "Mr. Covey was one of the few slaveholders who could and did work with his hands. He was a hard working man. He knew by himself just what a man or boy could do. There was no deceiving him" (63).

Douglass recalls in addition Covey's severe, hair-trigger temper and his seeming ubiquity: "His work went on in his absence almost as well as in his presence; and he had the faculty of making us feel that he was ever present with us. This he did by surprising us. He seldom approached the spot where we were at work openly, if he could do it secretly. . . . This being his mode of attack, it was never safe to stop a single minute. . . . He appeared to us as being ever at hand" (63–64). By invisible, omnipresent threat Covey imposes an internalization of discipline imposed first upon himself. But like the "institution" of slavery generally, Covey's inducement in the slaves of a state of "conscious and permanent visibility that assure the automatic functioning of power"[21] must in addition be backed by actual violence.

This requirement culminates in an encounter that comprises Douglass's pivotal insight into the syntax he must master before his already achieved mastery of linguistic syntax can take effect. If Douglass's quest for literacy can be seen in some sense as a displaced attempt to relocate and reunite with his mother (a mother tongue), then his struggle with Covey is effectively a victorious oedipal struggle, the critical, epiphanic instance when he "touches the Father" of slavery's patriarchal violence and overcomes it, thereby reinvigorating his urge for escape and the utilization of literacy. "As soon as I found what he was up to, I gave a sudden spring, and as I did so, he holding to my legs, I was brought sprawling on the stable floor. Mr. Covey seemed now to think he had me, and could do what he pleased; but at this moment—from whence came the spirit I don't know—I resolved to fight; and, suiting my action to the resolution, I seized Covey hard by the throat; and as I did so, I rose. He held on to me, and I to him" (73).

It is perhaps no coincidence, recalling the Gore-Demby incident, that this face-off reemerges here, but with the terms of the equation being equal in this figuration. For the moment, Douglass's choke-hold in effect seizes Covey's ability to utter "a single word." Briefly there is only the political-allegorical sound of two men struggling as slavery's "moment of creation" reenacts itself. "We were at it for nearly two hours. Covey at length let me go, puffing and blowing at a great rate, saying that if I had not resisted, he would not have whipped me half so much. The truth was, that he had not whipped me at all. I considered him as getting entirely the worst end of the bargain; for he had drawn no blood from me, but I had from him" (74). Douglass's victory and his writing of it cancel the whip's inscription: ". . . he had not whipped me at all." Covey, master of surveillance, is afterwards unwilling to be surveyed by an incorrigible slave: "Mr. Covey enjoyed the most unbounded reputation for being a first-rate overseer and negro-breaker. It was of considerable importance to him. That reputation was at stake; and had he sent me—a boy about sixteen years old—to the public whipping post, his reputation would have been lost; so, to save his reputation, he suffered me to go unpunished" (75). As a consequence of his inversion of the power equation, Douglass writes that "however long I might remain a slave in form, the day had passed forever when

I could be a slave in fact. I did not hesitate to let it be known of me, that the white man who expected to succeed in whipping, must also succeed in killing me" (74). Douglass hence continues to exist as a figure in slavery's power equation but only "in form," since "in fact" he has converted the fundamental term of slavery—whipping—into the cancellation of the equation altogether—killing. Or, metaphorized differently, in his willingness to die rather than suffer physical coercion, Douglass has assumed the dimension of the invisible, that of the surveillant-overseer.

The other more complex and enduring way in which Douglass surveys the surveillant, and one essential to this movement in mastering the whole discourse of slavery, is his early, largely autodidactic grasp of literacy. Since the dominant discourse is the form of control most invisible, most scrupulously guarded, in cracking its code Douglass begins the process of both appearing to himself as a historical entity and disappearing from the brutally dehistoricizing scene of slavery.

Though she does so only briefly, no other woman in the *Narrative* comes as close to filling the gap left by Douglass's mother as Sophia Auld. On first meeting her Douglass writes: "And here I saw what I had never seen before; it was a white face beaming with the most kindly emotions; it was the face of my new mistress, Sophia Auld. I wish I could describe the rapture that flashed through my soul as I beheld it. It was a new and strange sight to me, brightening up my pathway with the light of happiness" (32–33). The contrast between Douglass's real mother ("I do not recollect ever seeing my mother by the light of day. She was with me in the night" [2]) and this beatific white face "brightening up" Douglass's existence with "the light of happiness," is complete. And since Mrs. Auld is inextricably connected to his acquisition of literacy (a fact that accounts in part for the radiance of his description), one feels compelled to restate the mother-identified valence of literacy suggested earlier. Indeed, it is only with difficulty that this connection can be overlooked when the paternalism of Hugh Auld erupts into this blissful scene of pedagogy.

> Very soon after I went to live with Mr. and Mrs. Auld, she very kindly commenced to teach me the A, B, C. After I had learned this, she assisted me in learning to spell words of three or four letters. Just as this point of my progress, Mr. Auld found out what was going on, and at once forbade Mrs. Auld to instruct me further, telling her, among other things, that it was unlawful, as well as unsafe, to teach a slave to read. To use his own words, further, he said, "If you give a nigger an inch, he will take an ell. A nigger should know nothing but to obey his master —to do as he is told to do. Learning would *spoil* the best nigger in the world. Now," he said, "If you teach that nigger (speaking of myself) how to read, there would be no keeping him. It would forever unfit him to be a slave."
> (36)

In this way Auld (father/slavery) articulates the dangers attendant upon giving a slave (son) access to knowledge of the dominant discourse (mother/literacy). And surely the most emblematic and most savory example of what Baker calls the *Narrative*'s "enfolding ironies"[22] can be isolated in this citation: " 'Now,' he said, 'If you teach that nigger (speaking of myself) how to read, there would be no keeping him.' " Here Douglass inscribes paternalism's naming of itself, the barrier it presents, and its blindness to the presence of the very subject who will eventually reconstruct his experience in the forbidden discourse. In its quiet but masterful compression of Douglass's victorious trespass, this sentence stands in antithetical relation to the passage depicting Aunt Hester's whipping. There the narrator's confrontation of violence and its connection to a discourse rooted in the social-material relations of power traces a slippage of confidence in a discourse whose terminus is the determinate fact of literacy. Whereas in the Aunt Hester passage the terrible spectacle of the whip-wielding master threatens to drain the *Narrative*'s powers of self-signification, in the above sentence all meaning issues from a narrator embedded, clandestine like his autobiographical self, in parenthetical enclosure, in several senses a kind of textual *deus abscondens*.

Indeed, concealment, secretiveness, stealth—these are the techniques Douglass utilizes in his acquisition of literacy. And necessarily so: "From this time I was most narrowly watched. If I was in a separate room any considerable length of time, I was sure to be suspected of having a book, and was at once called to give an account of myself" (40). One hardly knows whether to laugh or cry at these absurd attempts at suppression; but in any case, Douglass writes, "All this was too late. The first step had been taken. Mistress, in teaching me the alphabet, had given the *inch,* and no precaution could prevent me from taking the *ell*" (40).

Taking *ell* and *inch*—and literally, in the sense of building vocabulary— Douglass shrewdly utilizes a class adjacent to his own (as in a different way and to different, but ultimately related ends, he would utilize Covey): "The plan which I adopted, and the one by which I was most successful, was that of making friends of all the little white boys whom I met in the street. As many of these as I could, I converted into teachers" (40). Having been given the "gift" of the alphabet from a "naive" mistress, Douglass invests this minuscule amount of cultural capital in the exchange economy of America's harshly stratified society: "I used also to carry bread with me, enough of which was always in the house, and to which I was always welcome; for I was much better off in this regard than many of the poor white children in our neighborhood. This bread I used to bestow upon the hungry little urchins, who, in return, would give me that more valuable bread of knowledge" (41).

To learn to write Douglass takes similar advantage of the debris of dominant discourse inevitably cast off in the turmoil of its industry. In a historically prophetic way he consumes, as it were, the materially liberating difference between urban and agrarian economies. Observing that shipbuilders wrote letters on hewed timber to designate whether the boards were meant for starboard ("S"), larboard ("L"), with combinations of aft ("A") and forward ("F"), Douglass learned the four letters, copying them out with chalk at the shipyard. "After that, when I met with any boy who I knew could write, I would tell him I could write as well as he. The next word would be, 'I don't believe you. Let me see you try it.' I would then make the letters which I had been so fortunate as to learn, and ask him to beat that. In this way I got a good many lessons in writing, which it is quite possible I should never have gotten in any other way" (45). The *Narrative* thus presents two ways of extracting words—cultural capital and means of empowerment—from a hostile society, and these are in direct keeping with that society's laws of operation: exchange and competition, bread and bluff.

Douglass is almost immediately made to feel the weight of this acquired wealth. Of his avid reading in the abolitionist *Columbian Orator* he writes: "The reading of these documents enabled me to utter my thoughts, and to meet the arguments brought forward to sustain slavery; but while they relieved me of one difficulty, they brought on another even more painful than the one of which I was relieved. The more I read, the more I was led to abhor and detest my enslavers. I could regard them in no other light than a band of successful robbers, who had left their homes, and gone to Africa, and stolen us from our homes, and in a strange land reduced us to slavery" (42). That he believes himself to have already been in possession of the thoughts this reading enables him "to utter" is perhaps an index of the extent to which Douglass does in fact subsume the terms of his overall articulation in those of the dominant discourse. Abolitionist formulations of his condition are in any case made retroactively to appear as an unproblematic "perfect fit," ideally (if painfully) accommodating Douglass's inchoate sensations of injustice. But whether a portion of Douglass's reflective misery has its source in his seemingly uncritical acceptance of an "outsider's" expression of slavery must remain speculative at best; for, as we have seen in the analysis of Baker's position, at its logical extreme an argument of this sort posits the requirement for a nonexistent alternative mode of articulation, if not tradition of inculcation.

Yet the excruciating helplessness Douglass experiences as a consequence of this formation by abolitionist writings may at the very least stand as testimony to the fact that slaves were not the readership anticipated by Caleb Bingham, *et al.* "A Variety of Original and Selected Pieces; together with Rules; Calculated to improve Youth and Others in the Ornamental and Useful Art of Eloquence"—as its subtitle makes clear, the *Columbian Orator* is hardly a "guerrilla warfare" manual; and in the absence of truly "Useful" information, such passages as the following from the slave-master dialogue cited in the *Narrative* would understandably frustrate "Others" like Douglass:

MASTER: You were a slave when I purchased you.

SLAVE: Did I give consent of the purchase?

MASTER: You had no consent to give. You had already lost the right of disposing of yourself.

SLAVE: I had lost the power, but how the right? I was treacherously kidnapped in my own country, when following an honest occupation. I was put in chains, sold to one of your countrymen, carried by force on board his ship, brought hither, and exposed to sale like a beast in the market, where you bought me. What step in all this progress of violence and injustice can give a *right?* Was it in the villain who stole me, in the slave-merchant who tempted him to do so, or in you who encouraged the slave-merchant to bring his cargo of human cattle to cultivate your lands?[23]

This dialogue, which concludes quite implausibly with the sheer rhetorical force of the slave's argument compelling manumission from the master, is nevertheless a kind of dream-text for the *Narrative*. Its enactment, purely on the linguistic plane, of a liberating speech act in the dominant discourse comprises the subtextual ideal for Douglass's literary enterprise as a whole. Read in this way, Douglass's remark on the dialogue is instructive: "The slave was *made to say* some very smart things in reply to his master—things which had the desired though unexpected effect; for the conversation resulted in the voluntary emancipation of the slave on the part of the master" (42, my emphasis). Whereas he portrays abolitionist discourse as effectively the midwife to his own nascent conceptions of slavery, above Douglass's construction of the dialogue's slave is that of a puppet or mechanical device being spoken through by abolitionism. The anxiety involved in having taken up (or having been taken up by) an already operative foreign and hegemonic discourse, the fear that he might somehow stand in relation to abolitionism as larynx to voice, are thus displaced onto the literary figure of the dialogue's slave. In a gesture that is the inverse of concealing his listening autobiographical self within parentheses, here Douglass "inoculates" the *Narrative* against the germinal figure of the abolitionist puppet by exposing it on the surface of his text. Both are mastering gestures. But the latter additionally salvages the dialogue as an ideal paradigm of verbal suasion by isolating its strategy of ventriloquism, thereby implicitly setting its own narrativity against this false (though thematically model) text.

This dialogue from the *Columbian Orator* would thus fall into the category of texts with which Douglass vies for overall structural control of his *Narrative*.[24] The various and often subtle ways in which Garrison's preface, Phillips's Letter, and Douglass's own appendix ultimately place the dominant discourse within the *Narrative*'s control are very amply set forth in the Stepto article. I would only add that Garrison's windy oratorical flourishes ("under the lash of the driver, with the chains upon his limbs!") contrast favorably with Douglass's terse, controlled range of literary powers in this matter of authentication. Further, Phillip's allusion to the fable of "The Man and the

Lion" ("I am glad the time has come when the 'lions write history.'"), though memorable, effectively reinscribes the "brute" metaphor that Douglass struggles to dissolve in the *Narrative*. Phillips displays a comparably subversive-perverse streak (however contextually mitigated) in his "*I am free to say* that, in your place, I should throw the MS. into the fire" (xxiii, emphasis added)—a remark whose rhetorical emptiness is filled by the difference between the social privilege of the literary elite and the newly literate, such as Douglass, who can never afford the luxury of destroying the sole trace of their struggle in a fit of literary *pudeur*.

I have attempted to underline certain movements of the *Narrative*'s internal dialectic: this conflict within, and also always about, its project of representation that occurs between the spectacle of violences (both physical and symbolic) and the acquisition of literacy. Their synthesis *in* the *Narrative* comprises the *Narrative*, while simultaneously standing for Douglass's mastery of the only terms available—those of the dominant discourse. Crucially, this discourse, in the hands of a former slave, is no longer an undifferentiated dominant, one in the hands only of those deemed fit for the reproduction of already existent social relations. And Douglass repeatedly reveals the plasticity of this dominant in controlled narrative signatures. What remains, as disclosed by the centrifugal force exerted by the *Narrative*'s depictions of violence, is the unstable ensemble of social-material relations—never simply reducible to violence. Of these Douglass takes shrewd advantage in his acquisition of literacy, portrayals of which express themselves centripetally, empowering the *Narrative* with reflections of its origins. From the conflicted field of action traced by the *Narrative*, Douglass consolidates his autobiographical "I," an interface mediating antitheses.

Notes

1. G. W. F. Hegel, *Phenomenology of Spirit* (Oxford: Oxford University Press, 1977), 111.
2. Hegel, *Phenomenology*, 114.
3. Hegel, *Phenomenology*, 115.
4. Houston Baker, *The Journey Back* (Chicago: University of Chicago Press, 1980), 42.
5. Baker, *Journey*, xxi.
6. Baker, *Journey*, 42.
7. Baker, *Journey*, 38.
8. Baker, *Journey*, 38–39.
9. The "prison-house of language" alludes to Fredric Jameson's book, *The Prison-house of Language* (Princeton University Press, Princeton University, N.J., 1971) whose title derives from the following passage in Nietzsche's *The Will to Power* (section 522 (1886–87): "We have to cease to think if we refuse to do it in the prison-house of language; for we cannot reach further than the doubt which asks whether the limit we see is really a limit . . ."
10. Baker, *Journey*, 43.
11. Baker, *Journey*, 39.
12. Douglass recounts this seemingly whimsical association of himself with the Sir Walter

Scott character as follows: "Mr. Johnson [the Abolitionist with whom Douglass stayed after arriving in New Bedford] had just been reading the 'the Lady of the Lake,' and at once suggested that my name be 'Douglass.' From that time until now I have been called 'Frederick Douglass;' and as I am more widely known by that name than by either of the others, I shall continue to use it as my own." Frederick Douglass, *Narrative of the Life of Frederick Douglass, An American Slave, Written by Himself* (New York: Anchor Books, 1973), 110; hereafter cited in the text.

13. "Political unconscious" refers to a book by Fredric Jameson whose subtitle, "Narrative as a Socially Symbolic Act," succinctly states the work's Marxist thesis. My use of the term here is ironic insofar as it is meant to invoke "political unconsciousness" as well as the possible solution in a more rigorously materialist approach.

14. Henry-Louis Gates, Jr., "Binary Oppositions in Chapter One of *Narrative of the Life of Frederick Douglass An American Slave Written by Himself,*" in *Afro-American Literature: the Reconstruction of Instruction* (New York: MLA, 1979), 223 (reprinted in this volume).

15. Gates, "Binary," 227.

16. Gates, "Binary," 227.

17. Pierre Bourdieu, *Reproduction in Education, Society and Culture* (London: SAGE Publications, 1977), 8.

18. Bourdieu, *Reproduction,* 4.

19. Gates, "Binary," 230.

20. Gates, "Binary," 230.

21. Michel Foucault, *Discipline and Punish* (New York: Vintage Books, 1979), 201.

22. Baker, *Journey,* 34.

23. Caleb Bingham, *Columbian Orator* (Boston: Manning & Loring, 1802), 240–41.

24. Robert B. Stepto, "Narration, Authentication, and Authorial Control in Frederick Douglass' *Narrative of 1845"* in *Afro-American Literature: the Reconstruction of Instruction* (New York: MLA, 1979), 181 & ff.

The Antilanguage of Slavery:
Frederick Douglass's 1845 *Narrative*

ANN KIBBEY AND MICHELE STEPTO

By comparison with his later autobiographies, Frederick Douglass's 1845 *Narrative,* published some six-and-a-half years after his escape from Baltimore, offers little detailed description of slave life. Rather, Douglass concentrates on the linguistic significance of bondage in the American South, characterizing events as stark paradigms, portraying masters and slaves in terms of their verbal discourse and the intervening violence of the lash, and charting his own relentless progress to freedom by means of his insights into the language of his masters. The *Narrative* is also a careful examination of the structure of meaning within a slave economy as well as an argument against its social viability. Douglass's presentation of slave life, then, is a profoundly rhetorical one: the reality he presents is the slave's confrontation with the structure of signification in slave society, a reality Douglass describes paradigmatically, in terms of its purest potentiality of meaning.

Douglass portrays the relation between master and slave as one in which all intersubjective utterance is, by economic necessity, impossible. By equating "slave" and "nonhuman," slavery systematically negates the real stature of the slave as a human subject, and, by physical violence, forces him to deny—in public utterance at least—personal will or desire and to live within the restrictions of this meaning. Likewise, slavery denies human stature to the master, since he must articulate his status as master in the form of the command—whose lack of pronominal inflection, invoking neither "I" nor "you," abjures discourse between subjects—and enforce his command with the nonverbal "utterance" of the whip. Failing to acknowledge in language the human referent of "slave"—that irreducibly other person distinct from the "slave" of mental creation—the master, in his acts of violence, is marked by the same sublinguistic status as the person he enslaves.[1]

The absence of intersubjective utterance—an absence definitive, for Douglass, of all master-slave discourse—constitutes the linguistic meaning of

This essay was written especially for this volume and is published here for the first time by permission of the authors.

enslavement. Each "economic" slave, that is, each person born into the economic condition of slavery, must also be linguistically enslaved, must be made by violence to discover and enter into a structure of meaning that contradicts his or her humanity. In this primary relation of slavery, where the humanity of both master and slave is concealed, the words that pass between them function as an antilanguage, creating a social territory marked by an unutterable "I" and "you." Their linguistic separation, which negates their mutual human stature, systematically destroys the meaning of words to preserve at any cost the meaning of the one word, "slave."

As Douglass understands slavery linguistically, so also does he understand freedom. Against his paradigm of slave society, Douglass places his own freeman's *Narrative,* whose final significance we apprehend from the narrative's last event, his speech to a Nantucket antislavery meeting. Drawn to the abolitionist movement by William Lloyd Garrison's newspaper, the *Liberator,* Douglass began to attend antislavery meetings, where, despite his freeman's status, slavery still had a hold on him. "I seldom had much to say at the meetings," he recalls; "the truth was, I felt myself a slave, and the idea of speaking to white people weighed me down."[2] At an antislavery convention in Nantucket in 1841, Douglass finally transcended this self-prejudice, leaving slavery behind linguistically as well as economically: "I felt strongly moved to speak, and was at the same time much urged to do so. . . . It was a severe cross, and I took it up reluctantly" (119). Douglass presents this moment of reluctance as his last slavish one: "I spoke but a few moments, when I felt a degree of freedom, and said what I desired with considerable ease. From that time until now, I have been engaged in pleading the cause of my brethren. . . ." (119). In speaking to the convention, Douglass both discovered and affirmed his freedom fully in the linguistic expression of his humanity. Although economic liberty was the precondition for this experience, the realization of his freedom was, as Douglass presents it, preeminently a linguistic event.

The speech that Douglass delivered to his Nantucket audience was presumably a version of the 1845 *Narrative.*[3] This correspondence suggests that what the Nantucket event offers is the social context in which to place the story of his life, which is to say that it is only in this final context that the narrative becomes intelligible as a social act. Douglass discovers his subjective humanity through his participation in the meeting, not prior to or apart from it. His narrative voice, then, is at once an individual voice and a social product, a subject that is intersubjective in its very constitution.[4] The form of the narrative reflects this sense of the paradoxically social nature of individuality, for the "I" who presents it is not a subject separated from the human society he describes. Just as Douglass's experience at Nantucket occurred in the social context of those who heard him speak, so the narrative of his progress towards this event is interwoven with the stories of others: his individual history appears only as one among many. Granted that this history is told more fully than any other, still it does not exclusively determine the meaning or purpose of the *Narrative.* Indeed, Douglass unmistakably interrupts his personal story in refusing to relate the means of his escape, thus making it impossible to follow the thread of narrative continuity by recourse to his life alone. However tempting it may be to cast Douglass's self-presentation in the heroic mold of the extraordinary individual, Douglass makes us acutely aware of the fortuitousness of his present condition, even while calling attention to himself as the free author of the *Narrative:* "It is possible, and even quite probable, that but for the mere circumstance of being removed from that plantation to Baltimore, I should have to-day, instead of being here seated by my own table, in the enjoyment of freedom and the happiness of home, writing this Narrative, been confined in the galling chains of slavery" (46). It was not simply that the Auld house in Baltimore offered more opportunities for escape than Colonel Lloyd's planta-tion. Rather, the move changed Douglass's status from field hand in a rural society to quasi-personal servant in the economically various world of urban society. Throughout the *Narrative,* Douglass never fails to describe the economic circumstances of his linguistic insights, carefully detailing his moves through all the gradations of slavery. Precisely because Douglass always felt himself subject to the economic and social conditions in which he lived, he defines freedom in terms of the intersubjective reality of the Nantucket meeting, as something achieved at a particular place and time, within a particular economic and social structure, and not as a sheer act of personal will by an isolated individual in defiance of his circumstances.

If we understand the Nantucket meeting in this way, it also becomes clear that Douglass's life story breaks with the notion that the slave narrative is a variant of the Protestant spiritual narrative.[5] Rather than assert a discontinuity between the slave and free author—as the narrative of spiritual regeneration necessarily does—Douglass insists instead that the author of his *Narrative* is the same man who was enslaved: "My feet have been so cracked with the frost, that the pen with which I am writing might be laid in the gashes" (43). Here, the symbolic "fit" of freedom to bondage repudiates the necessity for transformation inherent in the Protestant concept of spiritual regeneration. In recounting an experience that might be considered a conversion of sorts—his discovery of the word "abolition"—Douglass does recall the phrases of religious conversion, but with an ironic undertone that announces their inappropriateness. In language reminiscent of the Christian's yearning to hear the Word of God, he states that he "always drew near when that word was spoken," that word being "abolition" (56). "The light broke in upon me by degrees," he remembers, borrowing a favorite phrase of the new convert, but the light for Douglass is not the divine light: it is rather the human knowledge, gleaned from the stevedores on the Baltimore docks, that "abolition" denoted a social reality he might experience if he could escape. While the Nantucket convention might seem a religious moment, a kind of Quaker meeting in which

Douglass feels himself moved by an Inner Light to suffer the "severe cross" of bearing witness, its religious allusions, too, are ironic, and the enthralling charm of askesis, of suffering for a Christian cause, fades with the actuality of his words. Speaking freely and easily, he testifies not of the deity, but of his own humanity.

Douglass's critique of Christian conversion is part of his broader criticism of idealist thought. Although Douglass owed his initial conception of freedom to idealist antislavery tracts, he also became aware, in reading them, that his own dilemma could never be resolved at the level of signification alone. Indeed, the realization of the disparity between his social condition and the ideal of freedom was a painful one: "As I writhed under it, I would at times feel that learning to read had been a curse rather than a blessing. It had given me a view of my wretched condition, without the remedy" (55). In the anguish of this entrapment, Douglass's own voice fell silent. Like Scripture, the tracts shaped and articulated his conceptions for him: "They gave tongue to interesting thoughts of my own soul, which had frequently flashed through my mind, and died away for want of utterance" (55). In a similar metonymic displacement, the world around him promiscuously symbolized the freedom he could not have: "[Freedom] was heard in every sound, and seen in every thing. It was ever present to torment me with a sense of my wretched condition. I saw nothing without seeing it, I heard nothing without hearing it, and felt nothing without feeling it. It looked from every star, it smiled in every calm, breathed in every wind, and moved in every storm" (55–56). In this pathetic fallacy, Douglass has no voice of his own, for his commitment to an ideal of freedom has alienated him from his material and social existence. The world figuratively "speaks" his freedom only because, as a slave, he cannot literally speak it for himself. And while the pathetic fallacy implies that freedom, not slavery, is his "natural" condition, it implies as well that only the nonhuman—literally speechless—world about him "thinks" so.

Remembering his contemplation of the receding ships on Chesapeake Bay, symbols for him of freedom and the apparent impossibility of it in his own life, Douglass furnishes a magniloquent peroration as evidence of the sort of interior monologue that the sight regularly produced in him. "Thus I used to think," he comments, "and thus I used to speak to myself; goaded almost to madness at one moment, and at the next reconciling myself to my wretched lot" (77). The tension generated by idealism compelled him towards a raging lunacy, on the one hand, and an equally terrifying and suicidal passivity on the other. Like the boy who secretly read the antislavery tracts, the idealist who watched the symbolic ships sail away was a man still in the hell of bondage—whatever the condition of his soul—because his own humanity remained nothing more than an abstract proposition. It was not enough, finally, for Douglass simply to think his freedom or believe, however lucidly, in the justice of it. In this narrative, freedom is above all the social liberty *not* to have to live one's life as an act of thought or faith.

Douglass presents his desired freedom obliquely, however, for the Nantucket convention is hardly a way of life. On the contrary, it is the most paradigmatic event in the *Narrative,* described in the starkest terms possible. A kind of dramatic performance, it rhetorically conveys the meaning of freedom in history while maintaining a tension between that reality and the daily life Douglass experienced as a "working man" in the North. In short, while the Nantucket convention provides the conclusion of the *Narrative,* it also initiates a new dialectic.

In his description of the slave who sings in the woods on his way to the home plantation, Douglass offers an early and instructive paradigm of slavery's antilanguage. Only the most obedient slaves on the out-farms were chosen for this jaunt to pick up monthly provisions. Slaves competed for the distinction, since it was "associated in their minds with greatness. . . . They regarded it as evidence of great confidence reposed in them by their overseers; . . . a high privilege, one worth careful living for" (30). Momentarily free of the lash, alone in the woods, the slave who had thus won the approval of the overseer sang at once of his association "with greatness" and his abject condition, "revealing at once the highest joy and the deepest sadness" (31).

This slave song in the woods is the antithesis of the intersubjectivity Douglass discovers in speaking to the other members of the Nantucket meeting. Just as Nantucket offers him the social experience of himself as signified by the terms "human" and "free," so slavery systematically offers the slave a nonhuman and nonsocial meaning. The slave song epitomizes the condition of those who submit to this meaning, intoning the "dehumanizing character of slavery" (32). The songs were purely spontaneous, a free expression: "the thought that came up, came out—if not in the word in the sound" (31). But the only thoughts that came out in meaningful words were about the master's farm, the "Great House Farm" where the singer obtained provisions for the subsistence of himself and his fellow slaves. This was clearly articulated in the chorus—"I'm going away to the Great House Farm"—but the other words "to many would seem unmeaning jargon." Though "full of meaning to themselves," they meant nothing to anyone else (31). With the center of authority as his destination, both literally and linguistically, the slave's only intelligible words were those about his masters; in his careful obedience to the overseer, Douglass suggests, the slave had lost the power to articulate any social meaning but the slaveholder's. As the purpose of his journey suggests, the singer lives materially, socially, and linguistically at the pleasure of his master. Isolated in his social position, he can express his humanity only as a self-presence in the absence of other human beings. Though he lives in society, he sings like "a man cast away upon a desolate island" (32), and the words that express subjectivity have individual meaning but no social meaning. These "wild songs" speak the "horrible character of slavery" because they are subjective without being intersubjective: to submit to the dehumanization of slavery is to be enslaved in a purely private referentiality that limits the functional context of subjective utterance to a single mind, or to a series of single minds, for whom there is no mutual "other."

Such private, nonintersubjective referentiality is paradigmatic of the slave's linguistic performance within a society that demanded that he be reduced to the status of a brute beast whose will was entirely his master's. This reduction required a fracturing of the referentiality of the linguistic sign: signs functioned in disparate, even opposing ways, depending upon whether the assertion involved slave or slaveholder. Of course, any sign is capable of bearing a multiple reference in the material world, depending upon the context in which it is issued; but the slaveholder always ordered his exploitation of the sign's variable referentiality around slavery's fracture of the human world. This fracture in turn depended upon an invariable definition of the slave as nonhuman: without individual particularity, without subjectivity, incapable of generating meaning, and socially identifiable only in terms of his master's will. In short, the slave was identical with his sheer biological existence.

The linguistic fracture is Douglass's first subject. He presents it in chapter 1 as allied on the one hand to the slave's lack of verbal substance, and on the other to the impossibility of socially orienting himself with respect to his parents. Having announced himself in the conventional opening utterance of the genre, Douglass contrasts the subjectivity that allows him to make the utterance with the absence of defining language he experienced as a slave:

> I was born in Tuckahoe, near Hillsborough, and about twelve miles from Easton, in Talbot county, Maryland. I have no accurate knowledge of my age, never having seen any authentic record containing it. By far the larger part of the slaves know as little of their ages as horses know of theirs, and it is the wish of most masters within my knowledge to keep their slaves thus ignorant. I do not remember to have ever met a slave who could tell of his birthday. They seldom come nearer to it than planting-time, harvest-time, cherry-time, spring-time, or fall-time. (21)

The modulation here from "know" to "tell" suggests the slave's total lack of language as either an epistemological or an expressive instrument. It implies a muteness as well as a deafness. For such a being, as for the horse to whom he is compared, there is neither "self" nor "other." The silence is the double one of the nonverbal beast, who neither understands nor can utter a language of intersubjective meaning, but is consigned, rather, to the prelinguistic "pleni-tude" of the natural world. This world is differentiated in cyclical terms, to be sure, as "planting-time, harvest-time," and so forth. But for the slave who enacts this difference, hoe in hand, in the material world, that is not enough; for unless he regards his labor as a "human" activity, its linguistic signs will continue to function in a purely "nonhuman" context. Planting time, as a human and cultural activity, will always signify something other than breaking clods and raking hills.

The linguistic fracture is even more evident and more open to the charge of illogicality in the case of slave paternity and maternity, as Douglass defines them in relation to the system's economic exigencies. Paradoxically, the patriarchal structure of the slave system was sustained by the absolute denial of paternity in either a natural or social sense. Interracial selves such as Douglass followed the condition of their slave mothers, as if their free, white fathers simply did not exist. The master-father's relation to his children was purely economic: he owned his slave children because he owned their mothers. When he did not wholly deny his paternity, when he was willing to acknowledge a "paternal partiality" to his slave children, they suffered the bitter jealousy and hatred of the others on the plantation, especially the master's wife, "ever disposed to find fault with them . . . never better pleased than when she sees them under the lash" (23). The patriarch who attempted to sustain the contradictory "double relation of master and father" toward his slave children was "frequently compelled to sell this class of slaves, out of deference to the feelings of his white wife . . . it is often the dictate of humanity for him to do so" (23). Within the slave system, such fathers could be "humane" only by legitimating the commodity status of their children. For the master who declined to see a slave born on his plantation as totally nonhuman, the constraints of slavery nevertheless forced him to take this second opportunity to separate natural relations and cultural relations, to reiterate the meaning of slavery in the "language" of money. Conversely, maternity for her children as well as for the slave mother, had a strictly biological meaning, one which was often realized materially in the practice of separating mothers and children so as to prevent any social bond from developing between them. In the realm of maternal designation, this was the equivalent of that "dictate of humanity" whereby the master-father sold rather than "owned" his child.[6]

That slave parents, fathers as well as mothers, and their children often developed strong family bonds in the face of such definitions is beyond doubt; but the bonds were not "binding" in any written or customary sense. Whatever familial ties the slaves developed among themselves were neither recognized in the economic transactions in which they served as commodities nor encoded in the language by which the owners operated. Like their human births, the slaves' familial relations did not exist systematically, while the humane impulses that occasionally prevented slaveholders from separating families were literally unwritten, constituted only as a gestural aberration that had no bearing on the system of meaning whereby slavery transformed human beings into nonhuman commodities.

The force of Douglass's argument here is reiterated in his emphasis on the positive lack of any social bond between his mother and himself. In the later narratives, while he never fails to suggest the impossibility of their forming a lasting social bond, he nevertheless offers a fuller portrait of his mother that suggests his own greater familiarity with her in a more or less stable context.[7] In the 1845 *Narrative,* by contrast, he speaks of the acts that constituted social maternity—"soothing presence," "tender and watchful care," and the sacrifice of much-needed rest after a day of field-work—only to show that they took place in a vacuum, without the response on his own part that would mark the presence of a social bond:

> I never saw my mother, to know her as such, more than four or five times in my life; and each of these times was very short in duration, and at night. She was hired by a Mr. Stewart, who lived about twelve miles from my home. She made her journeys to see me in the night, travelling the whole distance on foot, after the performance of her day's work. She was a field hand, and a whipping is the penalty of not being in the field at sunrise, unless a slave has special permission from his or her master to the contrary—a permission which they seldom get, and one that gives to him that gives it the proud name of being a kind master. I do not recollect of ever seeing my mother by the light of day. She was with me in the night. She would lie down with me, and get me to sleep, but long before I waked she was gone. (22)

The social acts that rescue individuals from the solitude of beasts here take place furtively under the aegis of night, invisibility, and nonconsciousness. Douglass's mother is with him, but he is for the most part not with her: "long before I waked she was gone." Moreover, this recollection is ordered around certain facts of plantation life—the penalty for not being in the field at sunrise, the permission, and the assertion that this written document "gives to him that gives it the proud name of being a kind master"—that could only have entered his thought at a much later date. It is only in the light of this later knowledge that Douglass conveys to us his mother's single-mindedness and strength, played out at the expense of her existence. The details of her death follow hard upon his description of their nighttime encounters: "Death soon ended what little we could have while she lived, and with it her hardships and suffering. She died when I was about seven years old, on one of my master's farms, near Lee's Mill. I was not allowed to be present during her illness, at her death, or burial. She was gone long before I knew anything about it" (22). The final sentence, echoing "long before I waked she was gone," establishes her midnight presences as equivalent to her life, grounding both in "hardships and suffering," the privations of field work by day and maternity by night.

Implying that his mother paid for her social maternity with her physical life, Douglass shows that even his earliest experience of social relations was deeply determined by the division of humanity into the arbitrary categories of "nature" and "culture" inherent in "slave" and "master." Like the father's sale of his children, his mother's premature death signified that any social being was impossible for the slave within this structure of meaning. In consigning the slave wholly to a "natural" world without social dimensions, slavery cancelled his or her linguistic capacity to name and develop primary human relations. In the antilanguage of slavery, Douglass's father was not his father, and his mother, despite her efforts, was not his mother. For Douglass she is marked only by the negations of darkness and death. "Very little communication ever took place between us," he says, and in his final words about her, he offers himself as one who had succumbed to slavery's negations: "[N]ever having enjoyed, to any considerable extent, her soothing presence, her tender and watchful care, I received the tidings of her death with much the same emotions I should have probably felt at the death of a stranger" (22–23). Although the qualifier "probably" and the subjunctive mood of the final clause tell us that Douglass regards the death as unique—for there was no other, no second death, to react to—he describes a reaction that is potentially fitted to the death of any of an indefinite number of others, whose very interchangeability is the function of a reduction to the nonhuman, in which individual differences and distinctions are effaced in the paradigmatic equality of all slaves as chattel.

In the master's view, the slaves were ideally a repetition of identical forms, equal in their anonymity. Though Douglass was introduced to a sense of this perverse equality in the anonymity of his parents, the concept of the slave was most fully articulated for him in the slave market. To be sold, he explains, was "a condition held by us all in the utmost horror and dread" (60). It was not simply that the physical abuse was liable to be greater "down river." Rather, the experience of being priced and the prospect of being sold seem to have been peculiarly terrifying in themselves. Sent back from Baltimore to the home plantation to be "valued with the other property" in the inventory at his master's death, Douglass found himself "ranked with horses, sheep, and swine" in the juxtaposition of human and nonhuman chattel. It was a uniquely revealing event for him: "At this moment, I saw more clearly than ever the brutalizing effects of slavery upon both slave and slaveholder" (60). Where relatively kind treatment at the Auld house in Baltimore had engendered the illusion that "slave" marked a social status, however low, the inventory disclosed his real status as chattel, as property outside the social hierarchy altogether. Certainly the gross mixture of human being and animals is meant to suggest the degradation of the slaves into bestiality, but there is more to the inventory than this. The slaves were not only ranked with animals in the "scale of being"; they were also priced as commodities for potential sale on the market, an anonymity more profound than Douglass had yet experienced.

The command to sell the slave was the ultimate pronouncement in the antilanguage of slavery, the moment in which the idea of "slave" was transposed from a linguistic structure of meaning to the monetary system of exchange in the marketplace. Douglass's professed inability to render the "brutalizing effects" of the inventory in words conveys the slaves' acute sense of linguistic deprivation in the face of this aspect of the slave system: "I have no language to express the high excitement and deep anxiety which were felt among us poor slaves during this time. . . . We had no more voice in that decision than the brutes among whom we were ranked. A single word from the white man was enough—against all our wishes, prayers, and entreaties—to sunder forever then dearest friends, dearest kindred, and strongest ties known to human beings" (60). The rationale for this "division" of the slaves was the "valuation" that preceded it. That is, the division reconstituted the social world of the slave according to the purely economic concept of the slave as an object of property. But, since the slaves remained human nonetheless, they experienced the inventory as the creation of a new set of social relations: as Douglass says, "I had now a new conception of my degraded condition" (59).

The inventory produced a "new conception" of slavery because it redefined the slave purely in terms of exchange value. In the marketplace, exchange value expresses only the abstract equivalence of qualitatively different acts of labor that produce the objects exchanged, thus giving commodities a uniform social status. The rationale of the marketplace presupposes that the commodities exchanged have a use in the concrete world that is dependent on their particular, historical qualities. The acts of exchange, however, directly acknowledge only the abstract character of objects that makes it possible to equate them. This is why exchange value makes an object a "social hieroglyphic," for the commodity as a single entity conceals a contradiction between its use value and its exchange value, between its substantive particularity and its arbitrary social character.[8] Money, the medium of exchange, completes this mystification because it expresses only the abstract, exchange value. While people may have variable motives for entering into exchanges, motives that can depend on the use value of a commodity, the system of exchange functions only by ignoring these qualitative differences, by "translating" all objects into the same medium: money. It is important to note that, while exchange value is realized in the market, the conceptual transformation occurs sooner, when commodities are ideally transformed into money: "A particular exchange value must first be exchanged for exchange-value in general before it can then be in turn exchanged for particulars. . . . [C]ommodities are really exchanged for money, transformed into real money, after they have been ideally transformed into money beforehand—i.e., have obtained the *attribute of price* as *prices*.[9] This suggests why the process of inventory, short of being sold, was the moment of clarification for Douglass, the moment when he realized what chattel slavery really meant. It was sufficient to assign the slave the attribute of price to invoke the categories of the marketplace. When the slaves became commodities, the qualitative differences among them as human beings were concealed in the expression of their exchange value—just as the equivalence of objects is expressed at the expense of recognizing both their inherent qualities and the particular historical acts that produced them.

The slave-commodity was indeed a social hieroglyphic, and far more profoundly so than an object-commodity, for the market directly functioned to mystify the subjectivity—the human condition—of the participants in the exchange.[10] In the market, social relations by definition exist between buyer and seller only, so the slave—as the commodity exchanged—was merely an object mediating the relation between his seller and purchaser. The exchange both created a social relation between two masters based on the nonhuman status of the slave and eliminated the social relations of the human commodity who was exchanged. At the command of the master, the slave was torn from the social world of the plantation where he was born and raised, exchanging its relations for the single relation between himself and his owner. Yet this was not a social relation, but merely the phantasm of one, for the slave as commodity had been degraded to the status of a thing. The master's sale of his slave children, for example, asserted that although the father was human, these children were not. When the master asserted his social status by symbolically appropriating the market relations of free society, he negated the basis of language between himself and the slave, and among the slaves themselves. The slave's degradation to a commodity was thus a degradation into silence. As Douglass says, "there is no language" to express his condition. There is only the attribute of price.

Douglass's lack of concern with the actual prices the slaves received in their "valuation" evinces his own sense that it is the attribute of price, rather than any specific numerical figure, that exclusively distinguishes the slave in the social world. To assign a slave the attribute of price is more than a refusal to name his humanity, for the system of prices, unlike a linguistic system, precludes the possibility of naming the uniqueness of what is priced. Thus the attribute of price not only equates the slave with objects sold in the market; it reifies his being in a way that actively denies his individuality. Like the word "slave," money is an ideal form; but unlike the word that names the slave, price defines him with a signal that invariably symbolizes his exclusion from language. Iterable only as money, his humanity cannot be articulated. The human being at the foundation of the slave system, he is paradoxically not there.

It may seem at first glance that the categories of the market existed only on the boundary of slave society. In one sense this is true, of course, for if the master defined his relation to all his slaves by selling them, he would no longer be a master. To remind the slave of his attribute of price, short of selling him, however, could effectively extend the master's authority as the market defined it. Simply to assert the potential for commodity exchange could deeply influence the slave's conception of himself and make him behave as if the social relation between masters at the market defined his status as a slave: "When Colonel Lloyd's slaves met the slaves of Jacob Jepson, they seldom parted without a quarrel about their masters; Colonel Lloyd's slaves contending that he was the richest, and Mr. Jepson's slaves that he was the smartest, and most of a man. . . . They seemed to think that the greatness of their masters was transferable to themselves. It was considered as being bad enough to be a slave; but to be a poor man's slave was deemed a disgrace indeed!" (36–37). These slaves experienced their social identity as if they already had the status of commodities on the market; that is, their social identity was only a function of their masters' supposed attributes, one of which was the power to buy and sell people. The importance of the potential for commodity exchange is further suggested by Douglass's remark that these same slaves would "mutually execrate their masters when viewed separately" (36). When the slaves considered their own masters among themselves, outside the implicit relations of exchange, then real if secretive social bonds existed, and they shared a conscious sense of their common social position.

Douglass further indicates the endemic fear of the market in an apocryphal tale that circulated among the slaves on Colonel Lloyd's plantation. He recounts the story of a slave who unwittingly addressed his master as a fellow human when they met on the road. Colonel Lloyd owned perhaps a thousand slaves, so many at any rate, that he did not know them and they did not know him. When queried, the slave freely objected to the treatment he received from his master. The master made no response then, but several weeks later the slave suddenly discovered he was to be sold. The story clearly opposes the slave's humanity to his status as a commodity, which was the real meaning of his anonymity. This tale suggests that if the slave ever presumed that the slave market was distant or unreal, he was simply deluding himself. The potential for commodity exchange was always there, and the reality of the slave market could intrude into his life and transform it without warning.

In the *Narrative*'s existential cartography, the slave market and the Nantucket meeting are antipodes, for only at the latter can Douglass find—or indeed, have—his voice. This is not a question of self-presence, but rather of intersubjective self-presentation, dialectically related to an "other" of some sort. If, as the final paragraph of the *Narrative* suggests, to be free is to speak freely, with the assurance of making sense if only within a limited context that confers a shared meaning on one's terms, then Douglass's freedom has nothing to do with circumventing the necessity of its being constituted in an exterior form. Indeed, for Douglass freedom is a positive welcoming of this exteriority as that field in which and through which one's social being is made audible and visible. In the exile of an antilanguage, one's signifiers, derived from an exterior context, cannot be returned to it: this is what it means to see without being seen, to hear without being heard, to be the bearer of "dark secrets," or the mythicized "conscience" or "unconscious" of a ruling class. This, if anything, is self-presence, and it is the very aim of social systems that inscribe, in the world of men and women, a distinction between human and nonhuman.[11]

Such self-presence is, for Douglass, a hell. He enters it through the "blood-stained gate" of the beaten body of his Aunt Hester, in a second birth, from a second mother who is also a second self: "It was all new to me. I had never seen any thing like it before . . . I had . . . been, until now, out of the way of the bloody scenes that often occurred on the plantation" (26). The event brings Douglass to a terrified acceptance of his equality with his aunt—and all other slaves—as an object of gratuitous violence. "I expected it would be my turn next," he remembers, for here the metonymic difference between slave and slave falls in the space of time it takes the master to catch his breath or find a new whip. Otherwise, it is a hell of identical substitutions, the number of second selves being limited only to the number of slaves in existence anywhere at a given moment. Over its "blood-stained gate" is inscribed the tautology "A slave is a slave."

The formal opposite of a tautology is a contradiction, and this particular tautology "answers" certain questions riddled with contradictions: What mother is not a mother? What son is not a son? What father is not a father? The secret of such riddles is a contradictory doubling of the material world achieved through a language whose terms are always ordered around the economic necessity of slavery's original tautology. The fracture in the referential capability of the linguistic signifier—particularly terms constitutive of social and stative meanings—results in a language that exploits the iterability of the signifier, its capacity to mean only in context. A meaning is supplied that, depending upon whether the assertion involves slave or slaveholder, rigorously excludes one or the other. For example, the observably human acts of planting and harvesting are denoted by signifiers that, in turn and by fiat, are made to function in a context that systematically deprives them of any acknowledged human referent. Indeed, as nature's own "birth records," these particular signfiers can mark the birth of each slave into and as a brute creation. The question arises, then, in what way did Douglass the slave come to regard a term such as "human," bearing meaning only for the slaveholder, as referential to himself? If his language makes man, how could the slave escape the prison of this antilanguage, subvert the self-definition it offered him?

Douglass traces his first "glimmering conception of the dehumanizing character of slavery" (32) to the songs of the slaves on their way to "Great House Farm." In the contradiction between the words and tone of the songs, Douglass heard the inconsistency of slavery, its contradictory referentiality: "They would sometimes sing the most pathetic sentiment in the most rapturous tone, and the most rapturous sentiment in the most pathetic tone" (31). The social character of the songs, the meaning of their words and tone together, embodied for Douglass the contradiction of the "slave," the "dehumanized" human being. The assertion of humanity implicit in the term "dehumanizing" was not immediately apparent to Douglass, however: "I did not, when a slave, understand the deep meaning of those rude and apparently incoherent songs. I was myself within the circle; so that I neither saw nor heard as those without might see and hear" (31). The term "dehumanizing" embodies Douglass's later stance outside the "circle" of slavery; but as a child on Colonel Lloyd's plantation, the songs aroused only an acute feeling of imprisonment: "The hearing of those wild notes always depressed my spirit, and filled me with ineffable sadness" (31).

To make a "contented slave," Douglass explains later in the *Narrative,* "it is necessary to make a thoughtless one. It is necessary to darken his moral and mental vision, and, as far as possible, to annihilate the power of reason. He must be able to detect no inconsistencies in slavery; he must be made to feel that slavery is right; and he can be brought on that only when he ceases to be a man" (103–4). While the slave system necessarily reduced its victims to the status of chattel, equivalent to and exchangeable for each other or money, it could not reduce slaves to languageless chattel without entirely negating their economic value. While it sought to equate the slave with a material world that could not talk back or countermand the slaveholder's least assertion, it still had to find in him a human being of the most delicate understanding, if the business of plantation or household or shop was to be carried on without an unusual exertion on the part of the master; if, indeed, the business of slaveholding was to be economically justifiable at all. The very fact that the slave's will must be entirely his master's own, that he must do what the master wished and not what came naturally (as in the case of true chattel, whose natural being constitutes their economic value) necessitated a shared language. Conversely, the very acknowledgment of a separate will in the slave pointed to the dividing presence of language. From the slaveholder's point of view, the result of this double bind was, at best, the man or woman who hears but is not heard, sees but is not seen.

For Douglass, however, to hear and see were enough, since one cannot possess a language at all without possessing it entirely. The man who is a "slave" as opposed to a "human," being a creature of language, has access thereby to inconsistencies of predication as well as to predications that systematize such inconsistencies. Language thus makes the slave potentially free, since it gives him the ability to understand fully and systematically the requirements that bind him. It is, in short, his most powerful tool in the deconstruction of his bonds.

Consigned to the material world, the slave can nevertheless talk back, predicating, if only in the privacy of thought, his own semantic conjunctions between words and things. Such predication is echoed in the characteristically "naming" or "signifying" rhetoric of the *Narrative:*

"[A permission or pass] gives to him that gives it the proud *name* of being a kind master" (22).

"[Mr. Hopkins] was *called* by the slaves a good overseer" (30).

"Mr. Severe was rightly *named:* he was a cruel man" (29).

"He was *called* the smartest and most trusty fellow, who had this honor [of doing errands at Great House Farm] conferred upon him the most frequently" (30; emphasis ours throughout).

Over the course of the entire *Narrative,* such rhetoric—and we could cite many more examples—begins to suggest a certain deliberate thoughtfulness about predication and language in general, or a dialectical moment in which even the most ingrained naming impulses are subject to review in the light of an ongoing empirical observation.

This moment makes naming a perilous activity, from the slave's point of view—hence, the maxim among the slaves that "a still tongue makes a wise head"—for the owner and overseer possess, in their power over life and death, the ability to enforce their own code of predication: "Mr. Gore acted fully up to the maxim laid down by the slaveholders,—'It is better that a dozen slaves suffer under the lash, than that the overseer should be *convicted*, in the presence of the slaves, of having been at fault.' No matter how innocent a slave might be—it availed him nothing, when accused by Mr. Gore of any misdemeanor. To be accused was to be *convicted*, and to be *convicted* was to be punished; the one always following the other with immutable certainty. To escape punishment was to escape accusation . . ." (38–39; emphasis ours). "Convicted" bears a double meaning here: in the first use, it denotes a linguistic act of observation and predication, requiring for completion nothing beyond the mere "presence" of the onlooking slaves. In relation to Mr. Gore, however, it denotes an act that elides the rational progression of accusation, conviction, and punishment—an elision emphasized in Douglass's final phrase, where "convicted" disappears altogether—and issues with that hyperbolic "immutable certainty" of physical consequences. The modulation nicely suggests the differing sources of power of slave and master, the slave possessing an empirically tested but unspoken language, the master possessing a language of mispredication entirely enforceable at whip's length. The slaveholder acts as if his utterances were *performative*, but they are in fact only *imperative*, and always contain the possibility for disobedience.[12] To understand this is to entertain the possibilities of misdemeanor, insolence, rebellion, and escape. For in the gap that exists between material reality and language—a gap bridged, yet thereby also maintained, in the master's whip—there exists the certainty that slavery's antilanguage is not finally definitive, either of material reality or of the slave's subjectivity buried within it. Douglass makes this point succinctly in his characterization of Thomas Auld: "He wished to have us call him master, but lacked the firmness necessary to command us to do so" (67).

An elegant, if minor, fruit of this knowledge is Douglass's editorializing use of diacritical marks. "Nigger" always appears in quotations: "It was a common saying, even among little white boys, that it was worth a half-cent to kill a 'nigger,' and a half-cent to bury one" (42). Or again, Mr. Covey is said to have a "reputation as a 'nigger-breaker'" (70). Such a word is not for general use, not, certainly, in the self-effacing guise of thought. It is always attributable to particular speakers, the suggestion being that their use of it partakes of a private and highly questionable code. This potential gap between word and referent also gives us the rich irony of Douglass's parentheses: " 'Learning would *spoil* the best nigger in the world. Now,' said he, 'if you teach that nigger (speaking of myself) how to read, there would be no keeping him'" (49).

To understand the power that lay behind the slaveholder's command was also to understand his weakness, for a power instrumental to language-enforcement was not, therefore, *of language;* that is, it lacked the ultimate "command" of language, the ability to make reality, make it ineluctably and inside people's heads. And while Mr. Gore, the complete overseer, "spoke but to command, and commanded but to be obeyed . . . dealt sparingly with his words, and bountifully with his whip" (39), slavery's whip's-length grasp of the material world was often terribly frail.

This is the principal subject of the *Narrative*'s third chapter, where Douglass offers us three anecdotes of plantation life. The first concerns Colonel Lloyd's garden, an Edenic enclosure complete with forbidden fruit:

> This garden was not the least source of trouble on the plantation. Its excellent fruit was quite a temptation to the hungry swarms of boys, as well as the older slaves, belonging to the colonel, few of whom had the virtue or the vice to resist it. Scarcely a day passed, during the summer, but that some slave had to take the lash for stealing fruit. The colonel had to resort to all kinds of stratagems to keep his slaves out of the garden. The last and most successful one was that of tarring his fence all around; after which, if a slave was caught with any tar upon his person, it was deemed sufficient proof that he had either been into the garden, or had tried to get in. In either case, he was severely whipped by the chief gardener. This plan worked well; the slaves became as fearful of tar as of the lash. They seemed to realize the impossibility of touching *tar* without being defiled. (33)

The colonel's stratagems are, of course, the evidence of his lack of control over his material property, human and otherwise. He cannot, evidently, command "but to be obeyed." This hiatus in the length of his reach necessitates a linguistic makeshift whereby "tar" becomes a sign of having eaten forbidden property, even as Adam and Eve's fig leaves were. Simultaneously, "tar" signifies "lash": "the slaves became as fearful of tar as of the lash." Thus cutting two ways, the word not only suggests that "immutable certainty" with which punishment follows accusation, as under the overseership of Mr. Gore; it lays bare as well the essential predication of infraction-punishment that empowers slavery's original tautology. The "arbitrariness of the sign" is a little too apparent here, much to the slaveholder's peril, and Douglass's ironic detachment from this misnaming process is apparent in his own use of double predication, for it is impossible to tell whether he means us to consider resistance to the garden's temptations a "virtue" or a "vice."

Douglass makes great sport of this dangerously exposed linguistic arbitrariness in the second anecdote, which concerns the colonel's "splendid riding equipage," and the father and son, "old Barney and young Barney," who were responsible for maintaining it:

They never knew when they were safe from punishment. They were frequently whipped when least deserving, and escaped whipping when most deserving it. Every thing depended upon the looks of the horses, and the state of Colonel Lloyd's own mind when his horses were brought to him for use. If a horse did not move fast enough, or hold his head high enough, it was owing to some fault of his keepers. It was painful to stand near the stable-door, and hear the various complaints against the keepers when a horse was taken out for use. "This horse has not had proper attention. He has not been sufficiently rubbed and curried, or he has not been properly fed; his food was too wet or too dry; he got it too soon or too late; he was too hot or too cold; he had too much hay, and not enough grain; or he had too much grain, and not enough hay; instead of old Barney's attending to the horse, he had very improperly left it to his son." To all these complaints, no matter how unjust, the slave must answer never a word. (34).

It seems hardly necessary to point out the adventitious referentiality of the colonel's double-talk here. Amid the material poverty of the slave's existence, there existed reasons in abundance for finding fault with him—punishment being, in fact, the only thing not in short supply. As Douglass states elsewhere, "It would astonish one, unaccustomed to a slaveholding life, to see with what wonderful ease a slaveholder can find things, of which to make occasion to whip a slave" (87). With Delphic mysteriousness, the colonel reads the "looks" of his horses by the cipher of his mood, and while his meaning is riddled, unreadable for the slave beforehand, its outcome is a foregone conclusion. Douglass's ironic detachment from the entire process is again discernible in the direct quotation from the colonel, which collapses a series of complaints into a jumble of contradictory accusations and gives us, as it were, the "sound" of his years of silence and listening "near the stable-door." Mute attentiveness was the slave's first school, instruction in how the fragile tissue of slavery's antilanguage was nothing more than an illusory series of makeshift namings, imperiled by his utterance and validated only through violence.

The penalty for utterance, for the "simple truth," as Douglass calls it, is grave. The slave in the third anecdote, who meets his sphinx-like master on the road and, failing to recognize him, answers "incorrectly," pays dearly: "for having found fault with his master, he was now to be sold to a Georgia trader" (35). Silence, too, can be the "wrong" answer, as in the case of Demby, in the fourth chapter: "Mr. Gore told him that he would give him three calls, and that, if he did not come out at the third call, he would shoot him. The first call was given. Demby made no response, but stood his ground. The second and third calls were given with the same result. Mr. Gore then, without consultation or deliberation with any one, not even giving Demby an additional call, raised his musket to his face, taking deadly aim at his standing victim, and in an instant poor Demby was no more" (40). Although he utters no sound, in exposing slavery's only resource, its power to kill, Demby "asks" to die as surely as the slave in the third chapter "asks" to be traded.

The ultimate physicality of the slaveholder's command meant more than that he brutalized his slaves. It meant that the brute in slavery was none other than the slaveholder himself, a "signifying" that Douglass develops with fugue-like precision. Although Mrs. Auld, Douglass's Baltimore mistress, "at first lacked the depravity indispensable to shutting me up in mental darkness," once having received "some training in the exercise of irresponsible power," she proved an "apt woman": "The fatal poison of irresponsible power . . . soon commenced its infernal work. That cheerful eye, under the influence of slavery, soon became red with rage; that voice, made all sweet accord, changed to one of harsh and horrid discord" (52–53, 48–49). In the midst of describing Mrs. Auld's deterioration, Douglass turns momentarily to a Mrs. Hamilton, who lived across the street from the Aulds. Although Mrs. Hamilton is announced under the guise of another logic—as an exception to the rule that the city master is kinder than the plantation master—Douglass strongly implies that Mrs. Auld is well on her way to being just such a monster: "Mrs. Hamilton used to sit in a large chair in the middle of the room, with a heavy cowskin always by her side, and scarce an hour passed during the day but was marked by the blood of one of [her] slaves. The girls seldom passed her without her saying, "Move faster, you *black gip!*" at the same time giving them a blow with the cowskin over the head or shoulders, often drawing the blood. She would then say, "Take that, you *black gip!*"—continuing, "If you don't move faster, I'll move you!" (51). It would be hard to arrive at a more brutal image than the one achieved by the conjunction of whip and speech here, the latter being the very sound of the former as it bites flesh. This is the "horrid discord" that Mrs. Auld's voice is becoming, a language of dull grunts: move faster . . . black gip . . . black gip . . . move faster . . . move.

Douglass's term "irresponsible power" suggests the debasement of language among those who command without it. Eventually, it is replaced by a merely noisy gibberish, the fit accompaniment to the arrested tableau of the upraised-hand-with-whip that we find in the description of Mrs. Hamilton or in the following, concerning the overseer Severe: "The field was the place to witness his cruelty and profanity. His presence made it both the field of blood and of blasphemy. From the rising till the going down of the sun, he was cursing, raving, cutting, and slashing among the slaves of the field, in the most frightful manner" (29). Severe's successor, Hopkins, is something of an improvement, a "good overseer" who "made less noise" (30).[13]

The bestiality of the master is nowhere better expressed than in Douglass's lengthy portrayal of Mr. Covey, the "nigger-breaker" whose job of breaking the fractious slave's will makes him indispensable to the slaveholder lacking the proper command. So highly valued are his services that "Some slaveholders thought it not much loss to allow Mr. Covey to have their slaves one year, for the sake of the training to which they were subjected, without any other compensation" (70). By definition the ultimate enforcer of slavery's antilanguage, paid to perform the necessary acts of brutality that the armchair slaveholder found loathsome, the "nigger-breaker" realizes overtly in his person and character the implicit bestiality of the slaveholder's position. Mr. Covey attacks Douglass at one point "with the fierceness of a tiger," and Douglass describes his appearance after the beating as that of "a man who had escaped a den of wild beasts" (79). In tribute to his reptilian approaches, the slaves call Mr. Covey "the snake": "He had the faculty of making us feel that he was ever present with us. This he did by surprising us. He seldom approached the spot where we were at work openly, if he could do it secretly. He always aimed at taking us by surprise. . . . When we were at work in the cornfield, he would sometimes crawl on his hands and knees to avoid detection, and all at once he would rise nearly in our midst, and scream out, "Ha, ha! Come, Come! Dash on, dash on!" (73). The character of slavery's antilanguage is present in the mindless repetitions of Covey's words here, but Covey is no flat tableau figure. He is more than merely severe, more than merely steeped in gore. He is, like the snake, the most cunning beast of the field, a creature upon whom Douglass lavishes his most ironic religious language—"he was ever present with us"—and Covey succeeds for a time in reducing Douglass to a "beast-like stupor" (75).

It is the demonic Covey whom Douglass must finally wrestle for his true name, in a two-hour free-for-all that proves "the turning-point in [his] career as a slave" (82). Covey eventually begs out, indulging in a little "signifying" of his own, "saying that if I had not resisted, he would not have whipped me half so much" (82). But the truth is not lost on Douglass:

> He had not whipped me at all. . . . The gratification afforded by the triumph was a full compensation for whatever else might follow, even death itself. He can only understand the deep satisfaction which I experienced, who had himself repelled by force the bloody arm of slavery. I felt as I never felt before. It was a glorious resurrection, from the tomb of slavery, to the heaven of freedom. My long-crushed spirit rose, cowardice departed, bold defiance took its place; and I now resolved that, however long I might remain a slave in form, the day had passed forever when I could be a slave in fact. I did not hesitate to let it be known of me, that the white man who expected to succeed in whipping, must also succeed in killing me. (82–83)

By fighting Covey, Douglass declares within slavery, and in defiance of it, his own indivisible individuality as a human being. He returns to the slaveholder the signifiers of slavery in the only form that an overseer can understand: the physical act. His singular "me," governing both participles in the final clause, stands against slavery's doubling of the human world, against the fractured referentiality of the antilanguage of the "white man," and beyond the reach of the overseer's whip's-length grasp of his world.

In this confrontation, Douglass drives a wedge between the "form" and "fact" of slavery that established his own social being as an authentic referent of the term "human." He exposes the antilanguage for what it really is: a formal symbolism devoid of any intelligible referentiality in the human world, without any aspect of literal meaning "in fact" for Douglass himself. Put another way, Douglass frees himself from the bondage of slavery's metaphorical conception of the slave by discovering his own suppressed literal humanity. He introduces this "epochal" event by directing us to a symmetrical inversion of an earlier moment: "You have seen how a man was made a slave; you shall see how a slave was made a man" (77). The earlier moment is of course that of the "blood-stained gate," when he enters slavery through the metaphorical second self of his Aunt Hester, whose whipping he witnessed: "I never shall forget it whilst I remember anything. It was the first of long series of such outrages, of which I was doomed to be a witness and a participant. It struck me with awful force. It was the blood-stained gate, the entrance to the hell of slavery through which I was about to pass. It was a most terrible spectacle. I wish I could commit to paper the feelings with which I beheld it" (25–26). The metaphor of the gate, and the hyperbolic insistence on his own response to the event, suggest that something happened that was unique but that escaped literal articulation. Recounting his entrance into slavery's negation of subjectivity, Douglass insists figuratively on the unrepeatable nature of his own reaction to it. By contrast, in recounting his fight with Covey, Douglass invokes the literal sense that can convey his own subjectivity: the figurative language of his "resurrection" from the "hell" of slavery's figuration gives way to a conscious, literal stance. Indeed, the metaphor of the gate early in the *Narrative* already foretells his later escape. It depicts slavery as a condition one enters singly— paradoxically after having achieved a certain degree of critical awareness and detachment—and not en masse, by birth membership in an enslaved race. For the individual, enslavement always has a beginning in the individual conscious- ness, an originary moment that is distinct from the fact of being born into it—and thus, by implication, it has an end.

The way in which the fight with Covey reverses the entrance into "hell" becomes more apparent when we examine the context Douglass gives it. Having failed to get "protection" against Covey's repeated beating from his master, Thomas Auld, Douglass receives protection of a different sort from a fellow slave, Sandy Jenkins: ". . . a certain *root,* which, if I would take some of it with me, carrying it *always on my right side,* would render it impossible for Mr. Covey, or any other white man, to whip me. He said he had carried it for years; and since he had done so, he had never received a blow, and never expected to while he carried it" (80–81). Sandy has not given him a literal, material "root" with magical powers against the whip, as Douglass first imagines, but rather a talismanic *"root"* that symbolizes the power of the slave's unacknowledged human nature. Douglass uses italics to mark his own discovery of Sandy's real meaning. Initially, Sandy's idea seems to be a mere conjurer's trick, and Douglass goes along with it only to humor him. Much to his surprise, the "root" appears to work at first, but on the second day Covey attacks. Nevertheless, although the magical "root" fails, the symbolic *"root"* proves to have the power Sandy claimed for it. While carrying the *"root"* as Sandy directed (that is, symbolically), Douglass suddenly finds himself inspired to confront Covey: "At this moment—from whence came the spirit I don't know—I resolved to fight; and, suiting my action to the resolution, I seized Covey hard by the throat" (81). Thus, the human being within Douglass the "slave" is finally invoked neither by the Christian God nor by the abolitionists, but by a fellow "slave" who truly understands the power, and the limits, of human signification. As the slave's own sign, the *"root"* silently (and thus appropriately) signifies the capacity for authentically self-referential language in the slave. Douglass wears it on his symbolic *"right side,"* and the root comes from a natural world outside the structure of slave society, not from a Christian slaveholder's tarred, contaminated hoard—Douglass pointedly notes that "the virtue of the *root* was fully tested" on Monday, not Sunday (81).

In understanding both the significance and the insignificance of the root he obtained from Sandy, Douglass reorders the literal object world in relation to himself as fully human (and not "in fact" an object), and regains the literal-historical sense of himself and his own subjectivity. He regains what he had lost when he entered the "hell" of slavery at the whipping of Aunt Hester. In this larger context, then, Douglass's fight with Covey inverts the negative relation with Aunt Hester imposed by slavery—that infinite substitution of selves—and produces the positive intersubjective relation with Sandy Jenkins that proves to be his real protection against the slaveholder.

By locating the beginnings of his "free self," not in the passage into free territory, but in the terrified child who, watching his aunt beaten, understands the meaning of his own enslavement, Douglass refuses to allow the opposition of slavery and freedom to negate his own past life. Freedom is not a marked translation, a conversion, from one self to another. It is, like slavery, a condition of the self but not definitive of it. This is why Douglass's defiance of Covey within the slave system can be, as he says, "in defense of my self," and in the most profound sense, for here he first asserts his human self in a public way. To this assertion from a slave there can be no reply from the slaveholder, and there was none: "From this time I was never again what might be called fairly whipped, though I remained a slave four years afterwards" (83). We can hear both assent and refusal in the slaveholder's silence toward Douglass: though he is not whipped, he is not freed either. The contradiction between the "form" of slavery and the "fact" of his own humanity remained to be resolved.

Under his next master, Mr. Freeland, Douglass made his first attempt to escape from slavery's "form," the economic and social structure in which he was still imprisoned. Though he and his fellow slaves are betrayed, in planning their escape they nevertheless validate the conception of free men they have created among themselves.[14] When one of the slaves, Henry, refuses to submit at their capture, his defiance is ordered to the linguistic and social reality of his fellow conspirators, not to the form of slavery. Henry's self-referential "I" provokes a reciprocal "you" from the constable:

> They then turned to Henry, who had by this time returned, and commanded him to cross his hands. "I won't!" said Henry, in a firm tone, indicating his readiness to meet the consequences of his refusal. "Won't you?" said Tom Graham, the constable. "No, I won't!" said Henry, in a still stronger tone. With this, two of the constables pulled out their shining pistols, and swore, by their Creator, that they would make him cross his hands or kill him. Each cocked his pistol, and with fingers on the trigger, walked up to Henry, saying, at the same time, if he did not cross his hands, they would blow his damned heart out. "Shoot me, shoot me!" said Henry, "you can't kill me but once. Shoot, shoot,—and be damned! *I won't be tied!*" This he said in a tone of loud defiance; and at the same time, with a motion as quick as lightning, he with one single stroke dashed the pistols from the hand of each constable. (96)

Henry's pronouns ground his general stance of defiance in the particular social reality of his historical moment. His confrontation with the real possibility of his unique death in history is equally a validation of his own unique human life. With his words, he declares unmistakably his individual particularity— "you can't kill me but once"—giving the lie to the endless substitution of slave for slave, and with his attack on the constables, he defends his life. Henry refuses to submit in a far more active sense than the silent Demby, a sense inspired by a definite plan for escape. Although Henry extorts an unequivocal recognition from the slaveholders, and lives to tell of it, he does not obtain his freedom. He achieves a victory, but not the one he really wants. Douglass undoubtedly shared the sense of victory—he quotes the dialogue carefully— but his own means of resistance is silence, a silence that became increasingly articulate through the course of his progress toward freedom.

In a dialectic of speech and silence, Douglass counterposes Henry's words to his own mute defiance of Covey: Henry reiterates what Douglass "says" with his silence. Once captured, however, the slaves are imprisoned and interrogated, and in this context they fall back on the linguistic strategy of absolute silence: "Own nothing" is the word they pass along to each other (97). This retreat to silence, however, is not—indeed, cannot be—a return to the silence of the slave-commodity. The silence of these coconspirators is cognitively meaningful, an intelligible, conscious refusal to tell what they know they conceal: their plan of escape, and, in the articulation of that plan, their commonality as human beings. As Henry's worlds are the opposite of the meaningless lyrics of the slave songs, so the coconspirators' silence is the opposite of that of the slave child Douglass. Silence is not now the slave's degradation, but his defense: originally imposed by the master as definitive of the slave's condition, silence is finally turned against the master himself.

Nevertheless, the silence of the coconspirators is an exposed one which the slaveholders "hear" just as they hear Henry's words. It remained for Douglass to discover a disguised silence the slaveholder could not hear, the "correct" linguistic response to the master within the antilanguage, which would, at the same time, lead to a successful escape. Douglass found his opportunity when Thomas Auld took him from prison and sent him back to Hugh Auld in Baltimore, where he lived on his own as a tradesman with the agreement that he would pay his master a fixed sum each week. When Auld threatened to revoke Douglass's near-freeman status, Douglass countered by refusing to hire out his labor time the following week, and by refusing, as well, to explain or justify his action to Auld: "Saturday night, he called upon me as usual for my week's wages. I told him I had no wages; I had done no work that week. Here we were upon the point of coming to blows. He raved, and swore his determination to get hold of me. I did not allow myself a single word; but was resolved, if he laid the weight of his hand upon me, it should be blow for blow. He did not strike me, but told me that he would find me in constant employment in future" (109). Douglass does not have to resort to physical violence, since Auld does not miss the import of Douglass's linguistic and economic omission. Auld accedes to the linguistic defiance of his slave, settling for the compromise of a slave who is obedient economically if not verbally. Having won from Auld this recognition of the contradiction between his linguistic humanity and the economic structure of slavery, Douglass is spurred on to attempt another escape. This time, he adopts a new, successful strategy. His undisguised silence is replaced by a fully disguised one, for, to the master, the silence of the obedient slave and the silence of the slave intent on escape "sound" the same:

> Early on Monday morning, before Master Hugh had time to make any engagement for me, I went out and got employment of Mr. Butler, at his ship-yard near the drawbridge, upon what is called the City Block, thus making it unnecessary for him to seek employment for me. At the end of the week, I brought him between eight and nine dollars. He seemed very well pleased, and asked why I did not do the same the week before. He little knew what my plans were. My object in working steadily was to remove any suspicion he might entertain of my intent to run away; and in this I succeeded admirably. I suppose he thought I was never better satisfied with my condition than at the very time during which I was planning my escape. The second week passed, and again I carried him my full wages; and so well pleased was he, that he gave me twenty-five cents, (quite a large sum for a slaveholder to give a slave,) and bade me to make a good use of it. I told him I would. (109–10)

Unlike the previous silence of omission, Douglass's words here are the nonviolent yet physical act of one who has come to fully understand "abolition." His silence, in the form of speech, is a negation of the antilanguage of slavery, for the contradiction inherent in his utterance fully replies to the contradiction inherent in slavery. He does not quote his own words here as he quoted Henry's, since the particular words mean nothing. Or rather, they "mean" the articulate silence behind them, in accord with the linguistic reality of freemen. As the slave at the root of the slave system, Douglass is paradoxically not there. But his absence now is the opposite of that of the metaphorical slave whose condition is defined in the antilanguage and the slave market of slave society.

The ellipsis that follows this last scene with his last master is the silence within which Douglass finally made his escape: "According to my resolution, on the third day of September, 1838, I left my chains, and succeeded in reaching New York without the slightest interruption of any kind. How I did so,—what means I adopted,—what direction I travelled, and by what mode of conveyance,—I must leave unexplained"(111). This ellipsis is an audible and living silence in the *Narrative,* a kind of address to the reader that is the culmination of all the silences that precede it, un/written on behalf of Douglass's "brother slave" who is still in bondage but might yet escape. Potentially, this refers to everyone yet in slavery, and the ellipsis appropriately declares their invisible and unutterable presence better than any words could, for his silence truly "speaks" their condition. The ellipsis is, as well, a truly intersubjective gesture toward the slaveholder. With it, Douglass produces for the slaveholder, if only in part, the same blind fear that the silence of their antilanguage produced for him and every other slave: "Let him be left to feel his way in the dark; let darkness commensurate with his crime hover over him; and let him feel that at every step he takes, in pursuit of the flying bondman, he is running the frightful risk of having his hot brains dashed out by an invisible agency" (106). Thus, while the silence of Douglass's ellipsis leaves no "trace," it is resonant with meaning. Unlike the slaveholder's words, it bespeaks the presence of the human being concealed within the system of slavery.

Dialectically, the ellipsis and the narrative "say" each other, for this absence, this silence of omission, is the negative form of Douglass's speech and presence at the Nantucket meeting. The final event of the *Narrative* makes "abolition" fully intelligible at the level of linguistic-social reality. As slavery was the negation of his subjectivity, so the meeting of freemen proves to be the negation of this negation, that speech that transcends the silence Douglass brings to it. With the words he utters to his Nantucket audience, Douglass articulates his own subjectivity as it could never have been heard in the antilanguage of slavery.

Notes

Ann Kibbey would like to thank the Social Science Research Council for a fellowship that enabled her to complete the research for this paper. She would also like to thank the Capital *Reading Group at Yale University and Daniel Harris of Douglass College, Rutgers University, for discussion of several portions of this paper.*

1. We are indebted here to Emile Benveniste's discussions of linguistic subjectivity and the imperative form in *Problems in General Linguistics*, trans. by Mary Elizabeth Meek (Coral Gables, Fla.: Univ. of Miami Press, 1971), 223–30, 231–38.

2. *Narrative of the Life of Frederick Douglass. An American Slave. Written by Himself* (New York: New American Library, 1968), 118, 119. All quotations are from this edition and will be noted hereafter in the text.

3. In his preface to the *Narrative,* William Lloyd Garrison reports that in his first speech at the convention in Nantucket, Douglass "proceeded to narrate some of the facts in his own history as a slave, and in the course of his speech gave utterance to many noble thoughts and thrilling reflections" (vi–vii).

4. For a discussion of this concept of the subject, see V. N. Volosinov, *Marxism and the Philosophy of Language,* trans. by Ladislav Matejka and I. R. Titunik (New York and London: Seminar Press, 1973), 65–98.

5. Early narrators such as Gustavus Vassa (Olaudah Equiano) and James Pennington wrote of their bondage and freedom in the terms of spiritual narrative. In Vassa's autobiography, emancipation pales beside Christian conversion as the definitive event of his life. Pennington, even though he grants much more importance to his escape from slavery, similarly attributes definitive significance to his conversion, his freeman status merely leading to the discovery that he was "a slave in another and a more serious sense," a "slave to Satan" in spiritual bondage. By contrast, Douglass's relation to God is something he takes for granted, for he never speaks of any conversion in his own life.

6. It should be noted that, with the exception of "old Barney and young Barney—father and son" and the "miserable woman" and the "married man of Mr. Samuel Harrison [whom Covey] used to fasten up with her every night" for breeding purposes, Douglass is silent on the topic of slave fathers. The same omission occurs in his later narratives.

7. In the 1855 and 1881 autobiographies, Douglass offers an appreciation of his mother's physical appearance. The working is virtually the same in both texts: "She was tall, and finely proportioned; of deep black, glossy complexion; had regular features, and, among the other slaves, was remarkably sedate in her manners." *My Bondage and My Freedom* (1855; rpt. New York: Dover Publications, 1969), 52. See also *The Life and Times of Frederick Douglass* (1881; rev. ed. 1892; rpt. from the 1892 rev. ed. New York: Bonanza, 1962), 28–29. Douglass also relates in both of the later texts an incident in which his mother, on one of her visits to him, appeared in time to rescue him from further punishment at the hands of "Aunt Katy." Again, the wording is similar, and it suggests how his rhetorical use of his mothers—and his rhetorical purposes generally—had changed since the 1845 *Narrative:* "The friendless and hungry boy, in his extremest need—and when he did not dare to look for succor—found himself in the strong, protecting arms of a mother; a mother who was, at the moment (being endowed with high powers of manner as well as matter) more than a match for all his enemies. . . . That night I learned the fact, that I was not only a child, but *somebody's* child." *My Bondage and My Freedom,* 56. See also *The Life and Times,* 35–36. Finally, the following from *My Bondage and My Freedom,* 57, offers a striking contrast to the severe and dispassioned discussion of his mother in the 1845 *Narrative:* "It has been a life-long, standing grief to me, that I knew so little of my mother; and that I was so early separated from her. The counsels of her love must have been beneficial to me. The side view of her face is imaged on my memory, and I take few steps in life, without feeling her presence; but the image is mute, and I have no striking words of her's treasured up." Although the images of muteness and partial visibility are still here, the remote and nearly mythic sacrificial victim of the first narrative has given way to a more sentimental and motherly figure of lingering presence.

8. The definitions of exchange value and money follow Karl Marx's analysis in Frederick Engles, ed., *Capital: A Critique of Political Economy* (New York: International Publishers 1967), vol. 1, pt. 1. See especially 35–47, 55–62, 71–79.

9. Karl Marx, *Grundrisse: Foundations of the Critique of Political Economy,* trans. Martin Nicolaus (New York: Random House, 1973), 193. Marx explains in *Capital,* 95, that "the price or money-form of commodities is, like their form of [exchange] value generally, a form quite distinct from their palpable bodily form; it is, therefore, a purely ideal or mental form."

10. The slave-commodity was a social hieroglyphic in the usual sense, too. Like the commodity with which he was equated, the slave also contained a contradiction—between his abstract and invariable identity as a slave/commodity on the one hand, and, on the other hand, his particular human capacity to function in concrete social situations (precisely what made him valuable to the slaveholder).

11. The theme of inaudibility and its masking trope of invisibility is something of a staple in the Afro-American literary tradition. It occurs in Du Bois's famous metaphor of the "Veil"; in the racial quandaries of Johnson's Ex-Colored Man, who cannot make himself seen, or his music heard, except in the "passing" forms of whiteness; and, most notably, in Ellison's *Invisible Man,* an exhaustive treatment of the relation between in/visibility and in/authentic speech.

12. For a comparison of imperative and performative utterances, see Benveniste's critique of J. L. Austin's conflation of the two forms in Benveniste, 231–38.

13. It is not yet known whether the names Gore and Severe are historical or fictional, but it should be noted that, in Douglass's presentation, Hopkins is alone among those who filled the position of overseer to Colonel Lloyd in having a name that does not suggest his character.

14. Here Douglass recapitulates his own history, for the conspiracy is formed out of the "school" he began in order to teach his fellow slaves to read (89–90). This time, however, reading is a collective event in which the slaves mutually validate the legitimacy of their freedom.

In the First Place: Making Frederick Douglass and the Afro-American Narrative Tradition

Deborah E. McDowell

> Beginning is principally an activity of reconstruction, repetition, restoration, redeployment.
>
> —Edward Said, *Beginnings*

> The fragmenting of knowledge into periods—firsts—is humanly necessary, but the fragments are by no means intrinsically inevitable or experientially real.
>
> —Cathy Davidson, *Revolution and the Word*

> I regarded the selection of myself as being somewhat remarkable. There were a number of slave children that might have been sent from the plantation to Baltimore. There were those younger, those older, and those the same age. I was chosen from among them all, and was *the first, last,* and *only choice.* (Emphasis added)
>
> —Frederick Douglass, *Narrative of the Life*

Assertions that the slave narrative begins the African-American literary tradition are repeated so often that they have acquired the force of self-evident truth. Charles Davis makes the argument up front in titling one of his important essays: "The Slave Narrative: First Major Art Form in an Emerging Black Tradition."[1] James Olney echoes Davis, only more strongly, in stating, "the undeniable fact is that the Afro-American literary tradition takes its start, in theme certainly, but also in content and form from the slave narrative."[2] Making an even bolder claim, H. Bruce Franklin argues that the slave narrative was the "first genre the United States of America contributed to the written literature of the world."[3]

Of the estimated six thousand extant narratives, Frederick Douglass's 1845 *Narrative of the Life of Frederick Douglass, An American Slave, Written by Himself* is considered the first of a first. It is regarded as the prototypical, premier example of the form. It is also viewed as the text that "authorized"

This essay was written especially for this volume and is published here for the first time by permission of the author.

most subsequent slave narratives. Such claims of the narrative's priority can only be considered heuristic or factitious, what Paul de Man describes elsewhere as an "instance of rhetorical mystification,"[4] inasmuch as it is not chronologically prior, either to John Saffin's *Adam's Negro's Tryall* (1703), sometimes said to begin the slave narrative genre, or Briton Hammon's *A Narrative of the Uncommon Sufferings . . . of Briton Hammon, A Negro Man* (1760), which is more often considered the beginning.[5] Nevertheless, the *Narrative's* status of priority persists. John Sekora contends that it is "the first comprehensive, personal history of American slavery."[6] With its publication, says Benjamin Quarles, one of Douglass's biographers, Douglass "became the first colored man who could command an audience that extended beyond local boundaries or racial ties.[7] William Andrews notes that the sales of the *Narrative* made it "the great enabling text of the first century of Afro-American autobiography," the text that created a popular demand for other fugitive slave narratives.[8]

It should be clear, even from these brief and randomly chosen excerpts, that Frederick Douglass and his 1845 *Narrative* have achieved monumental status. As Peter Walker observes, Douglass's presence in American history as "the courageous paterfamilias of a race" has "loomed so large and has been so compelling that he has been drafted into service as a personified social program by such widely divergent ideologues as [the acommodationist] Booker T. Washington and [the Marxist] Philip Foner."[9]

Douglass's function in literary history and interpretation has been similarly protean. He has been remarkably adaptable, to be more specific, to what Houston Baker has described as the "generational shifts" in the interpretation of Afro-American literature. He has been useful and usable to scholars whose approaches run the gamut from a now-devalued liberal humanism to a currently more valorized poststructuralism. In fact Baker's own shifting treatment of the 1845 *Narrative* is an excellent case in point of Douglass's adaptability to changing critical moments and the vocabularies by which we recognize them.[10] But however adaptable and fluid Douglass's *Narrative* has been to diverse and sometimes mutually antagonistic critical theories and methods, the underlying beliefs in its priority and originary significance remain unchanged. It is this changing sameness that interests me here. Why has the interpretive history, particularly of the last two decades, so privileged and mystified Douglass's narrative as a beginning text?

In an approach to this question, Edward Said's meditation on beginnings is instructive. He argues that "what is first, *is* eminent." Designating an individual as a founder has appeal, Said explains, because "in dealing with a distant past the mind prefers contemplating a strong seminal figure to sifting through reams of explanation." And it is not that such a figure is "simply a hypostasis. Indeed, he must fulfill the requirements of an exacting and . . . inaugural logic in which the creation of *authority* is paramount . . . an original achievement that gains in worth, paradoxically, precisely because it is so often repeated thereafter."[11]

It is easy to find in Said's observations clear and direct implications for a consideration of the 1845 *Narrative* and its originary significance in the African-American narrative tradition. His remarks on the role of texts in the formulation of beginnings are especially appropriate. "Entire periods of history are basically apprehended as functions of a text," Said observes. That is, they are "either made sensible by a text or given identity by a text."[12] Albert Stone's is only one of many treatments of Douglass's *Narrative* to confirm Said's claims. To Stone, this text is "the *first* native American autobiography to create a black identity in a style and form adequate to the pressures of historical black experience."[13]

The *Narrative* then does double duty: not only does it make slavery intelligible, but the "black experience" as well. And in performing this monumental work, the text thus acts in two directions at once: the here and now and the there and then. It is the *Narrative's* actions in the here and now that interest me. I am concerned with pursuing the uses to which the present generation of critics and scholars have put the past, specifically this man and his texts and this man as a text. As Douglass himself noted in "Self-Made Men," considered his most famous address, "it is the now that makes the then."[14] I am interested in why the making of Douglass, particularly by this current generation of scholars, has had such widespread explanatory power and appeal, and why it is attached so solidly to the logic of beginning and origin.

These questions assume all the more importance because, as Patricia Parker well notes, "the logic of first and second, and hence of sequence . . . continues to inhabit the discussion of female difference."[15] Some of the most compelling critiques of that logic of beginning, at least as it has operated in Western culture, have come from feminist theorists like Parker who trace it back to the first of the Genesis myths. They have challenged this myth that inscribes Adam's ontological priority as well as his priority in human history and culture, noting that his "firstness" necessitates Eve's "secondariness" as well as her exile from creative or symbolic activity. This myth, associated with the male story, with the name and the Law of the Father, represses the name and the word of the mother. Increasingly literalized, it has been taken as given or fact and operates in both conscious and unconscious beliefs and in cultural structures. In other words, the myth that "Adam was formed first, then Eve" (I Timothy, 2. 11–15) has pervaded a variety of cultural texts—sacred and secular—that show the unmistakable trace of Genesis and the sex/gender economy it has produced in culture.

Perhaps one prerequisite question here is thus whether the force in the critical making of Frederick Douglass and his *Narrative* as founding texts is something yet more basic and powerful, an a priori structure and system of desire that preexists and determines both Douglass's narrative choices and those his critics have made. That structure authorizes and inscribes the relationship between sexual difference and creative activity.

I

This man shall be remembered . . . with lives grown out of his life, the lives fleshing his dream of the needful, beautiful thing.
                                         —Robert Hayden, "Frederick Douglass"

Students of the 1845 *Narrative* commonly designate the following as its key sentence: "You have seen how a man was made a slave, you shall see how a slave was made a man."[16] The clause that follows that pivotal comma—"you shall see how a slave was made a man"—captures with great prescience the focus of much contemporary scholarship on slavery. That focus is studiously on making the slave a man, according to cultural norms of masculinity. This accounts in part, as I will show below, for why Douglass is so pivotal, so mythological a figure. I am not out to argue for any distinction between Douglass "the myth" and Douglass "the man," but rather and simply to view him as a product of history, a construction of a specific time and place, developed in response to a variety of social contingencies and individual desires.

The process and production in literary studies of Douglass as "the first" have paralleled and perhaps been partly fueled by what revisionist historians have made of him. We might go even further to argue that "history" has operated as narrative, in the making of Douglass and his *Narrative*. And so we face constructions upon constructions. While the mythologization of Douglass and this text well antedates the 1960s, 1970s and 1980s, these decades are especially crucial in efforts to understand this process.

These years were characterized by revisionist mythmaking, much of it prompted by Stanley Elkins's controversial book *Slavery: A Problem in American Institutional and Intellectual Life* (1959). I need not rehearse in detail Elkins's now-familiar Sambo thesis emphasizing the effects of black male emasculation in slavery.[17] Historians, armed with a mountain of supporting data, came forth to refute Elkins's data and his thesis. Among the most prominent of these revisionists was John Blassingame, whose *The Slave Community* was rightly celebrated for its attempt to write history from the perspective of slaves, not planters. Blassingame rejects Elkins's Sambo thesis as "intimately related to the planters's projections, desires, and biases,"[18] particularly their desire to be relieved of the "anxiety of thinking about slaves as men."[19]

Blassingame sets out to correct the record to show that the slave was not "half-man," "half-child,"[20] as the Elkins thesis tried to show, but a whole man. Blassingame doesn't simply lapse into the reflexive use of the generic "he," but throughout his study assumes the slave to be literally male, an assumption seen especially in his chapter titled "The Slave Family." There he opens with the straightforward observation: "The Southern plantation was unique in the New World because it permitted the development of a monogamous slave family," which was "one of the most important survival mechanisms for the slave." He continues, "the slave faced almost insurmountable odds in his efforts to build a strong stable family . . . his authority was restricted by his master . . . The master determined when both he and his wife would go to work [and] when or whether his wife cooked his meals." "When the slave lived on the same plantation with his mate he could rarely escape frequent demonstrations of his powerlessness." "Under such a regime," Blassingame adds, "slave fathers often had little or no authority." Despite that, the slave system "recognized the male as the head of the family."[21]

Blassingame is clearly not alone in revising the history of slavery to demonstrate the propensities of slaves toward shaping their lives according to "normative" cultural patterns of marriage and family life. But *The Slave Community* must be seen as a study of the institution that reflects and reproduces the assumptions of a much wider discursive network—scholarly and political —within which the black male is the racial subject.

There have been few challenges to this two-decade-long focus on the personality of the male slave. In her book *Ar'n't I a Woman?* (which might have been more aptly titled, "Can a slave be a woman; can a woman be a slave?"), Deborah White critiques the emphasis on negating Samboism, which characterizes so much recent literature on slavery. She argues that "the male slave's 'masculinity' was restored by putting black women in their proper 'feminine' place."[22] bell hooks offers an even stronger critique of this literature, noting eloquently its underlying assumption that "the most cruel and dehumanizing impact of slavery on the lives of black people was that black men were stripped of their masculinity." hooks continues, "To suggest that black men were dehumanized solely as a result of not being able to be patriarchs implies that the subjugation of black women was essential to the black male's development of a positive self-concept, an ideal that only served to support a sexist social order."[23]

While I would not argue that students of Afro-American literature have consciously joined revisionist historians in their efforts to debunk the Elkins thesis, their work can certainly be said to participate in and reinforce these revisionist histories. And what better way to do this than to replace the Sambo myth of childlike passivity with an example of public derring-do, with the myth of the male slave as militant, masculine, dominant, and triumphant in both private and public spheres?[24]

But the Elkins thesis, and the revisionist histories it engendered, are only part of a larger chain of interlocking events that have worked to mythologize Frederick Douglass. These include the demand for African and African-American Studies courses in universities, the publishers who capitalized on that demand, and the academic scholars who completed the chain. A series of individual slave narratives has appeared, along with anthologies and collections of less-popular narratives. The more popular the narrative, the more frequent the editions, and Douglass's 1845 *Narrative* has headed the list since 1960. Scholarly interest in African-American literature has accelerated corresponding-ly and, again, the 1845 *Narrative* has been premier. Although in his 1977 essay, "Animal Farm Unbound," H. Bruce Franklin could list in a fairly short paragraph critical articles on the 1845 *Narrative,* scarcely more than a decade later the book had stimulated a small industry of scholarship on its own.[25] Thus Douglass's assumed genius as a literary figure is the work of a diverse and interactive collective that includes publishers, editors, and literary critics who have helped to construct his reputation and to make it primary in Afro-American literature.

A major diachronic study of the production, reception, and circulation history of Douglass's 1845 *Narrative* is urgently needed; but even more urgent is the need for a thoroughgoing analysis of the politics of gender at work in that process. One could argue that the politics of gender have been obscured both by the predominance of nonfeminist interpretations of the *Narrative* and by the text itself. In other words, those who have examined it have tended, with few exceptions, to mimic the work of Douglass himself on the question of the feminine and its relation to the masculine in culture.

For example, in his most recent reading of the 1845 *Narrative,* Houston Baker assimilates the text to Marxist language and rhetoric, but a more conventional rhetoric of family resounds. Baker's reading foregrounds the disruption of the slave family and offers the terms of its reunion: economic solvency. "The successful negotiation of such economics," says Baker, "is, paradoxically, the *only* course that provides conditions for a reunification of woman and sable man."[26] He continues, "the African who successfully negotiates his way through the dread exchanges of bondage to the type of expressive posture characterizing *The Life's* conclusion is surely a man who has repossessed himself and, thus, achieved the ability to reunite a severed African humanity."[27] A sign of that self-repossession, Baker argues, is Douglass's "certificate of marriage." "As a married man," he concludes, Douglass "understands the necessity for *individual* wage earning."[28] "In the company of his new bride," he goes to a New England factory village where he participates "creatively in the liberation of his people."[29] This reading's implication in an old patriarchal script requires not a glossing, but an insertion and a backward tracking. However important Douglass's wage-earning capacities as a freeman are, one could say that the prior wage, if you will, was Anna Murray's, Douglass's "new bride." A freedwoman, Anna "helped to defray the costs for [Douglass's] runaway scheme by borrowing from her savings and by selling one of her feather beds."[30]

Mary Helen Washington is one of the few critics to insert Anna Murray Douglass into a discussion of the 1845 *Narrative.* She asks, "While our daring Douglass . . . was heroically ascending freedom's arc . . . who . . . was at home taking care of the children?"[31] But such questions are all too rare in discussions of the *Narrative.* Because critical commentary has mainly repeated the text's elision of women, I would like to restore them for the moment, to change the subject of the text from man to woman.

II

I have said that the slave was a man.
—Frederick Douglass, *My Bondage and My Freedom*

To attempt to restore the occluded woman in Douglass's *Narrative* is to bring forth gender as a category of analysis. Such a discussion might properly begin by considering autobiography as genre, particularly inasmuch as gender and genre are etymologically related. As Jacques Derrida, among others, has noted, the question of the literary genre is not a strictly formal or esthetic one. It embraces, in addition, the motif and logic of generation in both natural and symbolic senses, as well as the sexual difference between the feminine and masculine.[32]

In choosing autobiography as a form, Douglass committed himself to what many feminists consider an androcentric genre.[33] In its focus on the public story of a public life, which signifies the achievement of adult male status in Western culture, autobiography reflects and constructs that culture's definitions of masculinity. Douglass's *Narrative* not only partakes of these definitions of masculinity, but is also plotted according to the myth of the self-made man to which these definitions correspond. As Valerie Smith has observed, "by mythologizing rugged individuality, physical strength, and geographical mobility, the [slave] narrative enshrines cultural definitions of masculinity." She continues, "the plot of the standard narrative may thus be seen as not only the journey from slavery to freedom but also the journey from slavehood to manhood" in cultural terms.[34]

In choosing autobiography as a form, Douglass also implicitly and explicitly committed himself to what is perhaps its most salient requirement: that he legitimize himself by naming and claiming a father.[35] Of course, the slave system prevented him from doing either, which may explain why his obsession with learning his origins or his "proper name" was to preoccupy Douglass literally until his dying day.[36] That he believed his master to be his father, engendering a double relation, only confounded this search for origins.

If we read that search symbolically as a secondary expression of the Genesis myth of origins, then Douglass's name changes acquire added significance. As noted above, that myth inscribes the name and the Law of the Father, while repressing the name of the mother. It can be argued, then, that in changing the name his mother gave him—Frederick Augustus Washington Bailey—Douglass, as Henry Louis Gates astutely notes, "self-consciously and ironically abandoned a strong matrilineal black heritage of five stable generations."[37] We might argue further that the abandonment of the mother's name can be read as a rejection of the mother's word, to a rejection of the feminine. Although over the course of his three autobiographies, Douglass shifted and refined his representation of his mother, her figuration in the first autobiography is that most commonly accepted by literary critics, when they discuss the mother at all.[38] Generally, critics merely restate as a given Douglass's early descriptions of his separation from her and his emotionless but rhetorically effective account of their short acquaintance: "I do not recollect of ever seeing my mother by the light of day . . . Very little communication ever took place between us." While critics, in the main, have not been slow to attend to the *Narrative* as rhetorical tour de force, few have delved underneath the surfaces of these descriptions of the mother to uncover their latent grammar.

In striking ways, Douglass's *Narrative* participates in a more basic, a priori narrative that silences and effaces the mother's story.[39] Such a position gains in force if the 1845 *Narrative,* the first of three, is not accepted as the "standard edition" overriding Douglass's accounts of his life in the two subsequent narratives. If the 1845 *Narrative* is not given priority as the first, last, and only word on Douglass, but is considered in relation to the following texts, his problematical relation to his mother emerges with greater and more disturbing clarity. She thus becomes a powerful presence even in her absence.

In *My Bondage and My Freedom,* for example, Douglass writes: "the side of my mother's face is imaged on my memory, and I take few steps in life without feeling her presence; but *the image is mute, and I have no striking words of hers treasured up"* (57, emphasis added). In *Life and Times,* Douglass repeats earlier accounts of his mother, but adds a reference to his selection of "the head of a figure" from Prichard's *Natural History of Man,* which he believed to be a fair likeness of his mother. Peter Walker offers a complex reading of Douglass's choice of this figure, concluding persuasively that Douglass "found his black mother in the form of a princely man who, as far as the picture showed, may have been white."[40]

Douglass's account of his mute mother remembered as a white man captures emphatically the discursive priorities of masculinity and its gendered relation to the feminine. That slavery so destroyed the possibility of a relationship with his mother, Douglass is keen to emphasize. That emphasis works well rhetorically with his general indictment of the institution's destruction of family, which was one of abolitionism's singular strategies. While that destruction was certainly widespread and real, in Douglass's case it was, as Walker has suggested, partly fictive. What, then, other than the generic requirements of the fugitive slave narrative as an abolitionist instrument, explains Douglass's decision to remake his beginnings? This question is less dependent on the first narrative than on the second, and it involves the complex affiliations of femininity and feminism and abolitionism. In other words, *My Bondage and My Freedom* reveals more clearly than the first narrative that Douglass's rewriting of his own origins does more than satisfy the dictates of abolitionism. It also makes intelligible Douglass's and the movement's problematical relation to the feminine.

Douglass is rightly concerned to show that "genealogical trees do not flourish among slaves," that while his mother "had *many children,"* "she had NO FAMILY!" (*My Bondage and My Freedom* 48, emphasis in text). Thus was slavery "an enemy to filial affection" that rendered him a stranger to his siblings, "converted the mother that bore [him] into a myth," and "shrouded [his] father in mystery, and left [him] without an intelligible beginning in the world" (60). And while none would expect anything but such stirring condemnation, I believe that Gregory Jay is right to argue that Douglass's appeal to the "sanctity of the family" is an emotional and moral verity that allied abolitionism "with the powerful conventions of domesticity." In thus using the "family against slavery," Douglass elides, as Harriet Jacobs does not, the fact that "the paternalism and property relations at the heart of the slave system might also play a part in the construction of domestic relations." That Douglass forges this unexamined connection between abolitionism and domesticity at the same moment that the link between slavery and feminism was "being forged by various reform figures, including Douglass himself," is "all the more puzzling and powerful."[41]

But the puzzle is solved in part if we consider that while Douglass rejected the paternalism and property relations buttressing the slave system, he appropriated those buttressing the structure and ideology of the family. Or, as Valerie Smith puts it, "Within his critique of American cultural practices . . . is an affirmation of its definitions of manhood and power" on which traditional domestic arrangements depend.[42]

Central to Douglass's condemnation is slavery's legal denial of family to slaves, especially its denial to male slaves the rights and privileges of patriarchy, which include ownership of their wives and children. In *My Bondage and my Freedom,* he lists among "the baneful peculiarities of the slave system" the fact that "in law, the slave has no wife, no children, no country, and no home" (429). And he laments that "the name of the child is not expected to be that of its father" (51–52). But however justified he is in condemning slavery for denying the slave the right to wife and children, the absurdity of its male bias should still not go unremarked. The fact that slave women could not take "wives" categorizes them, to borrow from Karen Sanchez-Appler, "not as potential free persons but rather as the sign and condition of another's freedom. The freedom so defined . . . is available to neither child nor woman."[43]

Here and throughout Douglass's autobiographies, his delineation of slavery's "baneful peculiarities" often rests on an implied equation of masculinity with subjectivity and textuality. Throughout, "slave" is conflated with "male." Near the end of *My Bondage* Douglass declares, with performative authority, "I have said the slave was a man" (431). Reflexive and anticipated arguments about the generic he/man, and the nineteenth-century context of the narrative's production, must be deflected here and should not foreclose a discussion of Douglass's tendency to construct the black male as paradigmatic slave. To be sure, that Douglass implicitly and explicitly arrogated subjectivity and primacy to himself is but a part of linguistic convention and a general cultural tendency to privilege maleness. It is also, however, a specific pattern in abolitionist discourse in which women occupied secondary places. The "Ladies

Department" of Garrison's *The Liberator,* cordoned off from and coming after the preceding matter, establishes this tendency plainly. Further, as Waldo Martin notes, Douglass lamented that abolitionism, "a grand philanthropic movement," had been "rent asunder by a side issue [women's rights], having nothing, whatever, to do with the great object which the American Anti-Slavery Society was organized to carry forward." According to Martin, though Douglass supported women's rights, he felt feminists "should have postponed their own protests," in his words, "for the slave's sake."[44] However understandable Douglass's position was, especially given the racism in the movement for women's rights, he misses the fact that some slaves were women and that however much their oppressions overlapped with that of male slaves, the particularities of each were such that they could not be merged.

When Douglass's *Narrative* moves from generic descriptions of slave life to focus on the more specific experiences of individuals, it seems, on the surface, that he is alert to the differences between the experiences of women and those of men. He chooses to highlight the most familiar mark of their difference in the discourse of slavery: black women's sexual oppression. But while such a move might be considered a radical act of resistance, it soon becomes implicated in the very situation of exploitation that it seeks to expose. Put another way, black women's backs become the parchment on which Douglass narrates his linear progression from bondage to freedom.

III

For heart of man though mainly right
Hides many things from mortal sight
Which seldom ever come to light
except upon compulsion.
—Frederick Douglass,
"What Am I to You"

Frances Foster is one of the few critics to describe the construction in the popular imagination of the slave woman as sexual victim, a pattern she sees in full evidence in male slave narratives. Foster observes a markedly different pattern in slave narratives written by women. Unlike the male narratives, which portray graphically the sexual abuse of slave women by white men, female narratives "barely mention sexual experiences and never present rape or seduction as the most profound aspect of their existence."[45]

The pattern that Foster describes is abundantly evident in all three of Douglass's autobiographies. One can easily argue that, with perhaps the exception of his mother and grandmother, slave women operate almost totally as physical bodies, as sexual victims, "at the mercy," as he notes in *My Bondage and My Freedom* "of the fathers, sons or brothers of [their] master" (60).

Though this is certainly true, slave women were just as often at the mercy of the wives, sisters, and mothers of these men," as Harriet Jacobs records in *Incidents in the Life of a Slave Girl.*[46] But in Douglass's account, the sexual villains are white men and the victims black women. Black men are largely impotent onlookers, condemned to watch the abuse. What Douglass watches and then narrates is astonishing—the whippings of slaves, one after another, in almost unbroken succession.

A scant four pages into the text, immediately following his account of his origins, Douglass begins to describe these whippings in graphic detail. He sees Mr. Plummer, the overseer, "cut and slash the women's heads" and "seem to take great pleasure" in it. He remembers being often awakened by the heart-rending shrieks of his aunt as she is beaten. He sees her "tie[d] up to a joist and whip[ped] upon her naked back till she was literally covered with blood. The louder she screamed, the harder he whipped; and where the blood ran fastest, there he whipped longest. He would whip her to make her scream, and whip her to make her hush; and not until overcome by fatigue, would he cease to swing the blood-clotted cowskin" (25).

Though the whippings of women are not the only ones of which Douglass's *Narrative* gives account, they predominate by far in the text's economy as Douglass looks on. There was Mr. Severe, whom "I have seen . . . whip a woman, causing the blood to run half an hour at the time" (29). There was his master, who he had seen "tie up a *lame* young woman, and whip her with a heavy cowskin upon her naked shoulders, causing the warm red blood to drip. I have known him to tie her up early in the morning and whip her before breakfast; leave her, go to his store, return at dinner and whip her again, cutting in the places already made raw with his cruel lash" (68–69). There was Mr. Weeden, who kept the back of a slave woman "literally raw, made so by the lash of this merciless, religious wretch" (87). As the *Narrative* progresses, the beatings proliferate and the women, no longer identified by name, become absolutized as a bloody mass of naked backs.

What has been made of this recital of whippings? William L. Andrews is one of the few critics to comment on the function of whippings in the text. In a very suggestive reading, he argues that Douglass presents the fact of whipping in "deliberately stylized, plainly rhetorical, recognizably artificial ways." There is nothing masked about this presentation. On the contrary, "Douglass's choice of repetition" is his "chief rhetorical effect." It constitutes his "stylistic signature" and expresses his "performing self." In the whipping passages, Andrews adds, "Douglass calls attention to himself as an unabashed artificer, a maker of forms and efforts that recontextualize brute facts according to requirements of self. The freeman requires the freedom to demonstrate the potency of his own inventiveness and the sheer potentiality of language itself for rhetorical manipulation."[47]

However intriguing I find Andrews's reading, I fear that to explain the repetition of whippings solely in rhetorical terms and in the interest of

Douglass's self-expression leads to some troubling elisions and rationalizations, perhaps the most troubling elision being the black woman's body. In other words, Douglass's "freedom"—narrative and physical alike—depends on narrating black women's bondage. He achieves his "stylistic signature" by objectifying black women. To be sure, delineating the sexual abuse of black women is a standard convention of the fugitive slave narrative, but the narration of that abuse seems to function beyond the mere requirements of form. A second look at the first recorded beating, his Aunt Hester's, forces out a different explanation. His choice of words in this account—"spectacle," "exhibition"—is instructive, as is his telling admission that, in viewing the beating, he became both "witness and participant" (25).

Critical commentary has focused almost completely on Douglass as witness to slavery's abuses, overlooking his role as participant, an omission that conceals his complex and troubling relationship to slave women, kin and nonkin alike. In calling for closer attention to the narration of whipping scenes, I do not mean to suggest that Douglass's autobiographies were alone among their contemporaries in their obsession with corporal punishment. As Richard Brodhead has observed, "Corporal punishment has been one of the most perennially vexed of questions in American cultural history," and it had its "historical center of gravity in America in the antebellum decades."[48] Both in antislavery literature and in the literature of the American Gothic, what Brodhead calls the "imagination of the lash" was pervasive. That much antislavery literature had strong sexual undercurrents has been well documented. As many critics have observed, much abolitionist literature went beyond an attack on slavery to condemn the South as a vast libidinal playground.

My aim here, then, is not to argue that Douglass's repeated depiction of whipping scenes is in any way unique to him, but rather to submit those scenes to closer scrutiny for their own sake. In other words, the preponderance of this pattern in antebellum literature should not preclude a detailed examination of its representation in a smaller textual sampling. Neither is my aim to psychoanalyze Douglass, nor to offer an "alternative," more "correct" reading, but rather to reveal that Douglass often has more than one voice, one motivation, and one response to his record of black women's abuse in his *Narrative.*

Freud notes in *Beyond the Pleasure Principle* that "repetition, the re-experiencing of something identical, is clearly in itself a source of pleasure."[49] If, as Douglass observes, the slave master derives pleasure from the repeated act of whipping, could Douglass, as observer, derive a vicarious pleasure from the repeated narration of the act? I would say yes. Douglass's repetition of the sexualized scene of whipping projects him into a voyeuristic relation to the violence against slave women, which he watches, and thus he enters into a symbolic complicity with the sexual crime he witnesses. In other words, the spectator becomes voyeur, reinforcing what many feminist film theorists have persuasively argued: sexualization "resides in the very act of looking."[50] Thus "the relationship between viewer and scene is always one of fracture, partial identification, pleasure and distrust."[51]

To be sure, Douglass sounds an urgently and warranted moral note in these passages, but he sounds an erotic one as well that is even more clear if the critical gaze moves from the first autobiography to the second. In a chapter titled "Gradual Initiation into the Mysteries of Slavery," Douglass describes awakening as a child to a slave woman being beaten. The way in which Douglass constructs the scene evokes the familiar male child's initiation into the mysteries of sexuality by peeking through the keyhole of his parents' bedroom:

> My sleeping place was the floor of a little, rough closet, which opened into the kitchen; and through the cracks of its unplaned boards, I could distinctly see and hear what was going on, without being seen by my master. Esther's wrists were firmly tied and the twisted rope was fastened to a strong staple in a heavy wooden joist above, near the fireplace. Here she stood, on a bench, her arms tightly drawn over her breast. Her back and shoulders were bare to the waist. Behind her stood old master, with cowskin in hand, preparing his barbarous work with all manner of harsh, coarse, and tantalizing epithets. The screams of his victim were most piercing. He was cruelly deliberate, and protracted the torture, as one who was delighted with the scene. Again and again he drew the hateful whip through his hand, adjusting it with a view of dealing the most pain-giving blow. Poor Esther had never yet been severely whipped, and her shoulders were plump and tender. Each blow vigorously laid on, brought screams as well as blood. (87–88)[52]

This passage in all its erotic overtones echoes throughout Douglass's autobiographies and goes well beyond pleasure to embrace its frequent symbiotic equivalent: power. It can be said both to imitate and articulate the pornographic scene, which starkly represents and reproduces the cultural and oppositional relation of the masculine to the feminine, the relation between seer and seen, agent and victim, dominant and dominated, powerful and powerless.[53]

Examining the narration of whipping scenes with regard to the sex of the slave reinforces this gendered division and illustrates its consequences. While the women are tied up—the classic stance of women in pornography—and unable to resist, the men are "free," if you like, to struggle. William Demby is a case in point. After Mr. Gore whips him, Demby runs to the creek and refuses to obey the overseer's commands to come out. Demby finally asserts the power over his own body, even though it costs him his life.

But clearly the most celebrated whipping scene of all is Douglass's two-hour-long fight with Covey, on which the 1845 *Narrative* pivots. Positioned roughly midway through the text, it constitutes also the midway point between slavery and freedom. This explains in part why the fight is dramatized and elaborated over several pages, an allotment clearly disproportionate to other reported episodes. When the fight is over, Douglass boasts that

Covey "had drawn no blood from me, but I had from him" and expresses satisfaction at "repell[ing] by force the bloody arm of slavery." He concludes, "I had several fights, but was never whipped" (81–83).

The fight with Covey is the part of the *Narrative* most frequently anthologized, and it is a rare critical text indeed that ignores this scene. I agree with Donald Gibson that "most commentators on the conflict have . . . interpreted it as though it were an arena boxing match." Gibson attributes such a view to what he terms the "public focus" of Douglass's narrative, "which requires that the slave defeat the slaveholder."[54] I would add to Gibson's explanation that this defeat serves to incarnate a critical/political view that equates resistance to power with physical struggle, a view that fails to see that such struggle cannot function as the beginning and end of our understanding of power relations.

The critical valorization of physical struggle and subsequent triumph and control finds an interesting parallel in discussion of Douglass's narrative struggles, among the most provocative being that of Robert Stepto in *From Behind the Veil*. In discussing the relation of Douglass's *Narrative* to the "authenticating" texts by William Garrison and Wendell Phillips, Stepto argues that these ancillary texts seem on the surface to be "*at war* with Douglass's tale for authorial control of the narrative as a whole."[55] While Stepto grants that there is a tension among all three documents, Douglass's "tale *dominates* the narrative because it alone authenticates the narrative" (Emphases added).[56]

In examining the issue of authorial control more generally, Stepto argues: "When a narrator wrests this kind of preeminent authorial control from the ancillary voices in the narrative, we may say he controls the presentation of his personal history, and that his tale is becoming autobiographical."[57] He continues, "Authorial control of a narrative need not always result from an author's defeat of competing voices or usurpation of archetypes or pregeneric myths, but is usually occasioned by such acts. What may distinguish one literary history or tradition from another is not the issue of whether such battles occur, but that of who is competing with whom and over what."[58]

This competition for authorial control in African-American letters, Stepto argues, does not conform to the Bloomian oedipal paradigm, for "the battle for authorial control has been more of a race ritual than a case of patricide."[59] Stepto is right to note that competition among African Americans is "rarely between artist and artist," but between "artist and authenticator (editor, publisher, guarantor, patron)."[60] Here, of course, Stepto could easily have inserted that these authenticators have generally been white males. Thus the battle for authorial control in Douglass's case was a battle between white and black males.

For Stepto, Douglass's ultimate control rests on his "extraordinary ability to pursue several types of writing with ease and with a degree of simultanei-ty."[61] But again, the explanation of Douglass's strength depends overmuch on a focus on style emptied of its contents. In other words, what is the "content" of Douglass's "syncretic phrasing," the "instrospective analysis," the "participant observations" that make him a master stylist in Stepto's estimation? But, more important, does Douglass's "defeat" of competing white male voices enable him to find a voice distinct from theirs?

Since Douglass's authorial control is the logical outcome of his quest for freedom and literacy, one might approach that question from the angle of the thematics of literacy, of which much has been made by critics. Revealing perhaps more than he knew in the following passage, Douglass describes one of many scenes of stolen knowledge in the *Narrative*. Because his retelling of this episode is all the more suggestive in *My Bondage and My Freedom*, I've selected it instead. "When my mistress left me in charge of the house, I had a grand time; I got Master Tommy's copy books and a pen and ink, and, in the ample spaces between the lines, *I wrote other lines, as nearly like his as possible*" (172, emphasis added).[62]

This hand-to-hand combat between black and white men for physical, then narrative, control over bodies and texts raises the question of who is on whose side? For, in its allegiance to the dialectics of dominance and subordination, Douglass's *Narrative* is, and not surprisingly so, a by-product of Master Tommy's copybook, especially of its gendered division of power relations. The representation of women being whipped, in form and function, is only one major instance of this point but the representation of women, in general, shows Master Tommy's imprint.

Abounding in this copybook are conventional ideas of male subjectivity that exclude women from language. The scenes of reading are again cases in point. Throughout the narrative Douglass employs what Lillie Jugurtha aptly terms "eye dialogue." That is, he presents personal exchanges that have the appearance of dialogue without being dialogue. In the following account, Douglass describes the scene in which Mrs. Auld is ordered to cease teaching Frederick to read:

> Mr. Auld found out what was going on, and at once forbade Mrs. Auld to instruct me further, telling her, among other things, that it was unlawful, as well as unsafe, to teach a slave to read. To use his own words . . . he said, "If you give a nigger an inch, he will take an ell. . . . Learning would spoil the best nigger in the world . . . if you teach that nigger (speaking of myself) how to read, there would be no keeping him. It would forever unfit him to be a slave. He would at once become unmanageable, and of no value to his master. As to himself, it would do him no good, but a great deal of harm. It would make him discontented and unhappy." (49)

In glossing this passage, Jugurtha perceptively notices that "there is no second speaker presented here, no Lucretia Auld responding to her husband . . . One pictures, though one does not hear, a husband and a wife talking . . . Unobtrusively, perspectives are multiplied. Monologue functions as dialogue."[63] That Sophia Auld was regarded by Douglass early on as a substitute mother figure, links her erasure in the foregoing passage to the erasure of his biological mother in the first part of the 1845 *Narrative* and, by extension, to the erasure of the feminine. In this secular rewriting of the sacred text, Mrs. Auld is exiled from the scene of knowledge, of symbolic activity. As a woman she is not permitted "to teach or to have authority over men; she is to keep silent" (I Timothy 2:11–12).

What critics have learned from and done with Douglass has often constituted a correspondingly mimetic process where the feminine is concerned. In other words, the literary and interpretive history of the *Narrative* has, with few exceptions, repeated with approval its salient assumptions and structural paradigms. This repetition has, in turn, created a potent and persistent critical language that positions and repositions Douglass on top, that puts him in a position of priority. This ordering has not only helped to establish the dominant paradigm of African-American criticism, but it has also done much to establish the dominant view of African-American literary history. In that view, Douglass is, to borrow from James Olney, "the founding father" who "produced a kind of Ur-text of slavery and freedom that, whether individual writers were conscious of imitating Douglass or not, wuld inform the Afro-American literary tradition from his time to the present."[64]

This dynastic model of Douglass and his progeny goes on ordering as if it were intrinsically inevitable and experientially real. According to Arna Bontemps, the *Narrative* contains "the spirit and vitality and the angle of vision responsible for the most effective prose writing by black American writers from William Wells Brown to Charles Chesnutt, from W. E. B. DuBois to Richard Wright, Ralph Ellison, and James Baldwin."[65] This model is being recast, but that recasting often takes the form of an annexation, and, not surprisingly, an annexation again of the feminine. Olney's otherwise brilliant essay is a case in point. His solution to the question of whether he would consider the implications of his literary history for an examination of black women was to attach a coda to the main body of the essay. There he writes,

> Putting aside the male exclusivity in the founding of the American nation and in the shaping of an Afro-American literary tradition (this latter taking the form in my essay of a line from Frederick Douglass, Booker T. Washington, W. E. B. DuBois, and James Weldon Johnson down to Richard Wright, Malcolm X, Ralph Ellison, and beyond), it is interesting and timely to speculate on another line in Afro-American writing, composed of black women writers, a line that runs parallel to the Douglass-Washington-Wright-Ellison line but that also signifies on and revises that exclusively male tradition.

Here, black women form a postscript or a tailpiece, if you like, lying outside the ambit of Olney's discussion proper, outside the "proper", which is to say, the prior discussion. They constitute a separate (but equal?) tradition. Olney seems to be still within the logic of the primary and the secondary. Further, he begins to construct yet another genealogy, one of critics of African-American sons descending from stalwart fathers in a kind of typological unfolding. Their status as sons who can then be fathers is clear in the utterance of their complete "entitles." Olney notes that "a number of critics of Afro-American literature—Houston Baker, Jr., Henry Louis Gates, Jr., and Robert B. Stepto—to name only three—have demonstrated brilliantly that it is precisely this revisionary playing off against or signifying on, previous texts that constitutes literary history and, specifically, the Afro-American literary tradition."[66]

Olney's drawing of the circle around the literary and critical tradition is an act of male performance, of naming, of setting priorities. This act goes on ordering and reordering our conceptions of African-American literary history and of American literature more generally. In the efforts to revise or reconstruct the so-called canon of American literature, Douglass's *Narrative* has been easily assimilated and given priority. Olney sees it as operating "both within and against the Franklinesque tradition."[67] Russell Reising sees the *Narrative* as "perhaps *the first* literary, political, and epistemological extension of ideas advanced in Emerson's major early essays."[68] And the editors of the second edition of *The Norton Anthology of American Literature* can be seen to have reinforced Reisling's claims in their decision to reprint the 1845 *Narrative* in its entirety. Their preface to the text ends with the assertion that "[Douglass's] life, in fact, has become the heroic paradigm for all oppressed people."[69]

It is this choice of Douglass as "the first," as "representative man," as the part that stands for the whole, that reproduces the omission of women from view, except as afterthoughts different from "the same" (black men). And that omission is not merely an oversight, but given the discursive system that authorizes Douglass as the source and the origin, that omission is a necessity. But if, as Said suggests, " 'beginning' is an eminently renewable subject,"[70] then we can begin again. We can begin to think outside the model that circumscribes an entire literary history into a genetic model and conscripts Douglass in the interest of masculine power and desire. In other words, we might start by putting an end to beginnings, even those that would put woman in the first place.

IV

What we call the beginning is often the end
And to make an end is to make a beginning
The end is where we start from.
T. S. Eliot—"Little Gidding"

Because of the contingencies of history, particularly those that have produced "black women writers" as a discipline or discourse object, we might say that the formerly secondary (black women) have become primary. In the opening sentence of his foreword to the excellent and timely Schomburg Series of Nineteenth-Century Black Women Writers, Henry Louis Gates, Jr., proclaims a new beginning: "The birth of the Afro-American literary tradition occurred in 1773, when Phillis Wheatley published a book of poetry."[71] Aptly titling his essay, "In Her Own Write," Gates goes on: "[that] the progenitor of the black literary tradition was a woman means, in the most strictly literal sense, that all subsequent black writers have evolved in a matrilinear line of descent" that includes Ann Plato, "the *first* Afro-American to publish a book of essays (1841)," Harriet E. Wilson, "the *first* black person to publish a novel in the United States (1859)," and Anna Julia Cooper, who "*first* analyzed the fallacy of referring to 'the black man' when speaking of black people" (emphases added).[72]

Gates does well to note that "despite this pioneering role of black women in the tradition," "many of their contributions before this century have been all but lost or unrecognized."[73] Seeking to redress this imbalance, he declares that the voices of black women must be uttered and to them we must listen. Indeed, such an appeal should not go and has not gone unheeded, but it need not hinge on a declaration of priority or firstness, a declaration allied to the very discourse and dialectic of dominance and subordination critiqued in the writing of so many black women.

If a genealogical model is to be used to explain the tradition of Afro-American literature and to explore either Douglass's or Wheatley's originary place within it, then such an exploration might begin with a reformulation or refocusing of genealogy as a concept of analysis. Such a reformulation would place greater emphasis on these authors' emergence as discourse objects than on determining either's priority in the tradition. Pursuing the former, we might ask, what has made Frederick Douglass so sacred a text with such overpowering influence and cultural authority? At whose expense and for whose gain has he been so made? What current situation enables his displacement by Phillis Wheatley, to some the now-reinstated "representative" black writer? In other words, the process of cultural production involved in making Douglass and Wheatley, or, for that matter, any "first" or "prior" figure, and the uses to which that production has been put, is the most urgent "genealogical" task.

Happily, such work has already begun. Though it still operates within the logic of first and second, one forthcoming essay by Henry Louis Gates is an example. Gates examines the abolitionist press and traces the process by which Frederick Douglass "as a standard bearer of Negro creativity and cultivation was marked by the simultaneous eclipse of the previously favored exemplar, Phillis Wheatley."[74] After the publication of Douglass's 1845 *Narrative,*

Wheatley disappeared almost completely from the abolitionist press, a disappearance not unrelated to the cultural identification of "manliness" with exemplariness.[75] Such an examination helps to redirect the conceptual methodologies and categories applied to the Afro-American literary tradition, particularly in discussions of the slave narrative. While the genre has been mainly examined taxonomically, that is, with a focus on its discrete, formal characteristics, a reconfigured genealogical model would examine the historical and cultural function of the slave narrative, both in the moment of its emergence and in contemporary scholarly discourse.

The cultural function of the slave narrative as genre and its relations to the inscription of gendered ideologies of masculinity and femininity represents a reordering of priorities in Afro-American literary study. With that shift we can begin to change the sequence and possibly set a new course for arrangements of gender and genre alike. Then, we will be able to rewrite the last lines of that familiar doxology: as it was in the beginning is now and ever shall be, world without end, Amen, Amen.

Notes

I would like to thank William L. Andrews, Janice Knight, Eric Lott, and Richard Yarborough for their helpful comments and suggestions.

1. Charles Davis, "The Slave Narrative: First Major Art Form in an Emerging Black Tradition," in Henry Louis Gates, Jr., ed., *Black is the Color of the Cosmos* (New York: Garland Publishing, 1982), 83–119.

2. James Olney. " 'I Was born': Slave Narratives, Their Status as Autobiography and as Literature" in Charles Davis and Henry Louis Gates, Jr. eds., *The Slave's Narrative* (New York: Oxford University Press, 1985), p. 168.

3. H. Bruce Franklin. "Animal Farm Unbound," *New Letters,* 43 (Spring 1977), p. 27.

4. Paul de Man, "Genesis and Genealogy," in *Allegories of Reading* (New Haven: Yale University Press, 1979), 102.

5. In *To Tell a Free Story* (Urbana: University of Illinois Press, 1986), perhaps the definitive study of the first century of Afro-American autobiography, William Andrews sees *Adam Negro's Tryall* as "a precursor of the slave narratives" and Briton Hammon's autobiography as the "first discrete narrative text in which an Afro-American recounts a significant portion of his life" (19, 18). Other students of the field see *The Interesting Narrative of Olaudah Equiano, or Gustavus Vassa, the African* (1789) as the originating text. In a recent article, Joanne M. Braxton argues for yet another beginning, *Belinda, or the Cruelty of Men Whose Faces Were Like the Moon* (1787). See her "Harriet Jacobs' *Incidents in the Life of a Slave Girl:* The Redefinition of the Slave Narrative Genre," *Massachusetts Review,* 27 (Summer 1986), 379–87.

6. John Sekora, "Comprehending Slavery: Language and Personal History in Douglass's *Narrative* of 1845," *College Language Association Journal,* 29 (December 1985), 169.

7. Benjamin Quarles. Introduction to *Narrative of the Life* (Cambridge: Harvard University Press, 1968), xix.

8. Andrews, *To Tell,* 138.

9. Peter Walker, *Moral Choices: Memory, Desire and Imagination in Nineteenth-Century American Abolition* (Baton Rouge: Louisiana State University Press, 1978), 212–13.

10. See Baker's "Revolution and Reform: Walker, Douglass, and the Road to Freedom," in *Long Black Song: Essays in Black American Literature and Culture* (Charlottesville: University Press of Virginia, 1972), in which he contrasts the forms and styles of David Walker's *Appeal* with Douglass's 1845 *Narrative*. He concludes that, while Walker was a revolutionary allied with "the declamatory poets of black America," Douglass was a reformer "allied with the formalists" (79). In "Autobiographical Acts and the Voice of the Southern Slave," in *The Journey Back: Issues in Black Literature and Criticism* (Chicago: University of Chicago Press, 1980), 27–52, Baker offers a different and very interesting reading of the *Narrative*, which employs theories of autobiography to problematize assumptions about the "self," to discuss its constructions in language, and to examine the implications of both for representing slavery and the slave. Most recently, in "Figurations for a New American Literary History," in *Blues, Ideology and Afro-American Literature* (Chicago: University of Chicago Press, 1984), Baker does a proto-Marxist reading of the property relations and the rhetoric and thematics of economics in the *Narrative*.

11. Edward Said, *Beginnings: Intention and Method* (New York: Columbia University Press, 1985), 32.

12. Said, *Beginnings,* 198.

13. Albert Stone, "Identity and Art in Frederick Douglass's 'Narrative'." *College Language Association Journal,* 17 (December 1973), 213.

14. Frederick Douglass, "The Trials and Triumphs of Self-Made Men: An Address Delivered in Halifax, England, on 4 January 1860," in John Blassingame, ed., *The Frederick Douglass Papers: Series One* (New Haven: Yale University Press, 1985), 290.

15. Patricia Parker, "Coming Second: Woman's Place," in *Literary Fat Ladies: Rhetoric, Gender, Property* (London and New York: Methuen, 1987), 190. For additional feminist critiques of the politics of origins, see Margaret Homans, *Bearing the Word* (Chicago: University of Chicago Press, 1986) and Christine Froula, "Rewriting Genesis: Gender and Culture in Twentieth-Century Texts," *Tulsa Studies in Women's Literature* 7 (Fall 1988), 197–220.

16. Frederick Douglass, *Narrative of the Life of Frederick Douglass, An American Slave Written by Himself* (New York: Signet/New American Library, 1968), 47. Subsequent references are to this edition and will be indicated in parentheses in the text. I will also make reference to *My Bondage and My Freedom* (New York: Dover, 1969) and *Life and Times of Frederick Douglass, Written by Himself* (New York: Pathway Press, 1941).

17. Perhaps as influential as the Elkins book in sparking revisionist histories of slavery was Daniel P. Moynihan's federally commissioned *Moynihan Report: The Case for National Action* (1965). While Elkins virtually ignored black women in his study, attributing the failure of black males to achieve "manhood" to a paternalistic slave system that infantilized them, Moynihan assigns blame to black women for being the predominant heads of household.

18. John Blassingame, *The Slave Community* (New York: Oxford University Press, 1979), xi.

19. Blassingame, *The Slave,* 230.

20. Blassingame, *The Slave,* xi.

21. Blassingame, *The Slave,* 172, 152.

22. Deborah Gray White. *Ar'n't I a Woman* (New York: W. W. Norton, 1985), 22

23. bell hooks. *Ain't I a Woman* (Boston: South End Press, 1981), 20–21.

24. Ronald Takaki's interpretation is an example of making Douglass a militant. In "Not Afraid to Die: Frederick Douglass and Violence," in *Violence and the Black Imagination* (New York: Capricorn, 1972), Takaki traces Douglass's rise to a political activist who advocated killing for freedom. In a forthcoming essay, "Race, Violence, and Manhood: The Masculine Ideal in Frederick Douglass's 'The Heroic Slave,'" Richard Yarborough discusses Douglass's obsession with manhood in his novella "The Heroic Slave." There manhood was virtually synonymous with militant slave resistance. In the popular realm, Spike Lee's controversial film *Do the Right*

Thing is structured according to this ideology of masculinity, which ranks black leaders (assumed to be male) according to their propensities for advocating violence.

25. For a bibliographic essay on the various editions of the Douglass narrative as compared to other slave narratives, see Ruth Miller and Peter J. Katopes, "Slave Narratives" and W. Burghardt Turner, "The Polemicists: David Walker, Frederick Douglass, Booker T. Washington, and W. E. B. DuBois," in M. Thomas Inge, Maurice Duke, and Jackson R. Bryer, *Black American Writers: Bibliographical Essays, Vol. 1* (New York: St. Martin's Press, 1978).

26. Houston Baker, *Blues, Ideology, and Afro-American Literature,* (Chicago: University of Chicago Press, 1984), 38.

27. Baker, *Blues,* 38.

28. Baker, *Blues,* 48.

29. Baker, *Blues,* 49.

30. Waldo E. Martin. *The Mind of Frederick Douglass* (Chapel Hill: University of North Carolina Press, 1984), 15.

31. Mary Helen Washington, "These Self-Invented Women: A Theoretical Framework for a Literary History of Black Women," *Radical Teacher* (1980), 4. In a recent study David Leverenz also notes that "Douglass's whole sense of latter-day self, in both the *Narrative* and its revision, focuses on manhood; his wife seems an afterthought. He introduces her to his readers as a rather startling appendage to his escape and marries her almost in the same breath." See Frederick "Douglass's Self-Fashioning," in *Manhood and the American Renaissance* (Ithaca: Cornell University Press, 1989), 128.

32. Jacques Derrida, "The Law of Genre," *Glyph* 7 (Baltimore: Johns Hopkins, 1980). Derrida notes that "in French, the semantic scale of genre is much larger and more expansive than in English and thus always includes within its reach the gender" (221). In his translator's notes to Derrida's essay, Avital Ronnell adds that " 'genre' enjoys a suppleness and freedom of semantic movement that is vigorously constrained in the English. . . . A genderless language, English by definition does not take well to the business of mixing with genres" (232).

33. See Sidonie Smith, *A Poetics of Women's Autobiography* (Bloomington: Indiana University Press, 1987). See also Domna C. Stanton, ed., *The Female Autograph: Theory and Practice of Autobiography from the Tenth to the Twentieth Century* (Chicago: University of Chicago Press, 1987) and Shari Benstock, ed., *The Private Self: Theory and Practice of Women's Autobiographical Writings* (Chapel Hill: University of North Carolina Press, 1988).

34. Valerie Smith, *Self-Discovery and Authority,* (Cambridge: Harvard University Press, 1987), 34.

35. See Annette Niemtzow, "The Problematic of Self in Autobiography: The Example of the Slave Narrative," in John Sekora and Darwin Tuner, eds., *The Art of the Slave Narrative* (Western Illinois University, 1982), 96–109.

36. See Peter Walker, *Moral Choices.* This search for the white father is a trope at least as powerfully paradigmatic as the more often discussed quest for freedom and literacy.

37. Henry Louis Gates, "Frederick Douglass and the Language of the Self," in *Figures in Black: Words, Signs and the 'Racial' Self* (New York: Oxford University, 1987), 114.

38. The historians Dickson Preston, in *Young Frederick Douglass: The Maryland Years* (Baltimore: Johns Hopkins, 1980), and Peter Walker, in *Moral Choices,* discuss the place of the mother in Douglass's autobiographies. Walker describes Douglass's "development of a 'fictive' kinship with his mother" and notes that "the more obvious and striking shift that Douglass made in the course of his autobiographical definition relates to his mother."

39. For a discussion of this pattern, see Margaret Homans *Bearing the Word* and Sidonie Smith, *A Poetics of Women's Autobiography* (Bloomington: Indiana University Press, 1987. See especially chapter 3, "Woman's Story and the Engenderings of Self-Representation."

40. Walker, *Moral Choices,* 254. Waldo Martin offers an alternative reading of Douglass's choice. While he acknowledges that the selection of this picture "could have suggested . . . the subconscious power of [Douglass's] racial ambivalence," the selection of an ambiguously

masculine figure "might have reflected the genderless dimension of his catholic vision of a common humanity transcending sex as well as race." *The Mind of Frederick Douglass,* 5.

41. Gregory Jay, "American Literature and the New Historicism: The Example of Frederick Douglass," Working Paper #10, Center for Twentieth Century Studies, University of Wisconsin-Milwaukee (Fall 1988): 19.

42. Valerie Smith, *Self-Discovery,* 20.

43. Karen Sanchez-Eppler, "Bodily Bonds: The Intersecting Rhetorics of Feminism and Abolition," *Representations* 24 (Fall 1988), 48.

44. Martin, *The Mind of Frederick Douglass,* 151. Martin notes also that "in his hierarchy of social reform priorities, Douglass viewed the abolition of black slavery as primary and the abolition of sexual slavery as secondary" (150).

45. Frances Foster, " 'In Respect to Females. . . . ': Differences in the Portrayals of Women by Male and Female Narrators," *Black American Literature Forum,* 15 (Summer 1981), 67.

46. See "The Jealous Mistress," in *Incidents in the Life of a Slave Girl.* Even Douglass himself says as much at another point. He notes that the mistress "is ever disposed to find anything to please her; she is never more pleased than when she sees them under the lash" (23).

47. Andrews, *To Tell a Free Story,* 134. Valerie Smith also offers an interesting reading of the whippings. They enable the reader to "visualize the blood that masters draw from their slaves . . . Passages such as [Douglass's Aunt Hester's beatings] provide vivid symbols of the process of dehumanization that slaves underwent as their lifeblood was literally sapped." *Self-Discovery and Authority,* 21–22.

48. Richard Brodhead, "Sparing the Rod: Discipline and Fiction in Antebellum America," *Representations* 21 (Winter 1988), 67. See also David Leverenz, *Manhood and the American Renaissance* for a discussion of beatings in Melville's *Moby Dick* and *White Jacket,* and in *Uncle Tom's Cabin.*

49. Sigmund Freud. *Beyond the Pleasure Principle,* Volume 18 of *Standard Edition of the Complete Psychological Works of Sigmund Freud* (London: The Hogarth Press, 1955), 36.

50. Jacqueline Rose. *Sexuality in the Field of Vision* (London: Verso, 1986), 112.

51. Rose, *Sexuality,* 27. See also Laura Mulrey, "Visual Pleasure and Narrative Cinema," *Screen* 16 (Autumn 1975), and Teresa De Lauretis, *Alice Doesn't: Feminism, Semiotics, Cinema* (Bloomington: Indiana University Press, 1984).

52. Such passages run throughout *My Bondage and My Freedom.* Even in the series of appendices to the text, Douglass keeps his focus riveted on the violation of the slave woman's body. In "Letter to His Old Master" [Thomas Auld], for example, he writes: "When I saw the slave-driver whip a slave-woman, cut the blood out of her neck, and heard her piteous cries, I went away into the corner of the fence, wept and pondered over the mystery." He then asks Auld how he would feel if his daughter were seized and left "unprotected—a degraded victim to the brutal lust of feindish overseers, who would pollute, blight, and blast the fair soul . . . destroy her virtue, and annihilate in her person all the grace that adorns the character of virtuous womanhood?" (427–28).

53. See Susanne Kappeler, *The Pornography of Representation* (Minneapolis: University of Minnesota, 1986), 104.

54. Donald Gibson, "Reconciling Public and Private in Frederick Douglass's *Narrative,*" *American Literature,* 57 (December 1985), 562.

55. Robert Stepto, *From Behind the Veil: A Study of Afro-American Narrative* (Urbana: University of Illinois Press, 1979).

56. Stepto, *From Behind,* 17.

57. Stepto, *From Behind,* 25.

58. Stepto, *From Behind,* 45.

59. Stepto, *From Behind,* 45.

60. Stepto, *From Behind,* 45.

61. Stepto, *From Behind,* 20.

62. Compare this passage with the same scene in the 1845 *Narrative:* "When left thus, I used to spend the time in writing in the spaces left in Master Thomas's copy-book, copying what he had written. I continued to do this until I could write a hand very similar to that of Master Thomas. Thus, after a long, tedious effort of .years, I finally succeeded in learning how to write" (58).

63. Lillie Jugurtha, "Point of View in the Afro-American Slave Narratives by Douglass and Pennington," in John Sekora and Darwin Turner, eds., *The Art of Slave Narrative* (Western Illinois University Press, 1982), 113.

64. Olney, "The Founding Fathers—Frederick Douglass and Booker T. Washington" in Deborah E. McDowell and Arnold Rampersad, eds., *Slavery and the Literary Imagination* (Baltimore: Johns Hopkins, 1989), 81.

65. Arna Bontemps, quoted in Charles Davis and Henry Louis Gates, Jr., eds., *The Slave's Narrative* (New York: Oxford University Press, 1985), xv.

66. Olney, "The Founding Fathers," 20.

67. Olney, "The Founding Fathers," 3.

68. Russell Reising, *The Unusable Past: Theory and the Study of American Literature* (New York: Methuen, 1986), 257.

69. *Norton Anthology of American Literature, Second Ed.* Vol. I (New York: W.W. Norton, 1985), 1867.

70. Said, *Beginnings,* 38.

71. Henry Louis Gates, Jr. "In Her Own Write," foreword to *The Schomburg Library Series of Nineteenth-Century Black Women Writers* (New York: Oxford University Press, 1988), xi.

72. Gates, "In Her Own," xiii.

73. Gates, "In Her Own," xi.

74. Henry Louis Gates, "From Wheatley to Douglass: The Politics of Displacement," forthcoming in Eric Sundquist, ed., *Frederick Douglass: New Literary and Historical Essays* (Cambridge: Cambridge University Press).

75. Also forthcoming in the Sundquist volume is an essay by Richard Yarborough, titled "Race, Violence, and Manhood: The Masculine Ideal in Frederick Douglass's 'The Heroic Slave.'" Yarborough subtly examines the connection that Douglass attempts to establish between manhood and violent resistance in Douglass's novel.

Index

♦